A Complete Book on
Medical Astrology

Principles and Case Studies
(Manage your health through preventive astral remedies)

The book helps you in understanding planetary influences through Systems' Approach predictive techniques for interpreting horoscopes.

BOOKKISH.com

UG-1, Arjit Arcade, Gali No. 12, Madhu Vihar Market
Main Road, I.P. Extension, Patparganj.
New Delhi-110092 (India)
Email: info@bookkish.com
Ph. 9313208110, 9871894538, 9953889373
Astrology | Self help | Spiritual

A Complete Book on
Medical Astrology
Principles and Case Studies
(Manage your health through preventive astral remedies)

The book helps you in understanding planetary influences through Systems' Approach predictive techniques for interpreting horoscopes.

Author:
V. K. Choudhry
M.B.A., Founder Chairman,
International Institute of Predictive Astrology,
Fairfield, USA, and Propounder of Systems' Approach for
Interpreting Horoscopes

Co-Author:
K. Rajesh Chaudhary
M.B.A., Vice President,
India Chapter, International Institute of Predictive Astrology,
Fairfield, USA

Sagar Publications
72, Janpath, Ved Mansion, New Delhi-110001
Tel.: 23320648, 23328245
E-mail: sagarpub@vsnl.com
Website: www.sagarpublications.com

1st Published 1997, Reprinted 2001
Revised Edition April, 2012
Reprinted 2016

Published and Printed by:
Saurabh Sagar for **Sagar Publications** New Delhi-110001

and

Printed at:
The Artwaves, New Delhi-110019, Telfax.: 41609709;
E-mail: theartwaves@gmail.com

ABOUT THE AUTHORS

Shri V. K. Choudhry

(Propounder of the Systems' Approach for Interpreting Horoscopes)

V. K. Choudhry

Shri V. K. Choudhry is well known in the field of Vedic Astrology through his many books and articles. His managerial background has enabled him to use modern communicative skills in so systematic a manner that the comprehension of predictive techniques has been greatly simplified. His book, "Self Learning Course in Astrology" makes learning of the "Systems' Approach" methodology a simple step-by-step process and has proved to be of great help to both the serious students as well as the practitioners still plagued by the confusing inconsistencies in the classical texts.

He was conferred the title of Jyotish Martund by the International Council of Astrological and Occult Studies, Hyderabad (India) in 1989; the title of Jyotish Kovid by the Indian Council of Astrological Sciences (ICAS), Madras, in 1991; and the title of Jyotish Bhanu by Astro Sciences Research Organization, New Delhi, in 1992. He has been a faculty member and Chapter Course Director (Astrology) with ICAS.

Shri Choudhry is the recipient of Pracharya Award (Professor of Astrology) conferred by Bharat Nirman in December, 1993, for his outstanding and excellent contributions in the field of Astrology.

In 1994, his name was listed in "Indo American Who's Who", in recognition of his contributions for predictive accuracy in Vedic Astrology.

Shri Choudhry participated in the 10th International Seminar of Astrology and Occult Science in June 1995, at Hyderabad and delivered lectures on "Timing of Events" and "Vastu Shastra". Shri Choudhry was conferred the title of "Master of Astrology" in this Seminar by International Council of Astrological and Occult Studies.

The Board of Directors of International Council of Alternative Medicines conferred the degree of Doctor of Alternative Medical Sciences on Shri Choudhry on 3rd of February 1996, at Bombay. The International Institute of Astrology and Occultism, New Delhi, conferred a Gold Medal and the honorary title of Jyotish Vachaspathi on Shri Choudhry in April 1996, at New Delhi.

International Foundation of Peace, Fraternity and Humanistic, Bombay, conferred the title of Dharam Yogi in 1995. International Council of Astrological Sciences, Bombay, conferred the title of Vastu Shastra Samrat in 1996, and Bhartiya Ved Jyotish Vigyan Sansthan, Modinagar (India), conferred the title of Sthapatya Ratna in 1996, on Shri Choudhry for his valuable contributions in the fields of Astrology and Vastu Shastra. Shri Choudhry participated in astrological conferences in London, Paris and U.S.A. In 2004 the first book of Shri V. K. Choudhry has been translated in Portuguese and published in Portugal. The Systems' Approach for Interpreting Horoscopes is applicable for mundane astrology predictions, as well. Shri Choudhry made many successful mundane predictions on Yahoo Groups – SAMVA, including twice predicting victory for Mr. George W. Bush as President of US and predicting natural disaster for US in August, 2005. Shri Choudhry guides students on Yahoo Group SATVA on the internet. The present membership of SATVA is around 1400.

United Cultural Convention, North Caroline, USA, sealed the nomination of Shri V. K. Choudhry for receipt of the 2002 Noble Prize for Outstanding Achievement and Contributions to Humanity. This nomination stems from extensive research on extraordinary leaders by the top officials of the United Cultural Convention.

Mr. V.K. Choudhry is Founder Chairman of the International Institute of Predictive Astrology, IIPA, Fairfield, USA. IIPA has more than 750 members spread across 40 countries. IIPA has 15 chapters.

American Biographical Institute inducted Mr. Vinod Kumar Choudhry to the Hall of Fame in July, 2009, for Distinguished accomplishments in Astrology and for dedication and efforts that have left an indelible mark on the lives of others.

Shri K. Rajesh Chaudhary

K. Raje sh Chaudhary

Shri K. Rajesh Chaudhary has contributed to the Systems' Approach for Interpreting Horoscopes under the guidance of his father, Shri V. K. Choudhry. He participated in the free Consultation Clinics organized in New Delhi by Bharat Nirman. Delhi Astro Study Circle (Registered) New Delhi, conferred the honorary title of Jyotish Martund on Shri Chaudhary in 2011. He is one of the Directors and Secretary of The Systems' Institute of Hindu Astrology, Gurgaon (India). He is Vice-President of the India Chapter of International Institute of Predictive Astrology, Fairfield, USA. He is co-author for the following successful books:

1. Predictive Techniques and the Application of Astrological Remedial Measures.

2. Systems' Approach for Interpreting Horoscopes

3. Select Right Profession through Astrology.

4. How to Study Divisional Charts

5. Application of Prasna Astrology.

6. How to Analyze Married Life.

7. Impact of Ascending Zodiac Signs.

Website: www.YourNetAstrologer.com
Website: www.JyotishRemedies121.com

SAGAR PUBLICATIONS

PREFACE

The world dreads today the fear of AIDS, cancer, cardiovascular diseases, psychiatric problems, etc. The modern system of medicine whether allopathic and/or alternative medicines offers us guiding factors for preventing these dreaded diseases or early detection of these so that these can respond to symptomatic treatment. The divine science of Vedic Astrology has the twin capacity to forewarn and forearm and offers the preventive remedies for such diseases wherever the possibility of such a disease is indicated by the predictive capacity of Vedic Astrology.

On persistent demand from the readers, we have taken up publication of this book. In the beginning the basic concepts, fundamentals and advance predictive techniques have been discussed so that the subject can be properly comprehended and the case studies are easily understood. We have taken up the significations of planets, signs and houses and the analytical techniques to identify the areas of health problems in the life of a person. We have also discussed application of preventive astrological remedial measures. The diverse case studies have been taken up on various types of health problems. We hope the readers will like the selection and the presentation.

The predictive techniques and the application of these techniques have been elaborated in the case studies included in this book for the practicing astrologers and the advance learners. We hope the readers will find the book to their satisfaction.

Some fundamental changes have been suggested in the background of solid reasons. The aim is to achieve predictive accuracy and for this, the Systems' Approach is dependable. Moreover, fundamental changes have been suggested to simplify analysis. This approach is universally applicable to all horoscopes with one single technique of analysis. This enables one to identify the area of a problem, the positive traits, the strengths and weaknesses of various planetary configurations right at birth without any explanation given by the person seeking astrological consultation.

Birth particulars have been withheld in some case studies out of respect for the privacy of the natives, even though the inclusion of such charts has been considered necessary.

V.K. Choudhry
K. Rajesh Chaudhary

105, A-Block, South City- II
Gurgaon-122018 (India)
Ph. : 91-9811016333, 91-9899417444
E-mail: vkchoudhry@gmail.com
Website: http//www.YourNetAstrologer.com
Website: http//www.JyotishRemedies121.com

CONTENTS

CHAPTER 1

CONCEPTS AND FUNDAMENTALS

The divine science of Vedic Astrology is a wonderful asset to the mankind. It unfolds the uncertainties in life, reduces tension, and enables one to move into the right direction. It deals with various aspects of human life such as health - physical and mental, business, social status, financial prosperity, name and fame, emotional stability, etc. The predictive tools of Systems' Approach to Vedic Astrology give us the firm indications in life pertaining to the future events right at birth. The astrological remedies at the same time help further by reducing the impact of malefic planetary influences and harness the significations ruled by functional benefic planets in a nativity.

HOW DO PLANETS AFFECT US

The basis of astrology is Karma theory. The planetary influences in the horoscope are based on the deeds of one's past life. Whatever we have to get or face in this life is based on the planetary influences arising in our horoscopes. The horoscope is map of the heavens (planets) plotted on a paper like a map in the twelve signs of zodiac placed in twelve number of houses. From this map of heavens we can read the planetary influences in the life of a person as also the amount of free will. The strength of Sun, Mars, Jupiter and the lord of the third house or the planets in the third house show the magnitude of free will.

The world dreads today the fear of AIDS, cancer, cardiovascular diseases, psychiatric problems, etc. The modern system of medicine whether allopathic and/or alternative medicines offers us guiding factors for preventing these dreaded diseases or early detection of these so that these can respond to symptomatic treatment. The divine science of Vedic Astrology has the twin capacity to forewarn and forearm and offers the preventive remedies for such diseases wherever the possibility of such a disease is indicated by the predictive capacity of Vedic Astrology.

We come across serious health problems even at birth, when the individual concerned has no role to play in abuse of his food habits, etc. Astrology relates it to the deeds of the past life based on the theory of Karma. We are not trying to create here any orthodoxy or blind faith or fatalism but we are trying to share with you our experience of application of the science of astrology and astrological remedies in timing of the diseases and timing of recovery. The exact or very close influence of Rahu or Ketu to the weak planets causes persisting infectious and allergic problems. These problems can be managed with the help of the preventive astrological remedies. This necessitates the astrological diagnosis right at birth.

The timing is done with the help of the horoscope which is a record of the planetary position prevailing at the time of the birth of a particular person at a particular place. This is the most valuable gift of Vedas to the mankind. All sciences depend on the experience by way of observations and analysis of hypothesis developed and tested based on these observations. It is really painful when such a useful gift to mankind is just termed as a superstition without even a trial by the so called rationalists and scientists.

Despite the phenomenal growth in the modern healing sciences, the permanent cure for the functional health problems, be it in the fields of psychological problems, cardiovascular problems, renal problems, asthmatic problems, liver problems, immunization power of the body, etc., has not been found. Astrology offers us the preventive diagnostic power and astral remedies both for preventive as well as curative purposes. Administering medicine is supported manifold when combined with astral remedies. The operating planetary periods and transit indicate the time frame for recovery. This in turn gives patience and results of the symptomatic treatment.

Major Constituents of Vedic Astrology

The divine science of Vedic Astrology has four major constituents, which are Signs, Houses, Planets and Planetary Periods. It will be in the fitness of things if the four constituents are briefly discussed for developing the understanding for learning Vedic Astrology.

A. SIGNS

The first constituent of Vedic Astrology is signs. They are twelve in number and are ruled by the planets indicated against each of them.

	SIGNS		LORDS	
1	Aries	(Mesha)	Mars	(Mangala)
2	Taurus	(Vrishabha)	Venus	(Shukra)
3	Gemini	(Mithuna)	Mercury	(Budha)
4	Cancer	(Karka)	The Moon	(Chandra)
5	Leo	(Simha)	The Sun	(Surya)
6	Virgo	(Kanya)	Mercury	(Budha)
7	Libra	(Tula)	Venus	(Shukra)
8	Scorpio	(Vrischika)	Mars	(Mangala)
9	Sagittarius	(Dhanu)	Jupiter	(Guru)
10	Capricorn	(Makara)	Saturn	(Sani)
11	Aquarius	(Kumbha)	Saturn	(Sani)
12	Pisces	(Mina)	Jupiter	(Guru)

The words within parenthesis indicate their nomenclature in Sanskrit. You will observe that the planets Mars, Venus, Mercury, Jupiter and Saturn rule over two signs. These planets have special attention to one of their signs and this sign is known as their mooltrikona sign. The signs Aries, Virgo, Libra, Sagittarius and Aquarius are the mooltrikona sign of the planets Mars, Mercury, Venus, Jupiter and Saturn, respectively.

The signs possess the positive and negative aspects of their lords according to their nature and according to the strength of their lords. The most important quality is that they lead us to infer the extent of fructifications of the significations of a particular house. For example, if the sign Libra falls in a house and its lord Venus is in full strength, the significations of that house in particular will flourish to a very affluent level of the society in which a particular native (person) is living.

B. HOUSES

The second constituent of Vedic Astrology is houses. These houses are twelve in number and each of the twelve houses of the horoscope deals with specific significations. The significations of the houses fructify under the planetary periods (sub-periods) connected with them. The houses are good and bad. The sixth, eighth and twelfth houses are known as bad (malefic) houses as these rule diseases, obstructions and losses, respectively.

C. PLANETS

The third constituent of Vedic Astrology is planets. In Vedic Astrology we consider the Sun, the Moon, Mars, Mercury, Jupiter, Venus, Saturn, Rahu and Ketu as planets. While the Sun and the Moon are the luminaries, Rahu and Ketu are the shadowy planets. As the planets Pluto, Neptune and Uranus neither have a lordship over a house nor have a planetary period of their own, they can in no way be considered for the predictive purposes.

The planets signify various things including the specific body parts and the functional system of health. For example, the Sun is personified as a king in the planetary cabinet. Persons having the Moon, the significator of mind, in the sign of the Sun would have the mental frame of enjoying life like a king i.e. of thinking big. The Sun signifies father, husband and male children. The Sun also rules heart, digestive system and vitality. The Moon rules the lungs, fluids in body, lymphatic system, etc.

Additionally, the planets govern the houses in a nativity where their mooltrikona signs fall. For example, if sign Libra falls in the eighth house, Venus would rule the significations of the eighth house.

The planets attain benefic or malefic functional nature in a horoscope based on the lordship of benefic or malefic houses containing mooltrikona signs. The planets may be weak or strong. The functional malefic planets when closely influence other planets or houses, cause afflictions to them.

D. PLANETARY PERIODS

The fourth constituent of Vedic Astrology is planetary periods. Though various types of planetary periods for specific planetary combinations are mentioned in classical texts, we consider only Vimshottari dasa system in this book as this is universally applicable for all sets of combinations in a nativity. Based on the longitude of the Moon in the natal charts, we calculate the operational major period of a particular planet and the balance period yet to be operational.

According to their strength in a horoscope, the planets give results of the general and particular significations ruled by them in their sub-periods.

For details the readers can refer to the book, "Self Learning Course in Astrology".

INTRODUCTION TO CHARTS

ASCENDANT / LAGNA / RISING SIGN

The revolution of the earth around its own axis causes rise of all the twelve signs in the east at different points of time during the period of 24 hours in a clock-wise motion. The signs rise in seriatim i.e. Aries first, and then Taurus followed by Gemini and so on and so forth.

The ascendant or lagna is that point in the zodiac which rises at the time of birth of a person with reference to the place of birth. The position of planets in zodiac is noted with reference to the earth. The ascendant is the first house in a horoscope and the rest of the houses are reckoned from it.

RASI CHART/NATAL CHART/MAIN CHART/HOROSCOPE

The rasi chart which is known as birth chart or natal chart can be drawn in many ways but for the purpose of our study, we will only take up the North Indian style, which is drawn as under:

NORTH INDIAN CHART STYLE

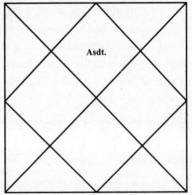

This is the best form of drawing a chart as it provides a very easy comprehension of the chart at a mere glimpse. It shows angles/ planets placed in angles without enumeration. Angular houses have been marked hereunder:

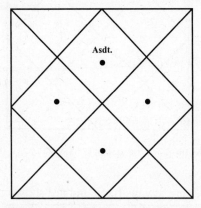

It shows whether any planet is posited in the malefic houses. The sixth, eighth and twelfth houses in a chart are known as malefic houses. Malefic houses have been marked hereunder:

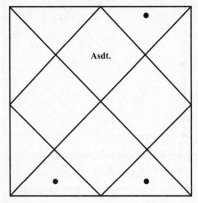

It shows the placement of planets in trines, if any, at a mere glimpse. The trine positions have been shown as under:

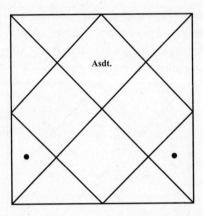

Even reckoning of the aspects is very easy in this form of a birth chart.

The houses are always fixed and are shown below:

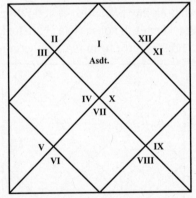

According to the Systems' Approach, the lordship of the houses is reckoned from the placement of a mooltrikona sign in a particular house. The lord of the mooltrikona sign placed in a particular house is called the lord of the house. The counting of houses is done in an anti clockwise direction. In the following chart, for example, the sign Gemini rises in the ascendant and the sign Libra is placed in the fifth house. So, Venus is the lord of the fifth house.

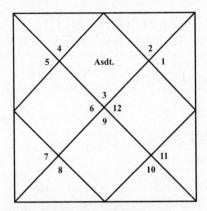

GRAPHICAL PRESENTATION OF
GENERAL SIGNIFICATIONS OF THE HOUSES

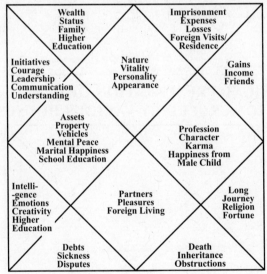

GRAPHICAL PRESENTATION OF
BODY PARTS RULED BY THE VARIOUS HOUSES

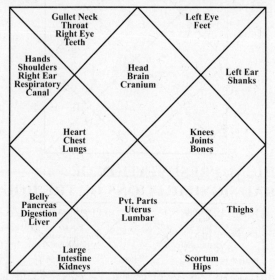

GRAPHICAL PRESENTATION OF
RELATIONS RULED BY VARIOUS HOUSES

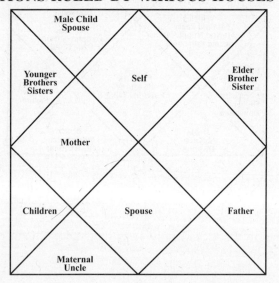

IMPORTANT TERMINOLOGY

NATAL CHART

Natal chart or radical chart or horoscope or natal positions are the positions of the ascendant and planets in various signs as noted for the time of the birth. Natal positions, therefore, are fixed. The planetary positions noted with reference to a particular chart for subsequent periods are known as transit or transit positions.

CONJUNCTION

Conjunction is the apparent coincidence or proximity of two or more celestial objects as viewed from the earth. The conjunction can be exact or close. If the difference in longitudes happens to be less than one degree, the resulting conjunction is known as an exact conjunction. If the difference in longitudes is within five degrees, the same is known as a close conjunction.

Example 1

This example is given for clear understanding of the exact or close conjunctions.

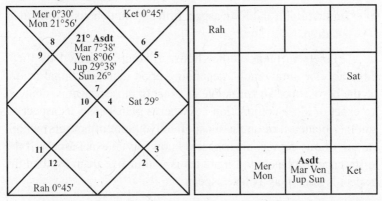

In this chart the planets Venus and Mars are in exact conjunction in the ascendant as their longitude difference is less than one degree.

The planets Sun and Jupiter are in close conjunction as their longitude difference is within five degrees.

The Moon is in exact conjunction to the most effective point of the second house.

Though Jupiter and Mercury are in the first and second houses, respectively, but they are in exact conjunction as their longitude difference is within one degree.

ASPECTS

The aspects are partial and full. In the Vedic system of Astrology, we are concerned with only full aspects. Each planet is believed to aspect fully the seventh house, reckoned / counted from the placement of the former.

In addition to this i.e. the seventh aspect, planets posited outside the orbit of the earth (Mars, Jupiter and Saturn) as well as Rahu and Ketu have additional special full aspects as under:

• Saturn aspects third and tenth houses from its location.

• Mars aspects fourth and eighth houses from its location.

• Jupiter, Rahu and Ketu aspect fifth and ninth houses from their location.

Planets influence other houses/planets aspected by them favorably or unfavorably, depending upon their functional nature in the horoscope. The principle of exact or close aspect is identical to exact or close conjunction i.e. when a planet casts its aspect on another planet(s) or on the most effective point of house(s) within an orb of one degree, the aspect is known as an exact aspect. If the difference in planetary longitudes is within five degrees, then the aspect is known as a close aspect.

Example 2

This example is given for clear understanding of the exact or close aspects.

Ket		Mar	**Asdt**
Ven			Mon
Mer Sun			
Sat	Jup		Rah

In this chart Rahu closely aspects the Sun with fifth aspect as the longitude difference of aspect is less than five degrees.

The planets Mars and Jupiter mutually form close aspect as their aspect longitude difference is within five degrees.

Mercury forms exact aspect to the most effective point of the second house. This is the seventh aspect of Mercury.

Ketu forms exact aspect to the Moon placed in the second house. This is fifth aspect of Ketu to the Moon from the tenth house.

Saturn forms exact aspect to Venus as the longitude difference is less than one degree between the longitude of the two planets. This is third aspect of Saturn from seventh house to Venus placed in the ninth house.

Saturn forms close aspect to the most effective point of the ascendant as the longitude difference is less than five degrees between the longitudes of Saturn and the ascendant. This is seventh aspect of Saturn from the seventh house to ascendant.

WIDE CONJUNCTIONS OR ASPECTS

The conjunctions or aspects with more than five degrees of longitudinal difference are wide conjunctions or aspects. These do not have permanent impact in life except the short lived transit influences on the planets involved in wide conjunctions or aspects. The wide aspects give their results in later part of life, say around 60 years or after.

The aspect of a functional benefic planet will be effective corresponding to the strength of the planet(s)/house(s) involved. If the aspecting functional benefic planet is weak due to any reason including debilitation its effectiveness will be weak and limited, but its close aspect will always act as a helping force. The close aspect of a functional malefic planet, except on the most effective point of its own mooltrikona house, will always act as a damaging force.

GENERAL AND PARTICULAR SIGNIFICATIONS OF PLANETS

The general significations of a planet mean the aspects ruled by that planet. For example, the Sun rules father, status of the native, heart, digestive system, etc., irrespective of the lordship of the Sun in a particular nativity.

The particular significations of a planet mean the significations of its mooltrikona sign house in the natal chart. It also touches the significations of the house where it is placed in the natal chart and the significations of the house where it is transiting in the natal chart.

The results of the significations of a weak planet fructify with delay and suffer whenever that weak planet is afflicted due to close aspect or conjunction with any functional malefic planet. The natal affliction causes damages in the entire sub-periods of the weak planet and the afflicting planets while the transit affliction causes short term damages during that effective transit influence.

PLANETARY STATES

The planetary states are the conditions in which a planet is placed. The prominent states and the results produced are as under:

1. **INFANCY:** Whenever the longitude of a planet in a particular sign is less than 5 degrees, it is said to be in infancy. Such a planet is incapable of fully promoting/protecting its general and particular significations.

2. **OLD AGE:** Whenever the longitude of a planet in a particular sign is more than 25 degrees, it is said to be in old age. Such a planet is incapable of fully promoting/protecting its general and particular significations.

3. **OWN SIGN:** A planet in its own mooltrikona sign is treated as strong and is capable of generating the expected results, provided it is otherwise strong and is a functional benefic planet.

The own signs of various planets are as under:

PLANET	OWN SIGN
SUN	LEO
MOON	CANCER
MARS	ARIES, SCORPIO
MERCURY	GEMINI, VIRGO
JUPITER	SAGITTARIUS, PISCES
VENUS	TAURUS, LIBRA
SATURN	CAPRICORN, AQUARIUS

4. **MOOLTRIKONA SIGN:** A planet in its mooltrikona (MT) sign is treated as very powerful, provided it is otherwise strong.

Under the Systems' Approach, the mooltrikona signs of various planets are as under:

PLANET	MOOLTRIKONA SIGN
SUN	LEO
MOON	CANCER
MARS	ARIES
MERCURY	VIRGO
JUPITER	SAGITTARIUS
VENUS	LIBRA
SATURN	AQUARIUS

5. **EXALTATION:** The planets are in exaltation in particular signs and give good results by promoting/protecting their general and particular significations, provided they are otherwise strong.

The exaltation signs of various planets are as under:

PLANET	EXALTATION SIGN
SUN	ARIES
MOON	TAURUS
MARS	CAPRICORN
MERCURY	VIRGO
JUPITER	CANCER
VENUS	PISCES
SATURN	LIBRA
RAHU	TAURUS
KETU	SCORPIO

6. **DEBILITATION:** The planets are in debilitation in particular signs. The debilitated planets becomes weak and fail to fully protect/promote their general and particular significations. Rather, there can be deterioration in their ruling sub-periods.

The debilitation signs of various planets are as follows:

PLANET	DEBILITATION SIGN
SUN	LIBRA
MOON	SCORPIO
MARS	CANCER
MERCURY	PISCES
JUPITER	CAPRICORN
VENUS	VIRGO
SATURN	ARIES
RAHU	SCORPIO
KETU	TAURUS

To study the aspect of debilitation of planets in detail, the readers may also refer to our book, "How to Study Divisional Charts."

7. **COMBUSTION:** Whenever a planet comes very near to the Sun, it is divested of its brightness (luster). The said state is called combustion. While in combustion, the planets fail to fully protect/promote their general and particular significations. If such a planet is weak on other accounts too, the significations ruled by them may not even take birth.

The planets are said to be combust when they are within the below mentioned degrees on either side of the Sun:

MOON	12	DEGREES
MARS	17	DEGREES
MERCURY	14	DEGREES
VENUS	10	DEGREES
JUPITER	11	DEGREES
SATURN	15	DEGREES

To study the aspect of combustion of planets in detail, the readers may refer to our book, "How to Study Divisional Charts."

8. **IN FRIENDLY SIGNS:** When planets occupy the signs of their friendly planets, they are happy and feel themselves free for producing results, if they are otherwise strong. The Sun, the Moon and Mars are friends and Jupiter is their preceptor. Saturn, Mercury, Rahu and Ketu are friends and Venus is their preceptor.

9. **IN INIMICAL SIGNS:** When planets occupy signs of their enemies, they do not find themselves comfortable to produce results expected of them. However, any sign from where a particular planet aspects its own mooltrikona sign is an exception to this rule and a planet in such a state does not find itself restricted to produce results.

CHAPTER 2

SIGNIFICATIONS OF SIGNS

1. **ARIES:** It is a fiery sign ruled by Mars, the significator of energy. This sign rules head (cranium and forehead) and brain. This sign rules pitta humor (bile) and makes the native born under this sign vulnerable to diseases resulting out of malfunctioning of bile. If Mars and Mercury are strong, the Arians enjoy good health. Otherwise, they have a sick constitution, suffer from wounds, headache, mental tension, fevers, short-temperedness, insomnia, diseases of impure blood, bilious diseases, inflammatory disorders, constipation, stammering, etc. Aries is the mooltrikona sign of Mars.

2. **TAURUS:** It is an earthy sign ruled by Venus. This sign rules face and its organs (nose, throat, mouth, teeth and eyes), neck, cervical region and bones, cerebellum and facial bones. This sign rules vata humor (acidity) and makes the native born under this sign vulnerable to diseases resulting out of acidity. If Venus, as lord of the sixth house, is strong the Taureans enjoy good health. Otherwise, they have a sick constitution, suffer from poor digestion, constipation, acidity, disorders of the throat, eyes, teeth, etc., and diseases mainly arising out of a weak venous system. Over-indulgence can be a cause for ill health.

3. **GEMINI:** It is an airy sign ruled by Mercury. This sign rules ears, lower neck, shoulders, arms, hands, respiratory and nervous systems, bronchial tubes, shoulder and collar bones, bones of arms and hands. This sign rules tri-dosha humor that is pitta, vata and kapha (bile, acidity and phlegm) and makes the native born under this sign vulnerable to diseases resulting out of imbalance of bile, acidity and phlegm. As both the

ascendant and the sixth house do not contain a mooltrikona sign in case of the Gemini ascendant, the Sun, the significator for vitality, is considered as the prime determinant of health for Geminians. If the Sun is strong, they enjoy good health. Otherwise, Geminians have a sick constitution and suffer from tonsillitis, teeth problems, lung disorders, hypertension, headaches, congestion and respiratory diseases, asthma, imbalances in the nervous system, depression resulting in partial paralysis, stammering, shoulder pain, etc.

4. **CANCER:** It is a watery sign, generally weak, ruled by the Moon. This sign rules the rib cage, chest, heart, lungs and breasts. This sign rules kapha humor (phlegm) and makes the native born under this sign vulnerable to diseases resulting out of imbalance of phlegm in the body. If the Moon and Jupiter are strong, the Cancerians enjoy good health. Otherwise, they have a sick constitution and unpleasant appearance and suffer from mental maladies, physical ailments of breast, chest, heart and epigastric region, lymphatic and circulatory congestion, jaundice and other liver complaints, etc. Under the Systems' Approach, Cancer is treated as the mooltrikona sign of the Moon.

5. **LEO:** It is a fiery sign ruled by the Sun. This sign rules upper belly, stomach, spine, spinal cord, back, liver, gall bladder, spleen and pancreas. This sign rules pitta humor (bile) and makes the native born under this sign vulnerable to diseases resulting out of malfunctioning of bile. If the Sun is strong, the Leos enjoy good health. Otherwise, they are vulnerable to the diseases of heart, spine, bones, spleen, pancreas, liver, stomach, weak digestion, fevers, etc., and lack stamina and will power. This is the mooltrikona sign of the Sun.

6. **VIRGO:** It is an earthy sign ruled by Mercury, the governor of nervous system. This sign rules the waist, abdominal umbilical region, nervous system, small intestine, upper part of large intestine, appendix and kidneys. This sign rules vata humor (acidity) and makes the native born under this sign vulnerable to diseases resulting out of acidity. If Mercury and

Saturn are strong, the Virgos enjoy good health. Otherwise, they become hypochondriac and are vulnerable to overexertion, nervous breakdown, appendicitis, constipation, etc. This is the mooltrikona sign of Mercury.

7. **LIBRA:** It is an airy sign ruled by Venus. This sign rules lumbar region and lumbar bones, skin, lower part of large intestine, urinary bladder, and inner sexual organs such as ovaries, uterus, testicles and prostate gland. This sign rules tri-dosha humor that is pitta, vata and kapha (bile, acidity and phlegm) and makes the native born under this sign vulnerable to diseases resulting out of imbalance of bile, acidity and phlegm. If Venus is strong, the Libras enjoy good health. Otherwise, they are vulnerable to diseases connected with parts ruled by this sign, skin diseases, diabetes, venereal diseases, renal problems, urination problems, arthritis, gout pains, etc. This is the mooltrikona sign of Venus.

8. **SCORPIO:** It is a watery sign ruled by Mars. This sign rules outer sexual organs, scrotum, rectum, anus and pelvic bones. This sign rules kapha humor (phlegm) and makes the native born under this sign vulnerable to diseases resulting out of imbalance of phlegm in the body. If Mars, as lord of the sixth house, is strong the Scorpios are well built and enjoy good health. Otherwise, they have a sick constitution and suffer from piles, fissure, urinary infections, boils, and operations, etc., in the parts ruled by Scorpio.

9. **SAGITTARIUS:** It is a fiery sign ruled by Jupiter. This sign rules hips and thighs, arterial system and nerves. This sign rules pitta humor (bile) and makes the native born under this sign vulnerable to diseases resulting out of malfunctioning of bile. If Jupiter is strong, the Sagittarians enjoy good health. Otherwise, they are vulnerable to anemia, poor digestion, flatulence, disorders of liver/gall bladder, jaundice, high fevers, diabetes, rheumatism and troubles in hips and thighs, etc. The native may also face troubles due to his tendency to overindulge in food and drink. This is the mooltrikona sign of Jupiter.

10. **CAPRICORN:** It is an earthy sign ruled by Saturn. This sign rules knees and kneecaps, skin, bones and joints. This sign rules vata humor (acidity) and makes the native born under this sign vulnerable to diseases resulting out of acidity. As both the ascendant and the sixth house do not contain a mooltrikona sign. the Sun, the significator for vitality, is considered as the prime determinant of health for Capricornians. If the Sun is strong, they enjoy good health. Otherwise, Capricornians have a sick constitution and suffer from joint pains/inflammation, arthritis, general weakness, emaciated body, skin diseases and allergies, etc. The native may also have troubles resulting from stress and nervous disorders.

11. **AQUARIUS:** It is an airy sign ruled by Saturn. This sign rules shanks, calves, ankles, shin bone, blood circulation, etc. This sign rules tri-dosha humor that is pitta, vata and kapha (bile, acidity and phlegm) and makes the native born under this sign vulnerable to diseases resulting out of imbalance of bile, acidity and phlegm. If Saturn and the Moon are strong, the Aquarians enjoy good health. Otherwise, they are susceptible to colds and infections, and suffer from fractures in lower legs, cancerous diseases and wounds, etc., in the parts ruled by Aquarius. Rheumatism and arthritis are also indicated with age. This is the mooltrikona sign of Saturn.

12. **PISCES:** It is a watery sign ruled by Jupiter, the significator of fortune and knowledge. This sign rules feet and toes, lymphatic system, bones of the feet and toe. This sign rules kapha humor (phlegm) and makes the native born under this sign vulnerable to diseases resulting out of imbalance of phlegm in the body. If the Sun, as lord of the sixth house, is strong the Pisceans are healthy. Otherwise, they have a sick constitution, suffer from phlegm disorders, lung infections, gout pains, joint pains, and disorders related with blood circulation, lymphatic system, feet, toes, bones of the feet/toes, etc.

CHAPTER 3

SIGNIFICATIONS OF HOUSES

Concerning the body, the significations of each house generally correspond to the significations of the equivalent sign of the zodiac in seriatim i.e. whenever we want to examine the condition of any part of the body, the concerned house and the same number of zodiac sign should both be examined. Afflictions to houses likewise cause diseases of the connected parts.

FIRST HOUSE: Represents physical constitution, head (cranium and forehead) brain, hair and pituitary glands. The weakness of the first house and/or afflictions to the first house or its lord result in a sick constitution, causing vulnerability to headache, mental tension, paralysis, giddiness, dementia, meningitis, wounds, scars, erratic activity of endocrine glands, derangement, brain fever, stupidity, nose bleeding, etc. A strong Sun and Mars, as significators for vitality and energy respectively, help as a protective cover.

SECOND HOUSE: Represents face and its organs (nose, throat, mouth, tongue, teeth and eyes, especially the right one), facial bones, upper neck and its bones, gullet, larynx, cerebellum, trachea, tonsils, thyroid gland, cervical region and cervical bones. The weakness of the second house and/or afflictions to the second house or its lord cause vulnerability to disorders of speech, throat, cervical, tonsils, gums, eyes, teeth, etc., and diseases mainly arising out of a weak venous system. Strong Mercury, as a significator of speech, helps as a protective cover.

THIRD HOUSE: Represents lower neck, shoulders, arms, right ear, hands, shoulders and collar bones, thyroid gland, respiratory and nervous systems. The weakness of the third house and/or afflictions to the third house or its lord cause vulnerability to problems of respiratory canal, disorders of thyroid, imbalances in the nervous system, depression resulting in partial paralysis, stammering, shoulder pains, fracture in the collar bone region, partial deafness, respiratory diseases, asthma, tuberculosis, etc. Strong Mercury, as a significator of communicative capability, helps as a protective cover.

FOURTH HOUSE: Represents the rib cage, heart, blood vessels, chest, lungs and breasts. The weakness of the fourth house and/or afflictions to the fourth house or its lord cause vulnerability to coronary problems, physical ailments of breast, chest, asthma, heart and epigastria region, lungs' disorders, mental disorders, lunacy and the problems connected to the circulatory systems. A strong Moon as a significator of blood, Venus as significator of vascular system and Mars as significator of muscles help as a protective cover.

FIFTH HOUSE: Represents upper belly, stomach, liver, gall bladder, pancreas, spleen, colon, diaphragm, spine and spinal cord. The weakness of the fifth house and/or afflictions to the fifth house or its lord cause vulnerability to diabetes, peptic ulcers, anemia, colic pains, stones in gall bladder, acidity, spinal cord disorders, dyspepsia, diarrhea, pleurisy, etc. A strong Sun, as significator of digestion - nourishing agent of the body, helps as a protective cover.

SIXTH HOUSE: Represents waist, navel, lower abdomen, kidneys, small intestine, upper part of large intestine, intestinal function and appendix. The weakness of the sixth house and/or afflictions to the sixth house or its lord cause vulnerability to problems of appendicitis, poisoning, colic, constipation, hernia, blood urea, psychiatric problems, exhaustion and nervous breakdown. Health is identified through this house. A strong Mercury and Mars, as significators for health, help as a protective cover.

SEVENTH HOUSE: Represents pelvic girdle, lumbar region, urinary bladder, lower part of large intestine, inner sexual organs such as ovaries, uterus, cervix, testicles and prostate gland, etc. The weakness of the seventh house and/or afflictions to the seventh house or its lord cause vulnerability to generative organs, venereal diseases, arthritis, gout pains, urination problems, menstrual disorders, impotency, sterilization, renal problems, etc. A strong Venus, as significator for kidney functioning, helps as a protective cover.

EIGHTH HOUSE: Represents scrotum and anus, outer sexual organs, excretory organs, pelvic bones, etc. The weakness of the eighth house and/or afflictions to the eighth house or its lord cause vulnerability to hydrocele, fissure, impotency, piles, urinary infections, boils, chronic diseases, etc. A strong Saturn, as significator for longevity, helps as a protective cover.

NINTH HOUSE: Represents thighs, left leg, thigh bones, bone marrow, hips, hip joints and the arterial system. The weakness of the ninth house and/or afflictions to the ninth house or its lord cause vulnerability to anemia, low productivity of blood, thalassemia, leukemia, high fevers, rheumatism and troubles in hips and thighs, etc. A strong Jupiter, as significator for liver, and a strong Sun, as significator for digestion, helps as a protective cover.

TENTH HOUSE: Represents knee and kneecaps, joints and bones. The weakness of the tenth house and/or afflictions to the tenth house or its lord cause vulnerability to arthritis, broken knees, inflammation of joints, general weakness, skin diseases and allergies, emaciated body, etc, besides giving setbacks in professional matters. A strong Sun, as significator for bones, helps as a protective cover.

ELEVENTH HOUSE: Represents shanks, ankles, shin bone, right leg, left ear and left arm. The weakness of the eleventh house and/or afflictions to the eleventh house or its lord cause vulnerability to circulatory problems, fracture of the lower portion of legs, pain in legs, problems of low productivity of blood, cancer of leg, etc. A strong Saturn, as significator for joints, helps as a protective cover.

TWELFTH HOUSE: Represents left eye, lymphatic system and feet. The weakness of the twelfth house and/or afflictions to the twelfth house or its lord result in problems to the body parts governed by this house, sleep disturbances, auto-immune disorder and weakens the immunization power. A strong Moon, as significator for immunization power, helps as a protective cover.

FRUCTIFICATION OF SIGNIFICATIONS

The signification of the houses fructify under the planetary sub-periods connected with them. The nature and extent of significations are dependent on three things, i.e. (1) the strength of the lord of the house in case of mooltrikona signs; (2) the strength of the significator of the house; and (3) the influences on the house itself. The significations of the houses containing mooltrikona signs suffer if their lords and significators are weak or they or their lords or significators are under the influence of functional malefic planets. The significations of the houses containing non-mooltrikona signs suffer if their significators are weak or they or their significators are under the close influence of functional malefic planets.

CHAPTER 4

SIGNIFICATIONS OF PLANETS

THE SUN

The Sun is significator for vitality and is a life giver in any birth chart because it rules the digestive system which provides nourishment to the whole body. It is bilious and has sturdy bones. It is hot, dry and constructive. It represents bone structure, constitution, blood, brain, stomach, bile, digestive fire, heart as life-centre, eyesight, gall-bladder, spine and belly. In case it is weak and/or afflicted in a birth chart, it makes the person vulnerable to weak eyesight, headaches, erratic blood circulation, heart trouble, bone fractures, overheating, fevers, blood pressure, baldness, neuralgia, bone cancer, weak immune system, etc.

THE MOON

The Moon is cold, moist and its constitution is a mixture of vata and kapha. The Moon represents fertility, emotional health and functional health as it governs fluids in body, good quality of blood and lymph, glands, tonsils, breasts, lymphatic system, face, lungs and chest. It also governs ovaries, menstrual cycle, uterus and generative organs. In case it is weak and/or afflicted in a birth chart, besides psychic problems it makes the person vulnerable to sleep disorders, lethargy, drowsiness, lung problems, mouth problems (including loss of taste), neurological disorders, epilepsy, digestive problems, water retention, blood disorders, anemia, blood-pressure problems, enlargement of spleen, diseases of the uterus and ovaries, tuberculosis, menstrual disorders, auto-immune disorder and the native is vulnerable to frequent cough and cold, fever, lack of appetite, general weakness, etc., and denotes hyper-sensitivity, over-reaction, inability to respond and difficulty in getting touch with feelings. The Moon is also general significator for sleep, emotional peace and immune power.

MARS

Mars is dry, fiery and pitta in nature. Mars represents the head, bone marrow, blood, bile, digestive fire, intestine, forehead, neck, muscular system, sinews, nose and external generative organs. In case it is weak and/or afflicted in a birth chart, it makes the person vulnerable to inflammations, overheating, inability to tolerate hunger, wounds, burns, accidents, fractures, piles, skin rashes, ulcers, lacerations, operations, all sorts of acute complaints, fevers (particularly eruptive), epilepsy, mental aberration, tumors, cancer in the muscular parts of the body when closely conjunct with Rahu, dysentery, typhoid, cholera, pox and boils, etc., and denotes anger, irritability, haste, impatience, inconstancy, lack of drive and courage, and an 'all-or-nothing' attitude.

MERCURY

Mercury is a mixture of vata, pitta and kapha. Mercury represents the lower part of abdomen, skin, mind, nervous system, lower neck, bronchial tube, gastric juice, intestines, tongue, mouth, hands and arms. In case it is weak and/or afflicted in a birth chart, it makes the person vulnerable to psychic diseases, insomnia, nervous breakdown, epilepsy, skin diseases, leucoderma, impotence, loss of memory or speech, vertigo, deafness, asthma, diseases of respiratory canal, disorders of intestines, dyspepsia, auto-immune, etc., and denotes difficulty in thought and communication, timidity, low self-esteem, aloofness, abnormality, expediency, over-intellectualization and poor discrimination.

JUPITER

Jupiter is a mild, temperate and warm planet and is phlegmatic in nature. Jupiter represents the hips, the fat tissue, blood, arterial system, glands, liver/gall bladder, pancreas gland, digestion, absorptive power, ears/hearing power, navel, feet, physical development, palate and throat. In case it is weak and/or afflicted in a birth chart, it makes the person vulnerable to lymphatic and circulatory congestion, thrombosis, anemia, tumors, jaundice and other liver complaints, ear problems, dyspepsia, flatulence, cough, cold, phthisis, diabetes and diseases of pancreas glands, etc.

VENUS

Venus is warm and moist planet and its constitution is a mixture of kapha and vata. Venus represents the pelvis and the sexual organs, reproductive parts, glands, the semen/ovum, private parts, kidneys, urinary bladder, face, eyes, upper neck, throat, chin, cheeks, skin, venous system, etc. In case it is weak and/or afflicted in a birth chart, it makes the person vulnerable to venereal diseases, diseases of urinary or reproductive system, diabetes, anemia, stones in bladder or kidneys, cataract, weakness of sexual organs, paralysis, sexual perversions, impotence or inability to have sexual relations, loss of bodily luster, etc.

SATURN

Saturn is a cold and dry planet. Its humor is predominantly vata. Saturn represents the nerve tissue, tendons, joints, spleen, teeth, knees, shin and part of leg between ankle and knee, phlegm and secretive system and bones. In case it is weak and afflicted in a birth chart, it makes the person vulnerable to painful diseases, all sorts of chronic and degenerative diseases, leg fracture, cancer, diseases of glands, skin diseases, paralysis, arthritis, rheumatism, gout, emaciation, rickets, consumption, flatulence, deformities, coldness of the body, nerve disorders, indigestion, dyspepsia, insanity, numbness, windy diseases, senility, impotence in men, pain and obstruction in the functions of the body like retention of urine, intestinal obstruction, etc.

RAHU

Rahu is mixture of kapha and vata. When afflicting, it causes diseases of phlegm, intestines, boils, skin, nervous system, ulcers, allergies, spleen, worms, high blood pressure, heart trouble, epidemics, psychic disturbances, hallucinations, hysteria, insanity, epilepsy, conditions resulting from all sorts of poisons, alcoholism, mysterious diseases, leprosy, indigestion, gas accumulation in stomach or intestines, insect bite, hiccough, swelling, pain or injury in the feet, cancer, etc. If afflicting or malefically disposed or afflicted by other functional malefic planets, it generates fears, phobias, nightmares, inertia, dullness and laziness.

KETU

Ketu is dry and fiery in nature and explosive in temperament. It rules the humor of bile (pitta). If afflicting or malefically disposed or afflicted by other functional malefic planets, it causes wounds, injuries, diseases in spine and nervous system, consumption, surgery, ulcers, inflammations, fevers, intestinal diseases, mental aberration, low blood pressure, deafness, defective speech, addictions, mental aberrations, skin diseases, stuttering, spasms, etc.

GENERAL

The impact of planets decrease or increase depending upon their weakness/affliction or strength and good influences on them in a particular nativity (birth chart) as also due to their placement in a particular house or in a particular sign.

CHAPTER 5

ADVANCED ANALYTICAL TECHNIQUES

SALIENT FEATURES OF THE SYSTEMS' APPROACH

For the benefit of the readers, the prominent features of the Systems' Approach are being discussed here. Events/indications in life are ruled by the interplay of the planets, houses, signs and planetary periods. The planets during their operating periods bless the native with the significations ruled by them depending upon their strength and placement in a particular horoscope. Identifying the weakness/affliction of planets is not at all a difficult job and can be learnt by beginners or non-astrologers in an easy manner. The Systems' Approach not only increases the accuracy of analysis but also speeds up the analytical process, helps in identifying the results of analysis in an unambiguous manner, consistently and without any confusion.

If the medical personnel learn Vedic Astrology, their dual competence will help humanity at large and will enhance satisfaction and personal eminence of the medical practitioners. Besides the protection from dreaded diseases through preventive astral remedies, the astral remedies tackle the problems of sterility, impotency, help in getting a healthy male child in addition to other areas of life governed by the same planet e.g. professional growth, harmonious married life, acquisition of wealth/property and status. For example, one with defects in the right eye suffers in his professional growth, suffers from loss of status, problems in married life and would be vulnerable to cardiovascular diseases, thyroid glands, etc. At the same time, one with phenomenal ambitions would be vulnerable to nervous breakdown, acidity and runs the risk of a paralytic attack. We hope this gives a clear understanding of the linkage between the planetary strengths and diseases, general problems in life, etc.

The key issues in horoscope analysis are:

(1) Identifying the functional nature of planets in a nativity;

(2) The techniques for judging the strength of a planet;

(3) The distinction between weak planets and afflicted planets;

(4) The impact of weak and/or afflicted planets;

(5) The orb of longitudinal difference for judging the impact of conjunctions and aspects;

(6) The most malefic influence;

(7) The most effective point of various houses in a horoscope.

FUNCTIONAL NATURE OF PLANETS

The functional nature of planets is the key analytical factor in the horoscope analysis. Besides Rahu and Ketu, the planets, whose mooltrikona signs are in malefic houses (sixth, eighth and twelfth) with reference to the ascendant, act as functional malefic planets in a nativity. For this purpose, under the Systems' Approach the sign Cancer is considered as the mooltrikona sign of the Moon.

For various ascending signs, the functional malefic planets are mentioned hereunder:

ASCENDANT	FUNCTIONAL MALEFIC PLANETS
1. Aries	Mercury, Rahu and Ketu.
2. Taurus	Venus, Jupiter, Mars, Rahu and Ketu.
3. Gemini	Rahu and Ketu.
4. Cancer	Jupiter, Saturn, Rahu and Ketu.
5. Leo	The Moon, Rahu and Ketu.
6. Virgo	Saturn, Mars, the Sun, Rahu and Ketu.
7. Libra	Mercury, Rahu and Ketu.
8. Scorpio	Mars, Venus, Rahu and Ketu.
9. Sagittarius	The Moon, Rahu and Ketu.
10. Capricorn	The Sun, Jupiter, Rahu and Ketu.
11. Aquarius	The Moon, Mercury, Rahu and Ketu.
12. Pisces	The Sun, Venus, Saturn, Rahu and Ketu.

The functional nature of any planet depends on the nature of the mooltrikona house of that planet. It is not related to the strength of the planet. A planet may be weak or strong but the functional nature will remain same as per the defined principle for identifying the functional nature of planets.

SPECIAL IMPACT OF RAHU AND KETU

In exceptional cases, when Rahu is well placed in a mooltrikona sign of a planet, without causing any conjunction or close aspect with other houses and planets and its dispositor is strong, Rahu gives good results during its sub-periods for materialistic prosperity. Rahu-Ketu, when exalted, give materialist benefits while debilitated Rahu involves the native in exposed scandals and acute physical sufferings.

The functional malefic planets for various ascendants, mentioned above, may appear to be at variance when seen in the context of the available classical texts, but when you analyze the charts based on the functional malefic planets brought out hereinabove, you would find that all of your confusions disappear at one stroke. The classical principles were laid down by Maharishi Parashara in Dwapara yuga and changes, mutatis mutandis (wherever necessary) have been suggested for the nativities in Kaliyuga.

The functional benefic planets for various ascending signs are as under:

ASCENDANT	FUNCTIONAL BENEFIC PLANETS
1. Aries	The Sun, the Moon, Mars, Jupiter, Venus and Saturn.
2. Taurus	The Sun, the Moon, Mercury and Saturn.
3. Gemini	The Sun, the Moon, Mars, Mercury, Jupiter, Venus and Saturn.
4. Cancer	The Sun, the Moon, Mars, Mercury, and Venus.
5. Leo	The Sun, Mars, Mercury, Jupiter, Venus and Saturn.
6. Virgo	The Moon, Mercury, Jupiter and Venus.
7. Libra	The Sun, the Moon, Mars, Jupiter, Venus and Saturn.
8. Scorpio	The Sun, the Moon, Mercury, Jupiter and Saturn.
9. Sagittarius	The Sun, Mars, Mercury, Jupiter, Venus and Saturn.
10. Capricorn	The Moon, Mars, Mercury, Venus and Saturn.
11. Aquarius	The Sun, Mars, Jupiter, Venus and Saturn.
12. Pisces	The Moon, Mars, Mercury and Jupiter.

It is necessary to understand the difference between afflicting planets and afflicted planets.

AFFLICTED PLANETS OR HOUSES

The afflictions to the planets or houses are caused by the close conjunction or aspect of the functional malefic planets. Whenever a planet or a mooltrikona house is already weak for any other reason and is under the close influence of any functional malefic, it is treated as an afflicted planet/house. But when the planet or the mooltrikona house is not weak for other reasons, it can be considered afflicted either under the exact influence of a functional malefic for normal afflictions or under the orb of influence of two degrees for special/multiple afflictions, becoming a weak planet/house for that reason. So whenever any planet or mooltrikona house is afflicted, it becomes weak not being capable of fully protecting/ promoting its significations. The significations of the houses having mooltrikona sign of an afflicted planet are harmed more when such planets are already weak for other reasons.

Whenever a non-mooltrikona house is under the close influence of any functional malefic, it is treated as an afflicted house.

If not placed in its own mooltrikona sign, any planet becomes afflicted just by mere placement in any of the dusthanas/malefic houses.

AFFLICTING PLANETS

The functional malefic planets act as afflicting planets.

A transit functional malefic planet will always afflict its natal position by conjunction or aspect, except when placed in its own mooltrikona house in rasi/birth chart. A natal/transit functional malefic planet never afflicts its own mooltrikona house, except when the functional malefic planet is already afflicted and afflicts from a dusthana/malefic house.

Dispositor weakness or bad placement affliction is not applicable in the case of placement of a planet in its mooltrikona house. The benefit of aspect to the mooltrikona sign of a functional malefic planet is limited to the proportion of the strength of the functional malefic planet.

THE MOST EFFECTIVE POINT OF A HOUSE

Besides the natal position of the planets, there is the most effective point (MEP) of each house known by the degree rising in the ascendant. The close impact of the planets in the case of houses is gauged through their closeness to the natal positions. Suppose an ascendant of 16 degrees rises. It means the most effective point of each house would be 16 degrees. In case the lord of a mooltrikona house is weak or in case of non-mooltrikona houses, a functional malefic planet having a longitude between 11 to 21 degrees will afflict these houses either by placement or by aspect. In case the lord of a mooltrikona house is "otherwise" strong, that house will only become afflicted under the single influence of a functional malefic planet having a longitude between 15 to 17 degrees, or under the multiple/special influence of functional malefic planet(s) having longitudes between 14 to 18 degrees. That "otherwise" strong lord will become weak for this reason. The influence of any functional malefic planet over its own mooltrikona house will never be malefic.

THE MOST MALEFIC INFLUENCE

Mostly, the people seeking advantage of Astrology remember it in the time of distress. Therefore, the first thing is to gauge the strength of the planets so that the influences of functional malefic planets on the weak planets can be analyzed. The most malefic influence in a nativity is that of the most malefic planet.

MOST MALEFIC PLANET

If there is a mooltrikona sign in the eighth house from the ascendant, its lord is called the most malefic planet (MMP). In case there is no mooltrikona sign in the eighth house then the role of the most malefic planet is played by the lord of the twelfth house containing a mooltrikona sign. And if there is no mooltrikona sign in the twelfth house, too, then the role of the most malefic planet is played by Ketu. For various ascendants the most malefic planets are as under:

ASCENDANT	MOST MALEFIC PLANET
Aries	Ketu
Taurus	Jupiter
Gemini	Ketu
Cancer	Saturn
Leo	The Moon
Virgo	Mars
Libra	Mercury
Scorpio	Venus
Sagittarius	The Moon
Capricorn	The Sun
Aquarius	Mercury
Pisces	Venus

If the planet or the lord of the house, with which the most malefic planet is forming a close conjunction/aspect, is strong, this most malefic planet creates tension(s) with regard to the matters represented by the house/planet involved. When the afflicted planet is weak, the significations suffer seriously. When the afflicted planet is badly placed, it results in tragic happenings. To understand the difference between tension, serious trouble and tragic happenings consider the situations of fever, jaundice and the loss of a limb ruled by the concerned planet, respectively. Any affliction caused by the triple transit triggering influence of a functional malefic planet can trigger the trouble, especially if it involves a slow moving planet in transit. When the affliction is close to the most effective point of the house, significations of all the houses involved, that is the house occupied and the house(s) aspected, suffer. In the case of the afflicted planets, besides their general significations, the significations of the house where their mooltrikona sign is placed, and the significations of the house where the planet is placed, also suffer.

THE MOST BENEFIC INFLUENCE

If there is a mooltrikona sign in the fourth house from the ascendant, its lord is called the most benefic planet (MBP). In case there is no mooltrikona sign in the fourth house, then the role of the most benefic planet is played by the lord of the second house containing the mooltrikona sign. In case there is no mooltrikona sign in the second house, then the role of the most benefic planet is played by the lord of the ninth house containing the mooltrikona sign. And if there is no mooltrikona sign in the ninth house, too, then the role of the most benefic planet is played by the lord of the third house containing the mooltrikona sign. For various ascendants the most benefic planets are as under:

ASCENDANT	MOST BENEFIC PLANET
Aries	The Moon
Taurus	The Sun
Gemini	Mercury
Cancer	Venus
Leo	Mercury
Virgo	Jupiter
Libra	Jupiter
Scorpio	Saturn
Sagittarius	The Sun
Capricorn	Mars
Aquarius	Venus
Pisces	Mars

EFFECTIVE ORB FOR JUDGING THE INFLUENCE OF NATAL/TRANSIT CONJUNCTIONS/ASPECTS

In the case of influence of functional malefic planets over the most effective points of mooltrikona houses/planets simultaneously strong in rasi and transit, the orb is one degree on either side for normal afflictions and two degrees on either side for special/multiple afflictions, while in the case of mooltrikona houses/planets either weak in rasi or in transit, the orb is five degrees on either side.

In the case of influence of strong functional benefic planets over the most effective points of mooltrikona houses/planets simultaneously strong in rasi and transit, the orb is five degrees on either side, while in the case of mooltrikona houses/planets either weak in rasi or in transit, the orb is one degree on either side. Under the influence of natal/transit functional malefic planets, all planets get malefically influenced.

The maximum influence of the transit or natal conjunction/ aspect is when it is within one degree on either side. As soon as the transit influence starts separating, the influence starts tapering down. It is very important to see the strength of the planet on which the transit influence is being studied. For example, if the Sun, being the lord of the fourth house, is placed in the fourth house and its longitude is eleven degrees and is strong, the functional malefic influence of Jupiter, the most malefic planet for the Taurus ascendant, will be effective when Jupiter is between 9 degrees and 13 degrees in the signs Leo, Sagittarius, Aquarius or Aries, while the single functional malefic influence of Mars will be effective when Mars is between 10 degrees and 12 degrees in the signs Leo, Capricorn, Aquarius or Taurus, because the Sun is strong in the natal chart. Please do not forget to consider the transit strength of this Sun. If the Sun in a Taurus nativity is placed in the sign Libra at a longitude of five degrees then the transit influence of Jupiter over it would be effective whenever Jupiter transits from zero degrees to 10 degrees in Libra, Aquarius, Aries or Gemini, and the transit influence of Mars over it would be effective whenever Mars transits from zero degrees to 10 degrees in Libra, Pisces, Aries or Cancer. However, once the longitude of the transit Jupiter or the transit Mars is 5 degrees, the transit influence would start separating and tapering down but it will clear the affliction only when their longitude is over ten degrees, assuming they are in direct movement. The orb of affliction for a non-mooltrikona house is five degrees on either side of the most effective point. We hope the readers are able to understand this dimension for better analysis.

MEASURING STRENGTH OF THE HOUSES

In case a mooltrikona sign falls in a house, the strength of the house is gauged through the strength of the lord and the nature of the conjunctions/aspects to the most effective point of the house. In the case of non-mooltrikona signs, the strength of the house is gauged only through the nature of the conjunctions/aspects to its most effective point. You will find in your experience that until and unless there is a close influence of a functional malefic planet on the most effective point of a house, the significations of the house containing a non-mooltrikona sign will not bother the person, at all. That is to say that the person will not seek astral consultation or remedies for the significations of the unafflicted houses containing a non-mooltrikona sign. The rising degree in the ascendant is known as the most effective point of all the houses.

DISPOSITOR

According to the Systems' Approach, the dispositor is a planet in whose mooltrikona sign another planet is located in the natal chart. Suppose in a natal chart the Sun is placed in the sign Libra ruled by Venus. In this case Venus will be the dispositor of the Sun. No planet which is in a non-mooltrikona sign will have a dispositor i.e. the planet(s) in Taurus, Gemini, Scorpio, Capricorn and Pisces have no dispositor. If a planet is posited in Aries, its dispositor would be Mars; if a planet is posited in Cancer, its dispositor would be the Moon; if a planet is posited in Leo, its dispositor would be the Sun; if a planet is posited in Virgo, its dispositor would be Mercury; if a planet is posited in Libra, its dispositor would be Venus; if a planet is posited in Sagittarius, its dispositor would be Jupiter; and if a planet is posited in Aquarius, its dispositor would be Saturn.

When a functional benefic planet becomes dispositor of an affliction, the results of such affliction will surface during the sub period and transit influence of that functional benefic planet. Similarly, when a functional benefic planet becomes dispositor of a benefic influence or blessing, the results of such benefic influence or blessing will surface during the sub period and transit influence of that functional benefic planet.

When a functional malefic planet becomes dispositor of a benefic influence or blessing, the results of such benefic influence or blessing will also simultaneously surface during the sub period and transit influence of that functional malefic planet provided the functional malefic planet is not involved in a close or exact affliction.

When a functional malefic planet becomes dispositor of an affliction, the results of such affliction will also surface during the sub period and transit influence of that functional malefic planet.

STRONG PLANETS

A strong natal planet protects and promotes its general significations and the significations of its mooltrikona house. Any planet is considered strong when its longitude is within 5 to 25 degrees and it is not in the state of weakness. It can increase its strength if:

a)   it occupies own or good navamsa and other divisions.

b)   it is under the close influence of functional benefic planets.

c)   it occupies its exaltation or mooltrikona sign.

d)   it is placed in the Sun-like houses, that is the second, third and ninth houses.

Any planet has capacity to bless the native with its results if its natal strength is at least 60% and it is unafflicted. In such a situation the results may come with some delay and of slightly lower order. With the help of the strengthening measures - gemstones or special power Kavach - the strength of the planets, where it is less than 60%, can be brought to the level of 60% so that it blesses the native with the significations ruled by it.

One can strengthen the weak planets (i) by way of a Kavach if the planetary strength is between 50% to 60%; (ii) by way of a special power Kavach if the planetary strength is between 35% to 50%; and (iii) by way of a special purpose Kavach with gemstones if the planetary strength is lower than 35%.

WEAK PLANETS

A weak natal planet is not capable of fully protecting/ promoting its general significations and the significations of its mooltrikona house during the course of its sub-periods and during the triple transit functional malefic influences. A planet becomes weak when:

1)   The most effective point of its mooltrikona sign is afflicted by a functional malefic planet within an orb of one degree.

2)   The most effective point of its house of placement is afflicted by a functional malefic planet, within an orb of one degree for mooltrikona signs or within an orb of five degrees for non-mooltrikona signs.

3)   It is conjunct or aspected by any functional malefic planet within an orb of one degree.

4)   It is combust due to its nearness to the Sun.

5) It occupies malefic houses from the ascendant, except if it is in its own mooltrikona sign.

6) It occupies its sign of debilitation.

7) It is in infancy or old-age.

8) It occupies its debilitated sign in navamsa.

9) It occupies the mooltrikona sign of a weak planet. However, its strength would be equal to the strength of its dispositor.

In case of special or multiple afflictions, the otherwise "strong" planet is considered afflicted (and weak), even when the orb of affliction is of two degrees.

The affliction is special or multiple i.e. when it comes from:

1) a conjunction with/ aspect from the most malefic planet,

2) an aspect from a functional malefic planet placed in a dusthana,

3) a conjunction with Rahu or Ketu (Rahu-Ketu axis),

4) an aspect of a functional malefic planet afflicted by other(s) functional malefic planet,

5) more than one functional malefic planet at the same time,

Fairly strong planet: A planet which has at least 70% power, is unafflicted and well placed, is considered as fairly strong planet.

Mild affliction: An affliction to the extent of 25% or less to a strong or fairly strong planet or the most effective point of a non-mooltrikona sign house is considered as a mild affliction.

The quantitative strength analysis for the planets can be obtained with the help of the following insights:

a) A planet will lose strength to the extent of 75% if its mooltrikona sign house is afflicted.

b) A weak planet placed in an afflicted house will lose strength to the extent of 75%.

c) An otherwise strong planet placed in a non mooltrikona sign afflicted house will lose strength to the extent of 50%. Such a planet may give good results in the first place and will cause setbacks later.

d) A closely afflicted weak planet will lose strength to the extent of 75%.

e) A closely afflicted otherwise strong planet will lose strength to the extent of 50%. Such a planet will give good results in the first place and will cause setbacks later.

f) A planet becoming weak due to close combustion will lose strength to the extent of 75% if the Sun is a functional malefic planet. Where the Sun is a functional benefic and it causes combustion to another planet, the planet will become 50% weak for the purpose of transit affliction. A combust planet in its sign of debilitation and placed in a malefic house will have only 10% power.

g) When planets are placed in the malefic houses, they generally lose strength by 50% besides suffering through the significations of the malefic house. The placement in the sixth house can involve the person in disputes, debts and can cause ill health. The placement in the eighth house can cause serious obstructions for the significations ruled by the planet. The placement in the twelfth house can cause expenses and losses for the significations of the planet.

h) When planets are placed in their signs of debilitation, they lose strength by 50%. When planets are placed in their signs of debilitation in birth chart and navamsa, they lose strength by 75%.

i) If in Rasi chart the planet is badly placed and at the same time debilitated in navamsa it would lose strength to the extent of 60%.

j) A badly placed planet in its sign of debilitation will lose its power by 75%.

k)   A planet debilitated in navamsa would lose power by 25%.

When the lord of the sixth house is in the ascendant the person gets involved in controversies. Discussing such a person also breeds controversies.

SUN-LIKE PLANETS

The second house rules the status of the person in the society or with the Government. The third house rules the communication power of the person which is an important aspect for leadership. The ninth house is the house of fortune and rules happiness from father and preceptor. The lords of the second, third and ninth houses, wherever other than the Sun, act like the Sun for the various ascendants:

ASCENDANT	SUN LIKE PLANETS
1. Aries	Jupiter
2. Taurus	The Moon
3. Gemini	The Moon and Saturn
4. Cancer	Mercury
5. Leo	Mercury, Venus and Mars
6. Virgo	Venus
7. Libra	Jupiter
8. Scorpio	Jupiter and the Moon
9. Sagittarius	Saturn
10. Capricorn	Saturn and Mercury
11. Aquarius	Mars and Venus
12. Pisces	Mars

Any planet placed in the sign Leo has comparatively more power and certainly up by 25% than the actual power of the said planet(s).

When being the lord of the second house a Sun-like planet is placed in Leo sign it gains additional strength.

When the Sun itself is placed in a Sun-like house, it also gains 25% additional strength. In case the Sun is a functional malefic planet when placed in a Sun like house, it should not afflict the house to gain the additional strength.

If the Leo sign is in a malefic house and the Sun is placed in this house, the bad placement of the Sun would not be applicable and the Sun would be strong if not in infancy, old age or debilitated in navamsa.

Let us take an example for understanding the calculation of the strength of the Sun-like planets. Suppose Libra is rising with 22.4 deg. The Sun is placed in the fourth House, close to the MEP and unafflicted. It is not in old age. The MEP of the eleventh house is also unafflicted. This Sun would be strong but not having any additional strength.

Suppose Aries is rising and if Jupiter is in 9th House (Sun-like) in its own mooltrikona sign but in infancy (2.5 deg) and Jupiter is unafflicted, then its strength would be 50% + 25 increase for its being a Sun- like planet which is equal to 62.5%. If Jupiter is placed in another Sun-like house, its strength will have a further rise of 25%. A planet by being lord of a Sun- like house and by being placed in another Sun-like house can achieve the strength up to 100% in commensuration to its weakness due to infancy or old age.

In the case of Sun-like planets, the lord of the second house gets the first place, the lord of the third house gets the second place and the lord of the ninth house gets third place in importance.

Any planet has capacity to bless the native with its results if its natal strength is at least 60% and it is unafflicted. In such a situation the results may come with some delay and of slightly lower order. With the help of the strengthening measures - gemstones or Kavach - the strength of the planets, where it is less than 60%, can be brought to the level of 60% so that it blesses the native with the significations ruled by it.

One can strengthen the weak planets (i) by way of a Kavach if the planetary strength is between 50% to 60%; (ii) by way of a special power Kavach if the planetary strength is between 35% to 50%; and (iii) by way of a special purpose Kavach with gemstones if the planetary strength is lower than 35%.

SIGNIFICATORS: In addition to ruling the houses containing their mooltrikona signs, the planets also act as Karakas (significators) for various houses. The various planets act as significators for the houses indicated against each:

PLANET	HOUSES
The Sun	First, second, third, ninth and tenth houses.
The Moon	Fourth house.
Mars	Third and tenth houses.
Mercury	Third, sixth and tenth houses.
Jupiter	Second, fifth, ninth and eleventh houses.
Venus	Fourth, seventh and twelfth houses.
Saturn	Ayushkaraka (longevity) i.e. the eighth house.

When strong, the various planets act as secondary significators for the following houses/matters:

PLANET	HOUSE/MATTER
The Sun	Fifth house, digestion, heart, leadership, job.
The Moon	Tenth house/Public relations.
Mars	First house/Energy.
	Fourth house/Real estate.
	Sixth house/Health.
Mercury	Second house/Speech.
	Third house/Communication ability.
	Sixth house/Health.
Jupiter	Ninth house/Spiritual fulfillment.
Venus	Twelfth house/Happy married life and comforts.
Saturn	Eleventh house/Easy income.

RAHU-LIKE PLANETS

The mooltrikona sign lords of the eighth and twelfth houses act as Rahu-like planets. The Rahu-like planets give inclinations for greed, over ambitiousness, encroachments, materialistic pursuits, lust, obstructions, mishaps and loss of patience.

Where there is no mooltrikona sign in the sixth house, afflicting Ketu acts as sixth lord being significator for injuries, financial constraints and losses through disputes.

RESULTS OF EXCHANGE OF HOUSES OR ASTERISMS

In classical works the situation, in which a planet 'A' is placed in a sign or nakshatra ruled by the planet 'B' and the planet 'B' is placed in a sign or nakshatra ruled by the planet 'A', is considered as exchange of houses or exchange of nakshatra (asterisms). For example, if the Sun is placed in the sign Scorpio and the planet Mars is placed in the sign, Leo, then the classical works consider this as exchange of houses by the Sun and Mars.

Under the Systems' Approach, we do not recognize this concept. Each planet is considered, separately, for its placement, strength, relationship with other planets, etc.

TRIPLE TRANSIT TRIGGERING INFLUENCE

The significant events are triggered by the interplay of the relationship between transit planets and natal planets/MEPs. The results generated depend upon the significations ruled by the planets involved, the significations ruled by their mooltrikona houses, the significations ruled by their houses of placement, either natally or in transit, and/or the significations ruled by the natal house(s) whose MEPs are under transit impact. This is called the triple transit triggering influence (TTT) as it is true for the three possible combinations of transit influence i.e. transit over natal, transit over transit, and natal over transit. In other words:

1) Whenever any weak natal planet/MEP is transited by FM(s), it triggers a significant undesirable incident concerning that weak natal planet or that weak house, whichever is the case. This is more so when the weak natal planet or the lord/ significator of the weak house is weak in transit too.

2) Whenever any strong natal planet/MEP is transited by FM(s), it triggers a mild unfavorable incident concerning that strong natal planet or that strong house, whichever is the case.

3) Whenever any weak natal FB/MEP is transited by FB(s), it triggers hopes or non-significant happy incidents concerning that planet or house, whichever is the case.

4) Whenever any strong natal FB/MEP is transited by FB(s), it triggers significant happy incidents concerning that planet or house, whichever is the case. This is more so when the planet or the lord/significator of the house is strong in transit too.

5) Whenever planets in transit form close conjunctions amongst themselves, the happenings occur depending upon their functional nature in connection with the houses with reference to a particular ascendant.

6) If the close conjunction or aspect(s) of planets in transit involve two or more FBs with reference to a particular ascendant, it triggers happy events pertaining to all the planets.

7) If one of the planets involved in close conjunction or aspect in a transit planetary movement is a FM, it harms the significations of the other FB(s) involved with reference to a particular ascendant.

8) If both or all the planets forming close conjunction in transit with reference to a particular ascendant are FMs, it harms the significations of all the planets involved.

9) Whenever any weak transit planet forms close conjunction with or become closely aspected by natal FM(s), it triggers a significant undesirable incident concerning that weak transit planet. This is more so when the planet is weak in rasi too.

10) Whenever any strong transit planet forms close conjunction with or become closely aspected by natal FM(s), it triggers a mild unfavorable incident concerning that strong transit planet.

11) Whenever any weak transit FB forms close conjunction with or become closely aspected by natal FB(s), it triggers hopes or non-significant happy incidents pertaining to that weak transit planet.

12) Whenever any strong transit FB forms close conjunction with or become closely aspected by natal FB(s), it triggers significant happy incidents pertaining to that strong transit planet. This is more so when the planet is strong in rasi too.

13) The transit effects are always seen with reference to the natal ascendant.

14) In setting the trends, the sub-period lord has maximum say. However, the transit impacts mentioned above supersede the trend results of the sub-period lord.

15) The malefic transit impact of slow moving FMs like Jupiter, Saturn, Rahu and Ketu is more pronounced when, during the course of their close conjunctions/aspects, they move more slowly as compared to their normal speed or become stationary. This is true both for natal and transit influences.

16) During the sub-periods of the FBs, the transit impacts of FBs are stronger while transit impacts of FMs are mild. If the sub-period lord is strong, then the transit influences of FBs cause significant happy events.

17) During the sub-periods of FMs, the transit impacts of FBs are mild while the transit impacts of FMs are more severe. If the

transit influences are from strong FBs, then the benefic results may be comparatively better but with some delay.

18) The duration of the transit results ceases to exist as soon as the transit close conjunction or aspect separates. The orb of separation as explained earlier would depend upon the strength of the planets on which the transit influences have been created.

19) Whenever a transiting FM transits the MEP of any house, it afflicts that house as well as the aspected house(s). A transit FM never afflicts its own mooltrikona house, except when the functional malefic planet is already afflicted and/or afflicts from a dusthana/malefic house.

20) A transit FM will always afflict its natal position by conjunction or aspect, except when natally placed in its own mooltrikona house.

21) A natal FM will always afflict its transit position by aspect even when transiting its own mooltrikona house.

22) A natal FM will always afflict its transit position by conjunction, except when placed in its own mooltrikona house.

The triple transit triggering influence will help you in understanding the impact of planetary influences more precisely. For further detailed study the interested readers may study our book, Triple Transit Influence of Planets.

RELATIVE IMPORTANCE OF PLANETARY INFLUENCES

Regarding afflictions, we can have:

1) Afflictions in rasi/natal chart.

2) Afflictions of transit on rasi.

3) Afflictions of transit on transit.

4) Afflictions of rasi on transit.

Afflictions in Rasi, being permanent afflictions, are more serious as they will manifest during all life as malefic tendencies present whenever the sub-periods of related planets are operating. They depend on the strength of the afflicted planets and the number/ proximity/maleficness of the afflictors. In the last three cases, as they are temporary afflictions, their degree of importance depend more on the lack of strength of the afflicted planets, the number/ duration of the afflictions, the proximity/maleficness of the afflictors, and the ruling sub-period in each case. The last ones, afflictions of rasi on transit, are even more important than the other two for all the ascendants containing fast moving planets as functional malefic planets i.e. almost all: Aries (Mercury), Taurus (Venus, Mars), Leo (the Moon), Virgo (the Sun, Mars), Libra (Mercury), Scorpio (Venus, Mars), Sagittarius (the Moon), Capricorn (the Sun), Aquarius (the Moon, Mercury) and Pisces (the Sun, Venus, Mars). These fast moving functional malefic planets, that in the previous two conditions are not so problematic, create here also serious problems whenever a slow planet in transit comes under their malefic influence. Unless astral remedies are earnestly performed, the problems may come up whenever the planet is weak and afflicted in any of these three transit conditions. The probability increases with the number of the transit conditions involved. The same reasoning applies to the triple transit triggering influences of functional benefic planets.

Regarding how to get the actual strengths of planets for a certain person at a specific time, the different kinds of strengths are:

1) Strengths of planets in rasi/natal chart.

2) Strengths of planets in transit.

3) Strengths of planets in rasi modified by the aspects from transits.

4) Strengths of planets in transit modified by the aspects from rasi.

The strength of planets in rasi is the most important. The last three conditions help and become more pertinent if condition 1) exists. If planets in rasi are weak, they will temporarily become strong only a little by the existence of the last three conditions if no strengthening measures have been used.

EXALTED FUNCTIONAL MALEFIC PLANETS

Exalted planets if functional malefic planets and at the same time afflicting by close conjunction or aspect other weak planet(s) or the most effective point of the house(s) do cause sufferings with regard to the significations ruled by the said afflicted planet(s) or house(s). The exalted planets, when badly placed, become weak and afflicted.

ROLE OF PLANETS

A planet plays its role in the following manner:

a)   As a natural significator for various things.

b)   As a lord of the house containing its mooltrikona sign to protect and promote the significations of that house depending upon its natal strength.

c)   Through its relationship with other planetary configurations in a nativity.

The strength of a planet governs the role of that planet for (a) and (b) above in protecting and promoting its general and particular significations. The functional nature of the planet governs its role as at (c) above.

ANALYZING RESULTS OF SUB-PERIOD LORDS

Events fructify in the sub-periods of planets. Therefore, it is very important that we understand the method of analyzing the dasa (main period) and bhukti (sub-period) results. The results of the general significations of the sub-period lord depend upon its strength, placement, conjunction and aspects to the same. The significations of the house of placement are touched when transit planets create benefic or malefic influences on the sub-period lord, depending upon their functional nature whether benefic or malefic. In the sub-period of a planet, the following significations are touched:

1) The general significations of the planet. For example the Sun rules father, social status, position with the government, male child, digestive system, heart, blood pressure, etc.

2) The significations of the house where the mooltrikona sign of the said planet is placed. In case in the mooltrikona house some functional malefic planet is placed close to the most effective point, or some functional malefic planet is closely aspecting the most effective point of the said house, or some planet is closely afflicted then during the sub-periods of the afflicting and afflicted planet(s) the significations of the mooltrikona house shall not prosper and shall face problems indicated by the afflicting planet depending upon its lordship. A natal/transit functional malefic planet never afflicts its own mooltrikona house, except when the functional malefic planet is already afflicted and/or afflicts from a dusthana/malefic house.

3) The significations of the houses where the planet is placed.

4) During the sub-period of a planet all the impacts on the house, which contains the mooltrikona sign of the said planet, also come into force. Due to such influences on the most effective point by a strong functional benefic planet even the sub-period of a weak planet would be blessing the native with good or

very good results. Similarly, a close impact of a functional malefic planet on the most effective point of a mooltrikona house may not allow the planet ruling that mooltrikona house to show good results in its sub-periods even if the said planet is strong in the natal chart.

Let us see the application of most malefic planet and most effective point while analyzing the results of sub-periods, with the help of an example.

Example 3

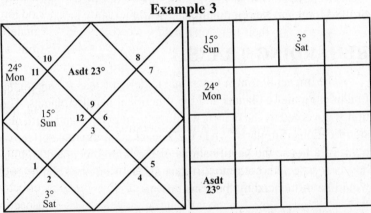

The 23 degree of Sagittarius rises in the ascendant. Therefore, the most effective point of all the houses will be 23 degree. Any planet conjunct within 5 degrees on either side i.e. within 18 degrees to 28 degrees in any house would be influencing the significations of the house in question in a pronounced manner depending upon the functional nature of that planet. The Moon is placed at 24 degrees in the third house in the sign Aquarius ruled by Saturn. As the Moon is the most malefic planet, this placement afflicts simultaneously the most effective point of the third and ninth houses, weakening their respective lords and itself. Since the Moon is conjunct with the most effective point of the third house, it not only destroys the initiatives of the person but during the sub-periods of both the Moon and Saturn it will not allow any ventures/initiatives of the person to succeed. The aspect of the Moon to the most effective point to the ninth house would also cause obstructions to the significations of the ninth house during the sub-periods of both the Sun and the Moon. The Sun is lord of the ninth house while the Moon is aspecting and malefically influencing the ninth house. In such cases if the weak Sun is well placed as in this case, the impact of the influence of the Moon would be a little bit milder than if the Sun is badly placed. As Saturn is very weak due to infancy, bad placement and the exact affliction of the most malefic planet on the most effective point of its mooltrikona house, during the sub-periods of the Moon and Saturn the impact would be quite grave.

REGARDING TRANSIT

The impact of transit functional malefic planets is on both the functional malefic planets and the functional benefic planets. The things governed by the planets would be their general and particular significations. Similarly, when the impact is on the most effective point of a house the significations of the house occupied and the house(s) aspected, both mooltrikona and non-mooltrikona houses would be influenced by the transit planet.

Transit of planets over the natal position of functional malefic planets or close aspect of natal functional malefic planets on planets in transit also spoil the significations of the planets in transit.

By transit strength we mean the planet should be strong in transit.

INTERACTION BETWEEN THE SUB-PERIODS AND TRANSIT

During the course of the sub-period of a planet the significations of the mooltrikona house ruled by the sub-period lord, the general significations of the planet and the significations of the house where the planet is placed would be touched.

The transit means when the planetary position on any given date subsequent to the date of the birth is studied with reference to the ascendant and the position of the planets in the natal chart.

For example, let us take a chart with the sign Sagittarius rising in the ascendant. In this chart the lord of the eleventh house, Venus, is placed in the twelfth house, ruling losses. During the sub-period of Venus trouble to elder brother, loss of income and trouble to friends is indicated. To cause a death-like event or some serious trouble to the elder brother the transit functional malefic planets Rahu/Ketu may form close conjunction or aspect with any of the three positions:

i)　Most effective point of the eleventh house.

ii)　Natal position of the sub-period lord, Venus.

iii)　Transit position of the sub-period lord, Venus.

The conjunction or aspect of natal Moon, Rahu or Ketu with transit Venus may also cause the same fatality if the natal Venus is weak.

Example 4

		Ven 10°25 Mer 29° Ket 29° 8	
7°6' Sat　10　11	Asdt 8°4' Sun 7°9'　9	7	
	12　6　3		
23°22' Jup　1　2		5　27°25' Mar	
29°37' Rah		4　22°17' Mon	

	Jup	Rah	
Sat			Mon
			Mar
Asdt Sun	Ven Mer Ket		

The example chart pertains to a lady born 22nd December 1964, at 0850 hrs at Copenhagen, Denmark 55N41' 12E'35 CE TIME (GMT + 1). In her case Venus main period (dasa) Venus sub-period (bhukti) started on 30th Oct 1981 and was to run up to 1st March 1985. Now from the horoscope we would see that an incident like loss of an elder brother is seen in the sub-period of Venus as Venus ruling the elder brother is placed in the house of losses. The transit Venus was of 1 degree in the sign Capricorn on 2nd February 1982. It apparently retrograded and came into contact with transit Ketu at 29 degrees in the sign Sagittarius on the 7th February 1982. Up to the 21st February 1982, the transit Venus and transit Ketu were within 3 degrees range. The sub-period lord was not only weak due to its being in infancy but it was also in close conjunction with Ketu. Being placed in the house of losses in the natal chart Ketu is having the inclinations of causing loss with whatever planet it forms close conjunction or aspect with. The native lost her elder brother.

The sub-period lord sets the trend according to its lordship, placement and other natal influences on itself in rasi while the transit/natal planets cause influence whenever they come into contact with the natal/transit position of the sub-period lord.

We hope this gives better understanding into the interaction between the transit results and the sub-period lord results with the help of the above example.

RELIABILITY OF TREATING A HOUSE AS ASCENDANT FOR SIGNIFIED RELATIONSHIP

We cannot treat a house as ascendant for the relation signified by that house. For example, ninth house for father and the seventh house for wife, etc. We can't decipher educational prospects of father, his assets, etc. from the twelfth house which is the fourth house from the ninth house. The status of father in general can be seen from the Sun and the ninth house. The detailed analysis of any relation can only be made from his/her own horoscope.

Regarding spouse, children, parents, elder/younger siblings and friends only general indications can be seen from the native's chart. For example, from the native's chart we can see whether the person will derive happiness from his/her children or at a particular time whether the child is enjoying or in trouble but we cannot identify in detail about the educational, professional or emotional matters of a child.

MEASURING CAPACITY OF PLANETS

While studying the impact of a planet, depending upon its strength, during the course of its sub-period both the natal and transit positions of the planet under operation are to be studied.

The result of a particular house will be influenced by a transiting planet when it is near to its most effective point depending upon its functional nature whether benefic or malefic.

A weak planet, too, has the capacity to protect its house if it is well placed, unafflicted, under the beneficial influence of functional benefic planets through close aspect/conjunction or aspects its own mooltrikona house.

Any planet has capacity to bless the native with its results if its natal strength is at least 60% and it is unafflicted. In such a situation the results may come with some delay and of slightly lower order. With the help of the strengthening measures - gemstones or Kavach - the strength of the planets, where it is less than 60%, can be brought to the level of 60% so that it blesses the native with the significations ruled by it.

One can strengthen the weak planets (i) by way of a Kavach if the planetary strength is between 50% to 60%; (ii) by way of a special power Kavach if the planetary strength is between 35% to 50%; and (iii) by way of a special purpose Kavach with gemstones if the planetary strength is lower than 35%.

BRIGHT RAYS

A planet with bright rays means a non-combust planet.

MEASURING STRENGTH OF PLANETS IN INFANCY/OLD AGE

The results of the planets in infancy or old age vary in degree of strength as per their longitudes as detailed below:

INFANCY

When	0	degree	power	is	zero
When	1	degree	power	is	20%
When	2	degrees	power	is	40%
When	3	degrees	power	is	60%
When	4	degrees	power	is	80%
When	5	degrees	power	is	100%

OLD AGE

When	30	degrees	power	is	zero
When	29	degrees	power	is	20%
When	28	degrees	power	is	40%
When	27	degrees	power	is	60%
When	26	degrees	power	is	80%
When	25	degrees	power	is	100%

Exaltation sign adds to the strength. The peak point of exaltation or debilitation has very little relevance.

DIVISIONAL CHARTS

The divisional charts are the charts which are drawn by division of houses for specialized analysis of a particular signification; for example navamsa for considering general fortune and marriage, etc., and dasamsa for considering professional aspects in a nativity. For a detailed study on this subject, you can read the author's book, "How to Study Divisional Charts".

CHALIT CHAKRA

This is a redundant concept so far as the Systems' Approach is concerned. The Systems' Approach identifies the functional nature of the planets on the basis of the ascendant. Each planet is treated in the house in which it is placed. A planet placed in the eighth house going to seventh or ninth house as per chalit chakra can never give good results. Its periods will bestow weak results because of the position of the planet being weak due to its bad placement and there will be obstructions and mishaps. The astrologers, who consider chalit chakra, fail in their predictions.

BAD PLACEMENT

The book, "Self Learning Course in Astrology" gives clear-cut guidance that, except when in its own mooltrikona sign, any planet placed in the sixth, eighth or twelfth house from the ascendant would be treated as badly placed. The planets are not called badly placed due to their position in a particular sign. In other words bad placement is referred to a malefic house and not to any particular sign. Any planet, even if exalted, becomes weak and afflicted due to bad placement.

IMPACT OF PLACEMENT IN FRIENDLY/ INIMICAL SIGNS

The friendly or inimical relationship of planets arising due to placement in the signs ruled by friendly planets or inimical planets only makes the planet comfortable or uncomfortable in doing its work, respectively. The planets work as per their functional nature and strength.

EVOLUTION OF THE SOUL

The evolution of the soul depends on the strength of the Sun, Jupiter and the lords of the tenth and first houses.

MEASURING AFFLICTIONS

The quantum of influence of the functional malefic planet (FM) on another planet or most effective point (MEP) of the house is gauged through the closeness of the conjunction or aspect. The afflictions to the planets/houses are caused by the close conjunction or aspect of the FMs in a nativity. Regarding otherwise "strong" planets and/or MT houses, the normal afflictions are effective within one degree range while the special/multiple afflictions are effective within two degrees range, becoming these otherwise "strong" planets/MT houses weak on this account. The normal afflictions to weak planets/MT houses are fully effective if they are within one degree range while afflictions are 80%, 60%, 40%, 20% and 0% if the afflicting planet is having a 1 deg, 2 deg, 3 deg, 4 deg and 5 deg longitudinal difference, respectively, from the weak planet/MEP of the weak MT house. The special/multiple afflictions to weak planets/MT houses are fully effective if they are within two degrees range while afflictions are 75%, 50%, 25% and 0% if the afflicting planet(s) is having a 2 deg, 3 deg, 4 deg and 5 deg longitudinal difference, respectively, from the weak planet/MEP of the weak MT house. It is most severe if the weak and afflicted planets are badly placed. The experience based on the feedback of the people indicates that these afflictions can be taken care of up to 80 - 90% with the help of the astral remedies i.e. Kavach, gemstones and charities, etc. If the planets/houses are strong, the damage is least. For non-MT houses, the impact of the affliction is 100% to 0% depending upon the longitudinal difference between the FM and MEP of the house as explained above for the weak planets/MT houses. If a planet being lord of a house is weak one should see the strength of the significator (karaka) and the supplementary houses.

IMPACT OF TRANSIT EXALTED RAHU AND KETU

The impact of well placed exalted Rahu over the well placed strong functional benefic planets is good for materialistic prosperity. The transit over the weak functional benefic planets gives small gains or creates false hopes. The transit over the functional malefic planets causes anxiety and delays with regard to the significations of the houses where the mooltrikona sign of the functional malefic planet under transit is placed. The impact of the transit of well placed exalted Ketu will be bad only on weak and afflicted planets when Ketu in transit is stationary.

When in dusthana houses the results of exalted Rahu/Ketu are as under:

a) When in the sixth house, it gives losses through theft and fire, debts, cheating and expenses on treatment of illness. If the lord of the sixth house is strong, Rahu can give some financial gains through manipulations.

(b) When in the eighth house, it can give inheritance, obstructions, manipulating tendencies and increased tendencies for sensual pleasures.

c) When in the twelfth house, it can give bad health, loss of sleep, craving for excessive gratification of senses, visits to far-off places or foreign lands.

IMPACT OF COMBUST PLANETS

When the Sun is a functional benefic planet its conjunction with other well placed functional benefic planets is good and gives exponential growth for the significations of the planets in close conjunction with the Sun. The combust planets suffer under the triple transit influences of functional malefic planets. This can, however, be guarded by application of the strengthening and propitiating astral remedies, to a large extent.

When the Sun is a functional malefic planet or a functional malefic planet or planets are closely and mutually influencing the Sun, the significations of all the planets involved suffer in their sub-periods as also during transit impacts.

For example see the following chart:

Example 5

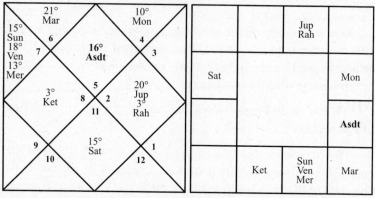

All the three planets in the third house are in close conjunction amongst themselves and the conjunction is good except the transit afflictions which will be short-lived if the influencing Rahu and Ketu during the transit do not become stationary. In this chart, the sub-periods of Venus, the Sun and Mercury in the main periods of the functional benefic planets will give good initiatives, increased income and happiness, involvement in writing, artistic pursuits, and status rise through such activities.

IMPACT OF RETROGRADE PLANETS IN ASTROLOGY

This is only a visionary phenomenon as this occurs due to different speeds of the planets in relation to the earth. The effects on a natal chart are due to fixed angular position of planets with reference to a particular place on the earth for a particular time, natal or transit.

Though the classical as well as some of the modern commentators have ascribed different views for the results of retrograde planets; the authors are of the firm view that retrograde planets are to be treated in a normal way as per their longitudes, so far as the natal planetary influences are concerned in a horoscope. However, the transit influences of a planet appearing to be in retrograde motion and then direct motion are prolonged on a specified degree(s).

However, for understanding the impact of a retrograde planet it is necessary that one learns predictive techniques and methodology for reading the triple transit influences.

IMPACT OF PLANETARY COMBINATIONS (YOGA)

The planetary combinations (yogas) in a horoscope are generated through close conjunctions, close aspects and placements. When two or more functional benefic planets form close relationship among themselves or with the most effective points of benefic houses, they generate good results related to their mooltrikona houses. This type of relationship caused due to the close conjunction/aspect is known as an auspicious yoga. If two functional malefic planets form a close relationship, they cause an inauspicious yoga and destroy the results related to their mooltrikona houses. If one functional benefic planet and one functional malefic planet form a close relationship, this causes an inauspicious yoga that destroys the results of the mooltrikona house ruled by the functional benefic planet. When a functional benefic planet occupies a malefic house, this causes yoga for misfortune related to the significations of its mooltrikona house. Similarly, when a functional malefic planet closely influences the most effective point of a house, it destroys the significations of that house, except if it is its own mooltrikona house.

The impact of Rajyogas and Dhanayogas accrues only if the planets involved are strong. Whenever, the planets ruling benefic houses conjoin or mutually aspect closely, they form good yoga (say Rajyogas) connected with the indications of both the houses involved, provided they are strong. The involvement of a planet ruling the house of income and/or wealth produces a Dhanayoga. In other words, mere location of a planet or a set of planets in a particular sign or house without creating a close relationship through a close conjunction or aspect does not result into any yoga. The planets involved in Rajyogas bless the native with name, fame, wealth, comforts, etc., during their sub-periods.

Similarly, until and unless any functional malefic planet forms a close conjunction or aspect with other planet(s) or house(s) they do not produce any Duryoga or even Kalsarpa yoga. The misnomer Kalsarpa yoga is being propagated by those persons who have failed to correctly identify the functional nature of planets in various nativities and have not been able to pin point the reasons for miseries. Any chart containing the so-called Kalsarpa yoga will not give bad results until and unless Rahu-Ketu or other functional malefic planets cause severe conjunctions or aspects with weak planets or houses in that particular nativity. Under the Systems' Approach, the analysis is always done with reference to the placement of planets, their strength and weaknesses and their mutual relationship with reference to the ascendant, and its most effective point in particular. The planets involved in Duryogas cause miseries/ tragedies as per their nature depending upon their lordships, during their sub-periods.

Another misnomer, 'Neechbhanga Rajyoga' is not coming from the propounding father but has found its place in the subsequent classical commentaries like Phaladipika, etc. The Systems' Approach does not believe in this concept and treats the debilitated planet as a weak planet.

HOW TO PROCEED WITH ANALYSIS FOR IDENTIFYING THE PROBLEM AREAS

For starting analysis, underline the functional malefic planets. Study the strength of the planets and identify the exact or close conjunctions/aspects. See also if any special/multiple affliction exits. Put a circle around the planets/houses which are afflicted. Now you can start the analysis.

The long-term problem is always with regard to the weak planets or the sub-periods of the functional malefic planets in the natal chart. The short-term problem is indicated by the (i) transit of functional malefic(s) over the natal planets, (ii) when transit planets come under the influence of natal functional malefic planets; and (iii) the close afflictions or bad placements of transit planets with reference to a particular ascendant. The good results should be indicated for the significations of the strong functional benefic planets having close benefic conjunctions/aspects.

The position of functional benefic planet(s) in dusthanas or malefic houses make them weak and afflicted but if they aspect the most effective point of the house containing their own mooltrikona sign then despite weakness they are able to protect the significations of their mooltrikona house to some extent. Also, if they are placed in the eighth house near the most effective point of the house then despite weakness it is good as they aspect the most effective point of the second house. In the case of a functional benefic Mars, Jupiter or Saturn posited in the eighth house they also aspect two other houses besides the second house. The detailed study of the functional malefic planets and the planets in malefic houses has been taken up in Chapter 3 of the book, "Predictive Techniques and the Application of Astrological Remedial Measures."

The case studies included here and in all our books bring out the techniques for quickly spotting the prominent events in life. For detailed study of the divisional charts, the readers may refer to our book, "How to Study Divisional Charts".

INSIGHTS

Fairly strong planet: A planet which has at least 70% power, is unafflicted and well placed, is considered as fairly strong planet.

Mild affliction: An affliction to the extent of 25% or less to a strong or fairly strong planet or the most effective point of a non-mooltrikona sign house is considered as a mild affliction.

Whenever Rahu-Ketu axis is placed exactly over the most effective points of houses containing odd signs besides afflicting the houses occupied and aspected, it turns the planets Saturn, the Sun, Venus, Mars and Jupiter weak by afflicting their mooltrikona houses.

Whenever Rahu-Ketu axis is placed exactly over the most effective points of houses containing even signs besides afflicting the houses occupied and aspected, it turns the planets the Moon and Mercury weak by afflicting their mooltrikona houses.

The close influence of the lord of the eighth house or Rahu or the lord of the twelfth house on the lord of the seventh house, and/ or the most effective point of the seventh house and/or Venus and the close influence of Rahu on the lord of the eighth house gives indulgence out of marital bond for excessive sensual pleasures and endangers the native with sexually transmitted diseases.

The close affliction of the nodes to weak planets makes one vulnerable to cancerous diseases. Ever since the author, V. K. Choudhry identified this planetary configuration giving cancerous results in the year 1989, our team had been very particular in watching the horoscopes with such planetary configuration for administering preventive astral remedies and we are very proud to say that in cases where the native had not started suffering from such a fatal disease, the preventive astral remedies proved to be of great help and the natives suspected for cancerous disease did not suffer in the sub-periods of such afflicting/afflicted planets.

Whenever the affliction is close to the extent of one degree, the problems surface in the first operating planetary period. When the affliction is close to the extent of two degrees, the problem may surface in the second operating planetary period. The affliction, with the longitudinal difference of three degrees or more gives problems in the third operating planetary period. Similarly, we should treat the afflictions of longitudinal difference of four and five degrees. This varies with the strength of the primary determinants. If the primary determinants are weak, it hastens the surfacing of problem.

A planet placed in the mooltrikona sign cannot exceed the strength of its dispositor.

During the sub period of a planet the results of planets placed in its mooltrikona sign also fructify simultaneously.

Prediction of unfavorable results can be/is made for the significations ruled by the weak planets even if there are no afflictions in the natal chart and no planet is badly placed.

A strong planet will give beneficial results of its general and particular significations throughout the life. If it is away from the MEP of the house of its placement, it may give results for the significations of the said house in the later part of life.

An FM planet does not afflict its own MT sign by conjunction or by aspect. An FM planet will afflict its own MT sign by aspect only if it itself is afflicted by another FM planet. Dispositor weakness or bad placement affliction is not applicable in this case. The benefit of aspect to the MT sign of FM is limited to the proportion of the strength of the FM.

The third house also rules learning, comprehension, vitality, leadership, vision and success.

The placement of the tenth lord in the second house gives professional education.

The strength of Sun or the Sun like houses or planets improve the results of other planets to some extent.

In Divisional Charts we see the influence of FMs of DCs.

The strong affliction of MMP to the significators of longevity, the placement of planets in the 8th house and the afflicted Moon cause short life span.

Close afflictions to MEP of the houses harm the main significations of the house.

The strong planets give results without any efforts while the weak planets need more efforts with little/delayed success.

Give due consideration to placement of the planets. The planets placed in the third house take the person to MBA / marketing like studies. The strong planets bring brilliance coupled with stability. The weak planets show their impact through instability.

The affliction depends upon the closeness of the functional malefic planet to the planet/house which is being afflicted.

The afflicting power of the functional malefic planet does not reduce due to its weakness. The afflicting power of the functional malefic planet increases when it is placed in a malefic house or it itself is under affliction.

If the planet/house under affliction is weak, the impact of affliction will be more.

For strong planet the orb of affliction is one degree.

The orb of affliction is two degrees for strong planets in the following cases:

-    multiple affliction;

-    affliction by the most malefic planet;

-    affliction by Rahu and Ketu both;

-    affliction from a planet placed in dusthana (malefic house),

For weak planets/houses the orb of affliction is five degrees.

The affliction to the MEP of houses is more severe in comparison to the affliction to a planet.

At the time of birth if the native is running the main period of the most malefic planet and the sub-period of Rahu or Ketu is in operation then the infant child may suffer from illness right at birth. Rahu or Jupiter or Saturn in the state of being stationary may be moving at a very slow speed. It means that the mutual malefic influence of transit affliction over natal affliction continues for a longer duration than the normal duration. For example, normally Rahu may travel the longitude of one degree in a period of ten or eleven days. But because of its slow movement it may take even three months to travel one degree. Such a situation gives prolonged illness at birth and even threatens life.

FATE VS FREE WILL

Fate is read through the birth charts. It is a reality. The birth chart is like a divine message. The incidence of free will is not an illusion. The free will is exercised through intellect, courage and by being blessed. People do exercise free will as they try to manage the situations. The chance of success again is fated. In astrology the free will is exercised through the fifth and third houses and the chance of success of management is seen through the incidence of strong birth planets. Let me show this by way on an example of prolonged transit influence which was one of the themes of the 7th IIPA International Conference of SA Astrologers.

Transit of Jupiter in Pisces for people born in the ascending zodiac sign of Libra led the others believe that they were aggressive in behaviour and they did not address the concerns of others or care of others. Similarly, the transit of Jupiter in Aries for the people born in the ascending zodiac sign of Scorpio resulted in conflicts in relationships as Jupiter ruling speech was having a prolonged stay in the house of conflicts. Therefore the advice for Scorpio ascendant born people is to follow the saying, "Silence is Golden" and exercise patience to save relationships. Those who follow the advice by exercising the free will gain and those who do not follow the advice fall prey to the fate which is seen through the prolonged transit influences in the sixth house.

BLACK MAGIC: Impact of nodes on fifth house, weak Mercury / Moon makes one vulnerable to black magic. The mooltrikona sign lords of the eighth and twelfth houses also act as Rahu.

The karma results manifest through the principles of divine justice. Jyotish/Astral remedies are the means for alleviating the karma results.

IMPORTANT TOOLS FOR PREDICTIVE ACCURACY

The important tools for predictive accuracy are the functional nature of planets, strength of planets, inter-relationships of planets, divisional charts, impact of Rahu & Ketu, planetary periods and triple transit triggers.

For differentiating between

- having issues in a particular area throughout life

- enjoying good results in a particular area but in some sub-periods facing issues and drawbacks

The guiding principles are that the planets give results as per their strength in their sub periods. Transit influences take precedence over sub period results. The strong/exact afflictions to natal planets are not easy things to be dealt with. The continuous propitiation with strengthening of afflicted planets help. Some other strong planets in the birth chart help in bringing down the impact of strong afflictions. The strong planets, in general, give good results for their significations throughout the life. Where there are no strong or well placed planets, there is limited hope of things turning good.

To answer question for timing of events, see the natal and transit planetary strengths, operating sub period and transit and answer these questions. For example, in a query for job, if the natal determinants of profession and the Sun are strong or well placed with at least 60% power and there is no transit affliction the person is likely to get work in a couple of months' time. Another month or so can be added if Rahu-Ketu are stationary. For rest of the people it may take longer time and they need strengthening of their planets and propitiation of the planets causing afflictions.

Whenever there are double or multiple close/exact afflictions, these take first priority in giving their results. In case such close/ exact afflictions of MMP and Rahu-Ketu axis are suffered by the prime significator of the marriage, the marriage can be delayed inordinately or even denied. In such cases the use of a special purpose Kavach and continuous special propitiatory remedies become absolutely essential.

Decade per degree rule: The impact of conjunctions and aspects is measured in terms of a decade per degree of closeness. If it is an exact aspect or conjunction between the two planets the impact is felt in the sub periods falling in the first ten years of life. If there is a close aspect or conjunction with a longitudinal difference of one to two degrees the impact is felt in the sub periods of the planets falling in the second decade. If there is a close aspect or conjunction with a longitudinal difference of two to three degrees the impact is felt in the sub periods of the planets falling in the third decade. If there is a close aspect or conjunction with a longitudinal difference of three to four degrees the impact is felt in the sub periods of the planets falling in the fourth decade. If there is a close aspect or conjunction with a longitudinal difference of four to five degrees the impact is felt in the sub periods of the planets falling in the fifth decade.

The results can be further influenced by stationary transit influence or the strength of the planets involved.

When any exalted functional malefic planet, other than Mercury, is conjunct with the MEP of the house of its placement, it becomes weak.

Strong Venus hastens marriage.

Strong Sun brings down the level of sufferings due to afflictions.

Metals ruled by planets: The Sun rules copper and gold. The Moon rules silver. Mars rules copper. Mercury rules brass. Jupiter rules gold. Venus rules silver and aluminum. Saturn rules iron, minerals and crude.

Planetary castes and Nature: Those with strong influence of Jupiter go in the learning, teaching, training, development and spiritual work - Brahmins. Those with strong Sun and Mars go for administrative / organisation profession, government assignments & security forces are fighters - Kshatriyas. Those with strong Moon, Mercury and Venus go for trading / business ventures - vaishayas. Those with weak planets and strong influences of Saturn and Rahu go for routine jobs – Sudra.

GENERAL

The balance sheet of past lives is in the form of the birth chart. Purva punyas (good deeds of past lives) are seen from the IX house. Karma of this life (deeds of this life) are seen through the fifth and tenth houses. The strong planets represent the good Karma from past lives, while the weak planets and afflictions to planets and houses represent the bad karma brought forward. Afflictions point to very bad Karma, whereas weaknesses represent milder bad karma.

Vedic Astrology is an ancient universal knowledge on which we offer our views as other authors/astrologers have done in the past and are doing in the present.

The items for propitiation suggested are based on the planetary tastes mentioned in the vedic literature and bhoota yagyam - one of the five great sacrifices. These have nothing to do with the remedies suggested in other books.

While we have expressed our views based on our experience, the readers are free for their own views and beliefs and for adopting the Systems' Approach brought out by us for interpreting the horoscopes.

The problems and mishaps are represented by the weak and weak and/or afflicted planets.

When the natal Moon is afflicted by Rahu, Rahu-like planets or is placed in the Rahu-like houses the person becomes more sensitive and especially to unfavorable incidents.

The exact affliction to badly placed lord of fourth or second or ninth or third house lord (most benefic planet) reduces the strength of other strong planets in the natal chart.

The weakness of the lord of the eighth house makes the father vulnerable to damage, both in terms of longevity and in terms of finances.

The weakness of the lord of the eighth house or fourth house curtails the financial resources or longevity of father. In Pisces ascendant there is no MT sign in the ninth and fourth houses. So, the eighth house becomes pertinent significator of the longevity of the father. We also consider the strength of the Sun in the natal chart as it is significator for father.

Affliction to the ascendant in any divisional chart by the eighth lord of the divisional chart is equally serious as the affliction to the prime determinants placed in eighth house of the divisional chart.

In divisional charts besides the affliction of R&K, the afflictions by the functional malefic planets of the divisional charts should be considered and the afflictions by the functional malefic planets of natal chart are not considered. Bad placements are also considered in the divisional charts.

The close influence of Rahu on the third lord makes the person adventurous.

The exact / close aspect of Rahu makes the person greedy and does not allow him/her to feel contented.

Suppose there is an exact conjunction/aspect of more than one planet in the birth chart or there is an exact conjunction/aspect of a planet with the most effective point of a house in the birth chart. When this position of exact conjunction or aspect develops prolonged malefic transit influence the person faces multiple challenges in his/her life simultaneously.

PLACEMENT IMPACT OF PLANETS

The placement of planets is an important factor in horoscope reading. The placement of a planet gives results connected with the significations of the house ruled by the planet with the house of placement despite its weakness or despite the planet being away from the most effective point of the house. If a functional malefic planet is on the most effective point of a house it causes problems but the problems may be connected with the significations ruled by the said planet. For example, if the lord of the second is placed in the twelfth house, the person may move to a distant place or a foreign land in connection with the professional status. If the second lord is placed in the tenth house the person may acquire status in life due to his/her professional achievements. If the second lord is placed in the fifth house, one may acquire professional qualification and acquire status through the same. If the second lord is placed in the seventh house one may attain status in a foreign land. If the second lord is placed in the fourth house one may attain status by being born in a resourceful family. If the second lord is placed in the eighth house one may attain status in life with some delay. If the second lord is placed in the ninth house one may be lucky to attain the status in life without much efforts with the help of parents and preceptor. If the second lord is placed in the eleventh house, one may acquire status in life because of good earnings in life and because of friendship with highly placed persons. If the second lord is placed in the second house, one may enjoy good status in life due to the appointment with the state or due to the family status. If the second lord is placed in the ascendant one may enjoy authoritative status. The placement of the Sun and Mars in the third house brings courage. The close influence of the fifth lord on the tenth house brings the element of intellect. The placement of the planets in the second house, which rules status, brings status as per significations ruled by them. The good placement of eighth lord in the house of status brings easy gains with small or little efforts. The planets in the first house influence the personality traits. The planets in the second house contribute to professional ventures. The planets in the third house bring entrepreneurial ventures and opportunities. The planets in the fourth house contribute to assets. The planets in the fifth house contribute to learning. The planets in the sixth house involve the person in debts, health problems and conflicts. The planets placed in the seventh house give rise to living in foreign lands, long journeys and associations. The planets placed in the eighth house cause easy gains, obstructions and delays. The planets placed in the ninth house involve the person in family or religious traditions or spiritual pursuits. The planets placed in the tenth house involve the person in professions connected with the planet. The planets placed in the eleventh house contribute to earnings through the significations ruled by the concerned planets. The planets placed in the twelfth house take one to distant places and foreign lands and can cause losses and expenses.

During the sub period of Mercury things work with stresses and strains even when Mercury is strong and or well placed in the natal chart. This is due to the volatile strength of Mercury in transit. When Mercury is weak in the natal chart the results in its sub period do create stresses and strains. The situation becomes further difficult when either of the Sun or Mercury is a functional malefic planet.

Whenever the lord of the twelfth house is placed in the sixth house or afflicts some planet from the sixth house closely, there are chances of problems with governement which may result in arrest, legal penalties, imprisonment, etc.

ECLIPSES:

Eclipses, in general, does not make a strong or prolonged impact for living persons until and unless some slow moving planet is stationary or moving utterly slow or appearing retrograde near the degree of some natal planet in the chart of an individual or nation.

For those who are taking birth, there are chances that there are strong close afflictions to the Sun and/or the Moon or any other planet in the natal chart. This can certainly cause prolonged problems for the native.

SA is an all pervasive framework, touching upon all aspects of predictive astrology - both natal and mundane.

Caution: Astrologers do not have a television set and cannot give running commentary. The best thing is in the shortest possible time, indicate the strong and weak areas in chart and prescribe appropriate remedies. One acquires credentials or good reputation as an astrologer with one's competence over a period of time.

CHAPTER 6

ASCENDANT-WISE TIPS FOR TRIPLE TRANSIT INFLUENCES

ARIES ASCENDANT

Every year during the months of September and October the transit Mercury, Venus and the Sun generally transit the sign Virgo and the native becomes vulnerable to health problems, disputes and financial constraints. Similarly, the transit planets in Scorpio during the months of October and November cause obstructions while the transit planets in the sign Pisces during the months of March and April cause additional expenses and problems in journeys/distant places.

When the slow moving planets Jupiter, Saturn, Rahu and Ketu transit in the sign Virgo, they make the persons born in Aries ascendant vulnerable to health problems, income problems, disputes and setbacks. When these slow moving planets transit in the sign Scorpio they cause setbacks, obstructions and difficulties to father and the sources of income. When these slow moving planets transit in the sign Pisces they cause loss of income, additional expenses, problems with law and setbacks. In such situations one should strengthen Jupiter and Saturn and continuously propitiate Rahu and Ketu.

TAURUS ASCENDANT

Every year during the months of October and November when transit Mercury, Venus and the Sun generally transit the sign Libra the native becomes vulnerable to health problems, disputes and financial constraints. Similarly, the transit planets in Sagittarius during the months of December and Januray cause obstructions while the transit planets in the sign Aries during the months of April and May cause additional expenses and problems in journeys/ distant places.

When the slow moving planets Jupiter, Saturn, Rahu and Ketu transit in the sign Libra, they make the persons born in Taurus ascendant vulnerable to health problems, job problems, disputes, accidents and setbacks. When these slow moving planets transit in the sign Sagittarius they cause setbacks, problems in job, obstructions and difficulties to father and the sources of income. When these slow moving planets transit in the sign Aries they may cause loss of income, additional expenses, problems with law, problems to father, job problems and setbacks. In such situations one should strengthen Saturn and continuously propitiate Jupiter, Rahu and Ketu.

GEMINI ASCENDANT

Every year during the months of November and December when transit Mercury, Venus and the Sun generally transit the sign Scorpio the native becomes vulnerable to health problems, disputes and financial constraints. Similarly, the transit planets in Capricorn during the months of January and February cause obstructions while the transit planets in the sign Taurus during the months of May and June cause additional expenses and problems in journeys/distant places.

When the slow moving planets Jupiter, Saturn, Rahu and Ketu transit in the sign Scorpio, they make the persons born in Gemini ascendant vulnerable to health problems, disputes and setbacks. When these slow moving planets transit in the sign Capricorn they cause setbacks, obstructions and difficulties to father and the spouse. When these slow moving planets transit in the sign Taurus they may cause loss of income, additional expenses, problems with law and setbacks. In such situations one should strengthen Jupiter and Saturn and continuously propitiate Rahu and Ketu.

CANCER ASCENDANT

Every year during the months of December and January when transit Mercury, Venus and the Sun generally transit the sign Sagittarius the native becomes vulnerable to health problems, disputes and financial constraints. Similarly, the transit planets in Aquarius during the months of February and March cause obstructions while the transit planets in the sign Gemini during the months of June and July cause additional expenses and problems in journeys/distant places.

When the slow moving planets Jupiter, Saturn, Rahu and Ketu transit in the sign Sagittarius, they make the persons born in Cancer ascendant vulnerable to health problems, disputes and setbacks. When these slow moving planets transit in the sign Aquarius they cause setbacks, accidents, obstructions and difficulties to father and the sources of income. When these slow moving planets transit in the sign Gemini they may cause loss of income, accidents, additional expenses, problems with law and setbacks. In such situations one should continuously propitiate Jupiter, Saturn, Rahu and Ketu. These slow moving planets near the most effective point of any house cause serious stress.

LEO ASCENDANT

Every year during the months of January and February when transit Mercury, Venus and the Sun generally transit the sign Capricorn the native becomes vulnerable to health problems, disputes and financial constraints. Similarly, the transit planets in Pisces during the months of March and April cause obstructions while the transit planets in the sign Cancer during the months of July and August cause additional expenses and problems in journeys/distant places.

When the slow moving planets Jupiter, Saturn, Rahu and Ketu transit in the sign Capricorn, they make the persons born in Leo ascendant vulnerable to health problems, disputes and setbacks. When these slow moving planets transit in the sign Pisces they cause setbacks, obstructions and difficulties to father and the sources of income. When these slow moving planets transit in the sign Cancer they may cause loss of income, additional expenses, problems to children, problems with law and setbacks. In such situations one should strengthen Jupiter and Saturn and continuously propitiate Rahu and Ketu. The slow moving planets Rahu and Ketu near the most effective point of any house cause serious stress.

VIRGO ASCENDANT

Every year during the months of February and March when transit Mercury, Venus and the Sun generally transit the sign Aquarius the native becomes vulnerable to health problems, disputes and financial constraints. Similarly, the transit planets in Aries during the months of April and May cause obstructions while the transit planets in the sign Leo during the months of August and September cause additional expenses and problems in journeys/ distant places.

When the slow moving planets Jupiter, Saturn, Rahu and Ketu transit in the sign Aquarius, they make the persons born in Virgo ascendant vulnerable to health problems, job problems, disputes and setbacks. When these slow moving planets transit in the sign Aries they cause setbacks, obstructions and difficulties to father and the sources of income. When these slow moving planets transit in the sign Leo they may cause loss of income, additional expenses, problems with law and setbacks. In such situations one should strengthen Jupiter and continuously propitiate Saturn, Rahu and Ketu. The slow moving planets Saturn, Rahu and Ketu near the most effective point of any house cause serious stress. The slow moving planet Jupiter near the most effective point of any benefic house brings happy events concerning the house transited and the houses aspected.

LIBRA ASCENDANT

Every year during the months of March and April when transit Mercury, Venus and the Sun generally transit the sign Pisces the native becomes vulnerable to health problems, disputes and financial constraints. Similarly, the transit planets in Taurus during the months of May and June cause obstructions while the transit planets in the sign Virgo during the months of Septemebr and October cause additional expenses and problems in journeys/distant places.

When the slow moving planets Jupiter, Saturn, Rahu and Ketu transit in the sign Pisces, they make the persons born in Libra ascendant vulnerable to health problems, disputes and setbacks. When these slow moving planets transit in the sign Taurus they cause setbacks, obstructions and difficulties to father and the sources of income. When these slow moving planets transit in the sign Virgo they may cause loss of income, additional expenses, problems with law and setbacks. In such situations one should strengthen Jupiter and Saturn and continuously propitiate Rahu and Ketu.

The slow moving planets Rahu and Ketu near the most effective point of any house cause serious stress. The slow moving planets Jupiter and Saturn near the most effective point of any benefic house brings happy events concerning the house transited and the houses aspected.

SCORPIO ASCENDANT

Every year during the months of April and May when transit Mercury, Venus and the Sun generally transit the sign Aries the native becomes vulnerable to health problems, disputes and financial constraints. Similarly, the transit planets in Gemini during the months of June and July cause obstructions while the transit planets in the sign Libra during the months of October and November cause additional expenses and problems in journeys/distant places.

When the slow moving planets Jupiter, Saturn, Rahu and Ketu transit in the sign Aries, they make the persons born in Scorpio ascendant vulnerable to health problems, disputes and professional setbacks. When these slow moving planets transit in the sign Gemini they cause setbacks, obstructions and difficulties to father and the sources of income. When these slow moving planets transit in the sign Libra they may cause loss of income, additional expenses, problems with law and setbacks. In such situations one should strengthen Jupiter and Saturn and continuously propitiate Mars,

Venus, Rahu and Ketu.

The slow moving planets Rahu and Ketu near the most effective point of any house cause serious stress. The slow moving planets Jupiter and Saturn near the most effective point of any benefic house bring happy events concerning the house transited and the houses aspected.

SAGITTARIUS ASCENDANT

Every year during the months of May and June when transit Mercury, Venus and the Sun generally transit the sign Taurus the native becomes vulnerable to health problems, disputes and financial constraints. Similarly, the transit planets in Cancer during the months of August and Septemebr cause obstructions while the transit planets in the sign Scorpio during the months of November and December cause additional expenses and problems in journeys or in distant places.

When the slow moving planets Jupiter, Saturn, Rahu and Ketu transit in the sign Taurus, they make the persons born in Sagittarius ascendant vulnerable to health problems, disputes and setbacks. When these slow moving planets transit in the sign Cancer they cause setbacks, obstructions and difficulties to father and the sources of income. When these slow moving planets transit in the sign Scorpio they may cause loss of income, additional expenses, problems with law and setbacks. In such situations one should strengthen Jupiter and Saturn and continuously propitiate Rahu and Ketu.

The slow moving planets Rahu and Ketu near the most effective point of any house cause serious stress. The slow moving planets Saturn and Jupiter near the most effective point of any benefic house bring happy events concerning the house transited and the houses aspected.

CAPRICORN ASCENDANT

Every year during the months of June and July when transit Mercury, Venus and the Sun generally transit the sign Gemini the native becomes vulnerable to health problems, disputes and financial constraints. Similarly, the transit planets in Leo during the months of August and September cause obstructions while the transit planets in the sign Sagittarius during the months of December and January cause additional expenses and problems in journeys/distant places.

When the slow moving planets Jupiter, Saturn, Rahu and Ketu transit in the sign Gemini, they make the persons born in Capricorn ascendant vulnerable to health problems, disputes and setbacks. When these slow moving planets transit in the sign Leo they cause setbacks, obstructions and difficulties to father and the sources of income. When these slow moving planets transit in the sign Sagittarius they may cause loss of income, additional expenses, problems with law and setbacks. In such situations one should strengthen Saturn and continuously propitiate Jupiter, Rahu and Ketu.

The slow moving planets Jupiter, Rahu and Ketu near the most effective point of any house cause serious stress. The slow moving planet Saturn near the most effective point of any benefic house brings happy events concerning the house transited and the houses aspected.

AQUARIUS ASCENDANT

Every year during the months of July and August when transit Mercury, Venus and the Sun generally transit the sign Cancer the native becomes vulnerable to health problems, disputes and financial constraints. Similarly, the transit planets in Virgo during the months of September and October cause obstructions while the transit planets in the sign Capricorn during the months of January and February cause additional expenses and problems in journeys/distant places.

When the slow moving planets Jupiter, Saturn, Rahu and Ketu transit in the sign Cancer, they make the persons born in Aquarius ascendant vulnerable to health problems, disputes and setbacks. When these slow moving planets transit in the sign Virgo they cause setbacks, obstructions and difficulties to father and the sources of income. When these slow moving planets transit in the sign Capricorn they may cause loss of income, additional expenses, problems with law and setbacks. In such situations one should strengthen Jupiter and Saturn and continuously propitiate Moon, Mercury, Rahu and Ketu.

The slow moving planets Rahu and Ketu near the most effective point of any house cause serious stress. The slow moving planet Saturn and Jupiter near the most effective point of any benefic house brings happy events concerning the house transited and the houses aspected.

PISCES ASCENDANT

Every year during the months of August and September when transit Mercury, Venus and the Sun generally transit the sign Leo the native becomes vulnerable to health problems, disputes and financial constraints. Similarly, the transit planets in Libra during the months of October and November cause obstructions while the transit planets in the sign Aquarius during the months of February and March cause additional expenses and problems in journeys/ distant places.

When the slow moving planets Jupiter, Saturn, Rahu and Ketu transit in the sign Leo, they make the persons born in Pisces ascendant vulnerable to health problems, job problems, disputes and setbacks. When these slow moving planets transit in the sign Libra they cause setbacks, obstructions and difficulties to father and the sources of income. When these slow moving planets transit in the sign Aquarius they may cause loss of income, additional expenses, problems with employer, law and setbacks. In such situations one should strengthen Jupiter and continuously propitiate Sun, Venus, Saturn, Rahu and Ketu.

The slow moving planets Saturn, Rahu and Ketu near the most effective point of any house cause serious stress. The slow moving planet Jupiter near the most effective point of any benefic house brings happy events concerning the house transited and the houses aspected.

CHAPTER 7

IDENTIFYING HEALTH PROBLEMS

Fortunate persons having "divine grace" make use of astrological advice to solve various life problems. Amongst all other problems, the problem of health is the one which affects a person both physically and mentally. The physical and mental disability or disturbance (temporarily or in a chronic way) touches each and every aspect of life. The medical diagnosis, preventive or actual, have become very complicated. In contrast to the medical science, Vedic Astrology offers human beings the advantage of advance knowledge of diseases from which a native may suffer during the course of his/her life. Again in contrast to the medical sciences it is Vedic Astrology which not only forewarns the native for the impending diseases but also helps in avoiding the same completely or partially by adopting suitable astral remedies, food habits, etc.

How to diagnose diseases is the question which comes up next. The houses which are weak and/or afflicted or the planets which are weak and/or afflicted give diseases connected with the significations ruled by them. This is the golden principle which provides us the key to diagnose the health problems and suggesting possible remedies. For example, when the prime determinant(s) of health, the additional prime determinant of health, and/or the Sun (being the significator of health) and the most effective point of the first/sixth house are afflicted by the conjunction/aspect of functional malefic planets and they are devoid of the aspect/conjunction of functional benefic planets, the native has weak constitution and during the period/sub-periods of the significator of health and the sub-periods of the afflicting planets the significations of diseases are aggravated.

The strength of the planets should also be seen in the relevant divisional chart with reference to the ascendant of the divisional chart. Debilitation, bad placement or affliction in the relevant divisional chart makes the planet weak regarding the significations of that divisional chart. The planets give us further hints. For example, weak/afflicted Mercury, being significator of health, may give suffering by way of nervous breakdown, skin infections or breathing problems, etc.

Whether the diseases would be temporary/permanent is revealed by the level of afflictions and the weakness of afflicted planets / houses. In case of natal afflictions with longer main periods like Venus, Saturn, Rahu, Mercury and Jupiter, the sufferings persist for a long time. In case of the natal afflictions the suffering is prolonged.

In case of transit afflictions by fast moving planets like the Moon, the Sun, Mercury, Venus, Mars and Ketu, relief is indicated comparatively early.

While the ascendant and the lord of the ascendant, the sixth house and its lord, the Sun (significator for vitality), the Moon (significator for mind) and Mercury (significator for nervous system) signify the physical and mental health in general, the individual planets indicate parts of the body governed by them. Moreover, the functional malefic planets in addition to their lordships cause sufferings by way of significations ruled by them. Mars afflicted by Rahu or a functional malefic Saturn may cause boils, wounds, muscular infections, irregular blood pressure, impurities of blood, etc. If the Sun is weak and in conjunction with Mars and one of these two planets is a functional malefic both the significations of Mars and the Sun suffer. The person, during mutual sub-periods of these planets, may have serious problems related with the general and particular significations of the Sun or Mars. The person, during mutual sub-periods of these planets, may have a fracture/operation of the part signified by the lordship of the Sun or Mars. Revolving around the foregoing general principles, numerous planetary combinations are seen which guide us towards possible diseases, a native may suffer.

Afflicted but otherwise strong planets give short duration health problems pertaining to their general and particular significations. If the lord of the ascendant is weak and there are severely afflicted planets or houses, a person is vulnerable to dreaded or critical diseases like cancer, skin infections, cardiac diseases, etc.

The health is ruled by the first and the sixth houses. Besides, these houses the lords of the ascendant and the sixth house containing a mooltrikona sign become the prime determinant(s) of health. In case both the ascendant and the sixth house do not contain a mooltrikona sign then the planet Sun, the significator for vitality, is considered as the prime determinant of health. For various ascendants, the following planets act as prime determinants:

PRIME DETERMINANTS

ASCENDANT	PRIME DETERMINANTS
Aries	Mars and Mercury
Taurus	Venus
Gemini	The Sun
Cancer	The Moon and Jupiter
Leo	The Sun
Virgo	Mercury and Saturn
Libra	Venus
Scorpio	Mars
Sagittarius	Jupiter
Capricorn	The Sun
Aquarius	Saturn and the Moon
Pisces	The Sun

If a mooltrikona sign rises in the shashthamsa (D-VI), the lord of the same becomes additional prime determinant of health. The Sun is the significator of health and vitality and Mars is the secondary significator of health and vitality. If the prime determinant(s), additional prime determinant and the prime and secondary significators are weak, badly placed and/or afflicted, then the native is vulnerable to serious health problems. In case the planets, mentioned here are strong or well placed and unafflicted, then the native enjoys good health except short term sufferings due to transit weakness and afflictions.

For various ascendants, the following planets become the afflictors:

ASCENDANT	AFFLICTORS
Aries	Mercury, Rahu and Ketu
Taurus	Venus, Jupiter, Mars, Rahu and Ketu
Gemini	Rahu and Ketu
Cancer	Jupiter, Saturn, Rahu and Ketu.
Leo	The Moon, Rahu and Ketu
Virgo	Saturn, Mars, the Sun, Rahu and Ketu
Libra	Mercury, Rahu and Ketu.
Scorpio	Mars, Venus, Rahu and Ketu.
Sagittarius	The Moon, Rahu and Ketu.
Capricorn	The Sun, Jupiter, Rahu and Ketu.
Aquarius	The Moon, Mercury, Rahu and Ketu.
Pisces	The Sun, Venus, Saturn, Rahu and Ketu.

SPOTTING THE HEALTH PROBLEMS

For spotting the health problems, we proceed as under:

1. Identify the strength of the planets.

2. Identify the concentrated malefic influence on the most effective points of various houses and the weak planets.

3. Identify the sub-periods of the afflicting and afflicted planets and the significators of the health problems.

4. Examine all the triple transit triggering afflictions, especially those with reference to the natal ascendant of slow moving or stationary functional malefic planets on the most effective points of various houses and the weak and afflicted planets, and those of natal functional malefic planets over slow moving or stationary weak planets.

The following are the significators of the health problems:

Weak Planets:

The weak planets are not in a position to protect their general significations and the significations of the houses containing their mooltrikona sign. Therefore, the native may have health problems due to malfunctioning of the significations ruled by the weak planets.

Afflicted Planets:

Those planets which are under the close influence of the functional malefic planets (afflictors as mentioned above) either by conjunction or aspect are treated as afflicted planets. The close influence of the lord of the sixth house and Rahu causes diseases which may respond to the symptomatic treatment. The close influence of the functional malefic planets ruling the eighth and twelfth houses and the planet Ketu gives chronic diseases. If the afflicted planet is weak and badly placed, the native suffers from fatal diseases and may have to undergo surgery, etc.

Planetary Periods:

The sub-periods of the afflicting or afflicted planets as mentioned above and the sub-periods of the planets placed in the sixth house and other malefic houses cause health problems. These sub-periods give rise to the trends which continue throughout the sub-periods and the trends can be reversed if the prime determinants are strong and the following sub-periods are of strong, well placed and unafflicted planets.

Transit Influences:

Sometimes, the illness is triggered by the close triple transit influences. The influence of slow moving malefic planets on the natal planets is generally long lived. If the afflicted planets are strong in the natal chart the symptoms of the illness end after the transit impact is over. If the afflicted planets are weak and badly placed in the natal chart and the sub-periods of the afflictors are in progress then the illness turns into chronic illness. The health problems caused by the transit to transit planetary influences are short lived and cease to exist when the transit affliction is over. The health problems caused by the natal over transit planetary influences can be long lived in case of slow moving transit planets.

TIME OF SURFACING

The problems of ill health start surfacing during the sub-periods of the following:

1. the lord of the ascendant; or
2. the lord of the sixth house; or
3. the planets placed in the sixth house; or
4. the planet causing affliction; or
5. the planet afflicted; or
6. the malefic transit influence on the weak natal positions.

UNDERSTANDING RULERSHIP OF PLANETS OVER FUNCTIONAL HEALTH

To identify the planets ruling various functional aspects of the health, it is necessary that we have the basic understanding of the functioning of the systems of the body. For the information of the readers, we shall discuss a few of the systems here:

Lymphatic System:

This system is the main line of defense of the body against the attack of the diseases. Lymphs is clear liquids containing white blood cells flowing in the lymphatic vessels. It is associated with the Moon. That is why the Moon has been identified as the significator for immunization system.

Skin:

A healthy and pink skin is indicative of good functional health. It reflects the personality of a person and focus on sexual feelings and expressions. That is why skin is represented by many planets including the lord of the ascendant, Venus, Mercury, Mars, Moon and even the Sun as the blood has a definite say in the formation of the skin.

Vision:

The beauty of eyes is governed by Venus while distant vision is governed by the Sun. The eyesight is governed by the Moon.

Hearing Power:

Mercury rules the power of communication and Jupiter rules the intelligence. Both these planets, thus play an important part as significators for the effective hearing power.

Osteoarthritis:

This is one of the diseases for which there is no fixed relationship of cause and treatment in medicine and the whole stress is on 'painkillers'. Our research reveals that osteoarthritis/gout pains are caused by the weakness of Mars, Venus and Saturn and the afflictions to the most effective point of the tenth house. The application of preventive astral remedies to cases with weak planets, mentioned in the preceding sentence, have shown encouraging results.

Diabetes:

It is another disease known for its dreaded mal-effects. The persons suffering from this disease become extremely weak, their body loses power of healing from any type of wounds/boils and it causes trouble to the eyes. It causes abnormal blood pressure if the patient is careless in the food habits. For analyzing the disease astrologically, let us first see the reasons of this disease in the medical science and the body parts involved. Our food is converted as digestible glucose in liver. Insulin released by pancreas is the main factor for conversion of glucose into the energy for whole of our body. The pancreas glands are behind stomach. If the discharge of insulin is not normal or less or suppressed due to any defects or reasons, the glucose is not converted into energy. The person suffers from hyperglycemia, meaning thereby that glucose level in the blood has increased. Further, if the filters in kidneys do not function properly the glucose starts passing through urine. If the fifth house, the significator of liver and pancreas glands, Jupiter, the significator of kidneys, Venus, and the significator of food digestion, Sun, are afflicted it holds the key for diagnosing diabetes.

Auto-immune Disease

Auto-immune disease is said to arise from an inappropriate immune response of the body against substances and tissues normally present in the body. In other words, the immune system mistakes some part of the body as a foreign antigen requiring elimination (any disease producing agent) and attacks its own cells. Auto-immune diseases are classified as hypersensitivity with different levels. In astrology, hypersensitivity is the result of the weakness of the Moon and Mercury and the immune system is governed by the Moon. Therefore, to check the vulnerability of a person to auto-immune diseases we have to analyze the planets Moon and Mercury and the twelfth house in a birth chart. The weakness of the prime determinants of health in the birth chart make things further difficult if the Moon, Mercury and the twelfth house are weak and afflicted. Strengthening the Moon and Mercury and remedial measures for the afflicting planets are likely to help a lot in offering protection against the vulnerability of a person to auto-immune diseases which can manifest in variety of ways.

While indicating the significations of houses, planets and signs, mentioned in the previous chapters, such types of functional aspects of the various systems of the body have been kept in view. The scope of this book is the astrological significators, their weakness and affliction, if any, and the application of the preventive astral remedies for enjoying good health by the natives.

Health problems surface when the significator houses and planets are weak and/or afflicted in a nativity besides the weakness of prime determinants and the periods and/or sub-periods of the afflictors and/or the afflicted significators are in operation.

CHAPTER 8

SERIOUS ILLNESS & TIMING RECOVERY OF PATIENTS

Identifying Serious Illness

The serious illness is governed by the following factors:-

i)   The sub-periods of weak and afflicted natal planets.

ii)   The sub-period of the planet whose mooltrikona sign falls in the sixth house and whenever such a sixth lord forms a close conjunction/aspect with another natal/transit planet or most effective point of a particular house.

iii) The illness is triggered by the triple transit malefic influence on the weak natal/transit planetary configurations.

Timing Recovery of Patients

Diverse applications of astrology include timing of events. Timing of events is done with the help of the sub-periods and the triple transit triggering influence of planets in the natal chart. Let us take up the study of timing recovery and survival of patients. In an atmosphere of suspense when medical attendants can't assure the querent (person asking question) about the condition of the patient, one is impelled to turn to astrology to know the likely end of the suspense and the timing.

To analyze recovery of the patient the horoscope is a must. Fairly accurate delineations can be worked out from a horary (prasna) chart, as well. The duration of recovery is worked out through the study of current sub-period, the natal strength of the planets and separating functional malefic transit influences. When the slow moving functional malefic planets like Rahu-Ketu, Saturn and Jupiter exercising affliction(s) are stationary, the duration of the critical condition of the patient is generally longer. The pace of recovery depends upon the general strength of the planets in the natal chart and transit

In this regard we have to proceed with the analysis in a systematic manner. Firstly, we have to work out the natal chart of the patient or one of the close relatives of the patient. In the absence of the birth particulars of the patient the analysis can be made from the horary chart or the chart of a close relative of the patient. After working out the chart, identify the slow moving functional malefic planet exerting malefic influence in the chart currently i.e. in transit and/or the slow moving planet under functional malefic natal influence. Rahu and Ketu work in a malefic manner for all the ascendants. After identifying the functional malefic planet(s) causing the serious condition and the strength of the natal position of the afflicted planet/house find out if the affliction is on the most effective point of a house ruled by a weak planet or on a weak natal planet. The transit strength of the identified weak and afflicted planet should also be identified. If the sub-period of a fairly strong or well placed natal functional benefic planet is running, the results may not be serious and the recovery depends on the separation of the functional malefic influence on the weak natal/transit positions. While the seriousness may go when the separating influence is one degree longitude apart, the recovery may be possible when the separating effect is five degrees longitude apart between the afflicting planet and the afflicted planet/house. The general strong position of transit planets hastens the recovery while the weak position delays the same. The strength of the Moon is a significant factor for consideration and transit affliction of the Moon gives the possible timing of setbacks indicating deterioration in condition. The brief spells of transit affliction of the Moon can be avoided for major medical remedies like starting of a new medication, operation, etc. to avoid immediate complications in the treatment.

For the benefit of the readers, we would now take up some illustrations so that the readers can comprehend the application of a systematic approach. The first three charts of this chapter pertain to serious indoor patients in the second fortnight of February, 1995. The general planetary position was not encouraging besides it being a dark half. Mars was in its sign of debilitation. The Sun was weak as its dispositor was weak and the Sun was under the close aspect of Rahu. Saturn was combust; Venus changed the sign and underwent old age and infancy. Jupiter was weak due to its being in the debilitated navamsa. The general weakness of majority of the planets kept the pace of recovery of patients quite slow and the transit afflictions of the Sun and the Moon increased intensity of seriousness.

CHART 1

Male born 14th October, 1929, 2306 Hrs. Lahore, India (Now Pakistan).

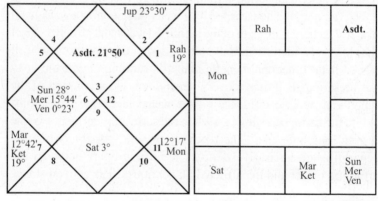

Rahu-Ketu axis afflicts the most effective points of the houses occupied/aspected in this nativity. During the main period of Ketu and the sub-period of Mars the functional malefic planets Rahu and Ketu, exercising close influence on the fifth house in the natal chart, came under their own transit influence and gave the problem of acidity and burning sensation in the food pipe. On the 18th January, 1995, the transit Rahu formed close conjunction with natal Mars. On 13th February, 1995, already in the sub-period of Rahu, the transit influence of Rahu and Ketu further intensified on natal Mars and the person was admitted to the hospital for an operation for removal of a suspected malignant growth in the food pipe. The person succumbed to the surgery on 6th March, 1995, when the transit malefic influence of Rahu and Ketu on weak natal Mars was exact, and transit Mars was debilitated. The speed of Rahu was quite slow and it took the toll. The sub-period of Rahu was indicative of such an eventuality in the main period of Ketu which is the most malefic planet for the natives born under the ascending sign of Gemini.

CHART 2

Horary chart for 27th February, 1995, 1545 Hrs. New Delhi, India.

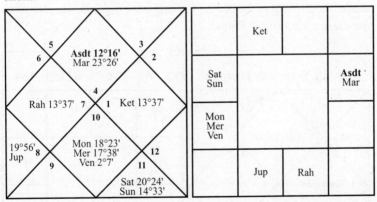

The query was regarding the illness of a relative admitted in the ICU. Rahu-Ketu axis was closely afflicting the most effective points of the houses occupied and aspected. The lord of the eighth house ruling death was severely afflicting the lord of the sixth house, Jupiter. The horary chart clearly indicates that the badly placed lord of the house of family, the Sun, is under the exact affliction of Rahu and was in the process of forming close conjunction with the lord of the eighth house in the eighth house. The conjunction of the lord of the second house ruling family was becoming further close with the lord of the eighth house and was also continuing under the close aspect of transit Rahu.

The lord of the ascendant of the horary chart was also entering the eighth house and coming under the close influence of Rahu indicating grief to the native. The patient died in the morning hours of the 1st March, 1995. The lord of the ascendant of the horary chart had also entered the eighth house and come under the close affliction of Rahu.

Appropriate astral remedies for the afflicting planets play a major role in toning down the severity of the afflictions. No astral remedies were being performed in this case.

During the second half of February, 1995, there were number of casualties in the ICU while the position of ICU patients reportedly started improving in the bright half and after the Sun was free from the close affliction of Rahu.

CHART 3

Male born 18th February, 1952, 1630 Hrs. New Delhi, India.

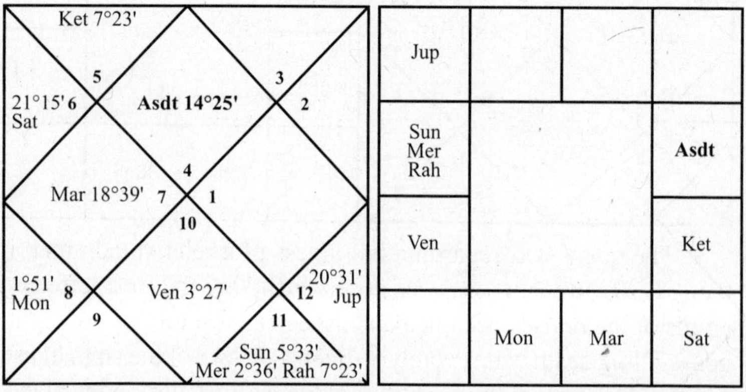

Jup			
Sun Mer Rah			Asdt
Ven			Ket
	Mon	Mar	Sat

Chart (South Indian / diamond style):
Ket 7°23'
5 ... 3
21°15' 6 Sat — Asdt 14°25' — 2
4
Mar 18°39' 7 — 1
10
1°51' Mon 8 — Ven 3°27' — 12 20°31' Jup
9 — 11
Sun 5°33'
Mer 2°36' Rah 7°23'

The lord of the ascendant is debilitated and weak but well placed and unafflicted. Mars, the lord of the tenth house, closely aspects the tenth house which is a positive factor for the longevity in view of the weakness of the prime factor of longevity, the lord of the ascendant. The functional malefic planets, Saturn and Jupiter, closely aspect each other giving rise to possibility of death through serious illness or an accident. Jupiter rules the house of illness and Saturn rules the house of death. The Sun and combust Mercury are placed in the eighth house and the Sun is suffering from the close affliction of Rahu-Ketu axis. The Sun is the significator for the vitality. The planetary configurations clearly deny the full life span. The native had just completed 43 years of age.

The native was admitted in the hospital for liver cirrhosis on 22nd February, 1995, and was in the sub-period of Saturn in the main period of Ketu. Jupiter is significator for liver. The sub-period was of a planet which is indicative of death. In transit, the Sun was in the eighth house, Jupiter had formed close aspect with the natal position of Jupiter and Rahu-Ketu axis was afflicting the most effective point of the eighth house besides the most effective points of the other houses occupied and aspected. Transit Saturn was exactly afflicting transit Jupiter. It was considered that the recovery of the patient was almost impossible. The patient breathed his last four days later when the transit Sun came under the exact aspect of Rahu.

CHART 4

Male born 7th July, 1994, 0704 Hrs. Bombay, India.

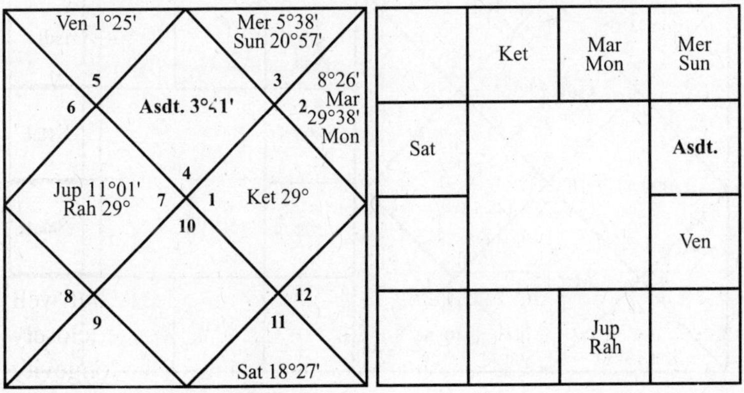

		Ket	Mar Mon	Mer Sun
Sat				Asdt.
				Ven
			Jup Rah	

Chart (diamond-style):

Ven 1°25'
Mer 5°38' Sun 20°57'
5
6   Asdt. 3°41'   3   8°26'
2 Mar 29°38' Mon
Jup 11°01' Rah 29°   7   4   1   Ket 29°
10
8
9   12
11
Sat 18°27'

The lord of the ascendant is in its sign of exaltation and unafflicted but very weak as it is in extreme old age. The lord of the eighth house is strong and is not creating any close affliction in the chart. In this way it strengthens the longevity and indicates gains to father but causes obstructions and ill health during its sub-period. Mercury and the Sun are badly placed but do not suffer from any close affliction. The functional malefic Jupiter, too, does not cause any close affliction in the chart. The child was reported to be suffering seriously from meningitis since 21st November, 1994. The native was running the sub-period of Mercury in the main period of Mars. The sub-period of a weak functional benefic planet was not considered to be dangerous for life. Transit Jupiter was afflicting the most effective point of the fifth house and the most effective point of the houses aspected, as well. Simultaneously, the transit Rahu had also formed close aspect with natal Sun and Saturn placed in the twelfth and eighth houses, respectively. Transit aspects were separating towards the end of the year 1994. Therefore, native's parents were advised for propitiatory measures for Rahu and Jupiter and strengthening measures for the weak functional benefic planets through the use of a Yantra (Kavach). The native responded to treatment completely by the end of December, 1994.

CHART 5

Male born 25th March, 1981, 1728 Hrs. New Delhi, India.

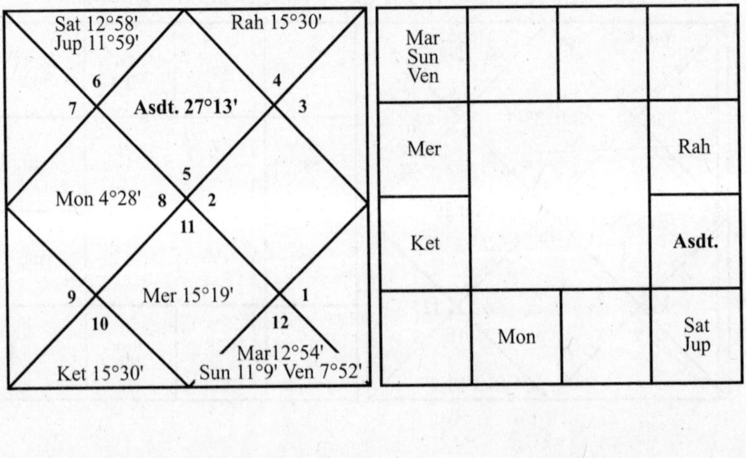

Sat 12°58' Jup 11°59' **6** **7**	Rah 15°30' **4** Asdt. 27°13' **5** **3**		
Mon 4°28' **8**	**2** **11**		
9 **10**	Mer 15°19' **12**		
Ket 15°30'	Mar12°54' Sun 11°9' Ven 7°52'		

Mar Sun Ven			
Mer			Rah
Ket			Asdt.
	Mon		Sat Jup

The lord of the ascendant is badly placed in the eighth house in close conjunction with the functional benefic planets, Mars and Venus. The Sun and Mars suffer from the close affliction of Rahu from the twelfth house. The Moon occupies its sign of debilitation.

Saturn and Jupiter are well placed and are closely conjunct with each other but both of them suffer from the close aspect of Ketu from the sixth house. Mercury is well placed but its dispositor is badly afflicted. The sub-period of Rahu robbed the courage of the native due to affliction of Rahu to the Sun and the combust Mars and the native developed fear phobia. The treatment from different sources proved to be of little help. On 25th of August, 1994, the astral counseling and remedies were sought. The native was suggested charities for Rahu, avoiding of the grey colored clothes and the use of protective disk, Kavach, for strengthening of the weak functional benefic planets which proved helpful and brought improvement in the general condition of the native. The full rehabilitation of the native was slow due to the following sub-periods of weak Jupiter and Saturn and as both of these planets were afflicted by Ketu by way of an aspect from the house of diseases.

CHART 6

Female born 15th December, 1982, 0835 Hrs. New Delhi, India.

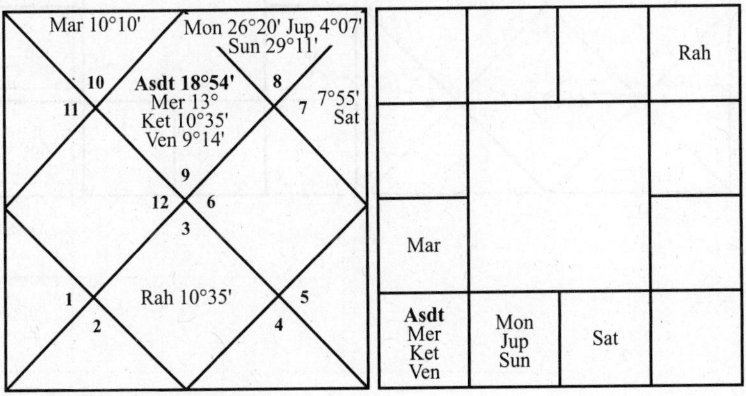

				Rah
			Mar	
	Asdt Mer Ket Ven	Mon Jup Sun	Sat	

North Indian chart:
- Mar 10°10'
- Mon 26°20' Jup 4°07' Sun 29°11'
- Asdt 18°54' Mer 13° Ket 10°35' Ven 9°14'
- 7°55' Sat (house 7)
- Rah 10°35'
- Houses: 10, 11, 8, 9, 12, 6, 3, 1, 2, 4, 5

The functional malefic Moon is debilitated, badly placed and is closely afflicting the weak Sun. The lord of the ascendant is badly placed. Rahu-Ketu axis closely afflicts Mercury and Venus. Rahu closely afflicts Saturn. Mars is the only strong planet. Mars is in the sign of exaltation and does not suffer from any affliction. The weak ascendant lord and afflicted planets make a native prone to ill-health. During the end of sub-period of Mercury in the main period of Ketu the native suffered from loss of memory. The astral remedies were sought towards the end of 1994 after trying medical and psychiatric treatment of all types. As the disease had not been the result of the transit influence but is indicative due to the affliction of Mercury which is closely conjunct with Ketu, no short term treatment gave relief. The astral propitiatory remedies for Rahu, Ketu and the Moon together with a Kavach for strengthening the weak and afflicted functional benefic planets were suggested. The use of the astral remedies started giving improvement.

CHART 7

Male born 20th March, 1992, 0733 Hrs. New Delhi, India.

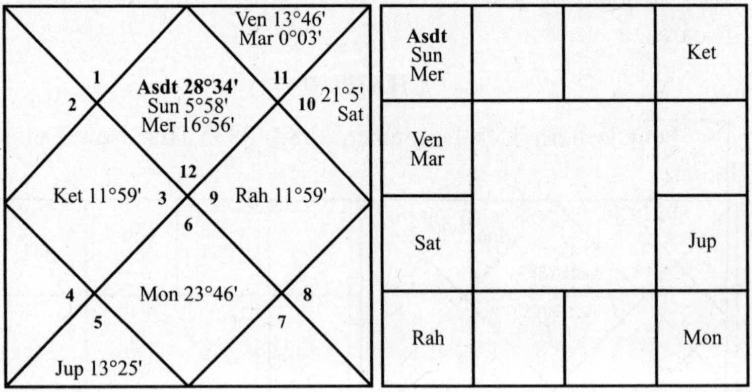

Asdt Sun Mer			Ket
Ven Mar			
Sat			Jup
Rah			Mon

No mooltrikona sign rises in the ascendant and therefore the lord of the eighth house governs the longevity. Mars is in extreme infancy and placed in the twelfth house. Jupiter is closely aspected and afflicted by Rahu and the most malefic planet, Venus. Venus is closely afflicted by the aspect of the functional malefic planet Ketu. Venus receives close aspect of the functional benefic, Jupiter, though it is of little help because of Jupiter's own bad placement and affliction. Mercury, the significator for speech and analytical power, is weak due to combustion and debilitation.

Mars, the main period lord at birth, rules the second house which inter alia other things also rules speech. Weakness of both, the lord of the house of speech and the significator for speech and the affliction of lord of the twelfth house to the significator of speech, Mercury, gave prominent results of the weak and afflicted planetary influences in this case. The native had almost no speech up to the middle of the year 1995 when the astral remedies were sought. In such cases, the astral remedies also cannot make significant improvement as none of the second house, its lord and Mercury has any beneficial impact on them nor is Jupiter strong.

CHART 8

Male born 15th July, 1994, 1029 Hrs. New Delhi, India.

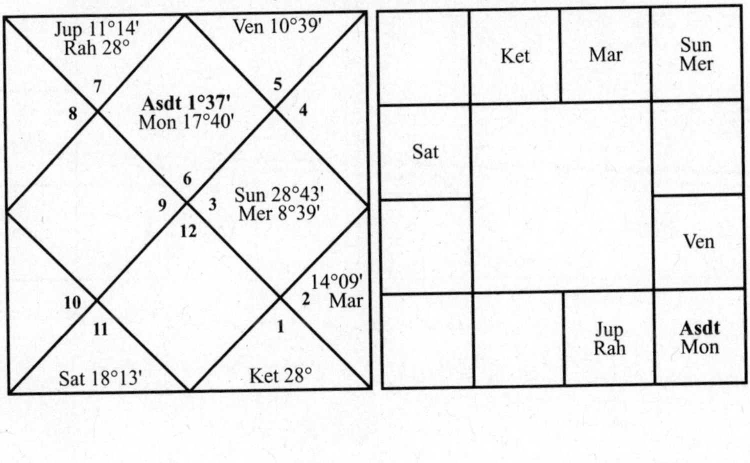

	Ket	Mar	Sun Mer
Sat			
			Ven
		Jup Rah	Asdt Mon

Rahu causes an exact aspect to the weak Sun. The most malefic planet, Mars, closely aspects the badly placed Venus. Rahu-Ketu axis afflicts the most effective points of the ninth, eleventh, first, third, fifth and seventh houses. Similarly, the Sun afflicts the most effective points of the eleventh and fifth houses, in the nativity. At birth the native was running the sub-period of Saturn in the main period of the Moon. Saturn rules the sixth house and is capable of giving diseases in its sub-period. The native was suffering from jaundice at birth. However, the sickness at birth was given by the close affliction of Rahu to the Sun which separated only in the end of August, 1994. Whenever, there is exact affliction of the functional malefic planets, the sub-period of a functional malefic is running at birth and the functional malefic being a slow moving planet is stationary or having a slower motion, the native suffers from ill health right at birth. If the prime significator for longevity is not weak, badly placed and afflicted, as in this case, the native recovers from the sickness prevailing at the time of birth as soon as the functional malefic planet's close conjunction with the afflicted planet separates. The natal and transit position of the planets at birth is same and the transit movement of functional malefic planets over the natal position of afflicted planets helps in arriving at the conclusions.

CHAPTER 9

APPLICATION OF PREVENTIVE ASTRAL REMEDIES

Medicine treats but Jyotish remedies prevent. The jyotish / astral remedies consist of a Kavach or a Special Power Kavach or a special purpose Kavach and the propitiatory astral remedies for the functional malefic planets. The application of astrological remedial measures is always advantageous in all aspects of life including health, education, profession and relationships. Astrology helps through predictions and astral remedies. Astrology enables wise people to charter and manage the course of success in life for health, career, love, relationships and financial matters. The interpretation and the effective jyotish remedies suggestion is based on the planetary influences in the individual horoscopes. Jyotish remedies act as panacea in all aspects of life and in harmony with medical remedies for various types of health problems. Jyotish remedies help in diagnosis of the health problems and application of medical remedies. The blessed ones are impelled by the divine forces for making use of the ultimate knowledge through application of jyotish remedies / astral remedies - both propitiating astral remedies for functional malefic planets and strengthening remedies for weak functional benefic planets through "Kavach" or a "Special Power Kavach" or special purpose Kavach or Gemstones. "Preventive Jyotish Remedies are best."

We all know that the full Moon with the entire starry host and even with all the mountains set on fire cannot fight the darkness of the night. Only the rise of the Sun can bring the night darkness to an end. Similarly, the planetary weaknesses and afflictions can only be reduced to a large extent or even removed with the help of the propitiatory and strengthening astrological remedial measures.

The problems in life are caused by weak planets and/or afflictions to them. To help people overcome their problems, the astrologer advises appropriate astral remedies, such as meditation and spiritual practices, color and gemstone therapy, the wearing of a Kavach or amulet as a protective shield, and the participation in pujas and yagnas, etc. Therefore, a two-way application of astral remedies is administered after diagnosing the problematic planetary influences in a chart. Firstly, the strength is provided to the weak functional benefic planets. The strength can be provided by various methods, e.g. gemstone, color therapy, Kavach (the protective shield containing mystical numbers of the planets) in an auspicious time. Secondly, the malevolence of the functional malefic planets is reduced through the regular practice of meditation, spiritual practices and offering propitiatory charities concerning these planets. The two-way application helps in reducing the impact of functional malefic planetary influences to a large extent. The preventive use of astral remedies is much more useful than the curative astral remedies.

Generally, people seek astral remedies advice in the end after trying all other therapies ignoring the distinct advantage of preventive diagnostic power of the astrological science. It is needless to stress that the benefit of preventive measures as against those of the curative measures is much better.

Whenever performed with faith and sincerity, the efficacy of astral remedies in terms of immediate results depends on many things including the ascendant and the strength of the natal planets. If the functional malefic planets are more in the natal chart, with multiple close afflictions, and the functional benefic planets are weak, one benefits with delay. For example, the people born in the Virgo, Cancer, Pisces, Taurus and Capricorn ascendants need lot of time for sincere and faithful performance of propitiatory remedies. Then the further factors to be seen are the strength of the planets and especially the lord of the operating sub-period and the transit influences.

WHEN TO GO FOR REMEDIAL MEASURES?

One of the frequently asked questions is what should be the timing of application of astral remedies. Prevention is better than cure. This saying is also true in case of application of astral remedies. No doubt, astral remedies are helpful in a problematic situation but if the native goes for preventive application, it not only proves to be a better tool to tackle various circumstances but also reduces the level of problems to a great extent. The problems are reduced to the level of tension and the potential damage is averted. In many cases we have found that their preventive application has averted dreaded diseases including cancer even when strong combinations for such diseases were present in the horoscope of the person.

To provide strength to the weak birth (natal) planets, we recommend use of gemstone or planetary Kavach as part of Astral or Jyotish remedies for the favorable planets in an auspicious time.

For both - curative and preventive remedies - the judicious mixture of the following astral remedies is applied.

GEMS: The ancient wisdom reveals that besides medicines the gemstones and colors are capable of providing good health and mental/spiritual happiness. The efficacy of the gemstones is even recognized by the Ayurveda, the ancient system of medicine.

The importance of time, which means the planetary influences at a particular point of time and at a particular place, has always been recognized since ancient times. The references have been found in the Hindu scriptures, Shakespearean era and the New Testament. It is also firmly believed that the potency of medicines and its curative power increase when the medicine is administered at a particular time of the day and in a particular season. This is also true for the jyotish/astral remedies.

Different planets represent the various colors. To provide strength to the weak natal planets, the divine science of astrology recommends use of gemstone for the favorable planets in an auspicious time. The strength of the planets is raised through the application of influence of concentrated rays of a particular color of a gemstone, which represents a particular planet. The gemstones represent the rays of light peculiar to different planets. The men and women use them for raising the power of planets besides wearing them for ornamental purposes.

Gemstones can be worn in a pendant or in a ring in an auspiciously elected time. Different gemstones are worn in a ring in the following fingers:

Ruby in left ring finger;

Pearl in left little finger;

Red Coral in left/right ring finger;

Emerald in right little finger;

Yellow Sapphire in right index finger;

Diamond in right ring finger;

Blue sapphire in left middle finger.

The gemstones are recommended to begin use in an auspicious time for particular weak planets if they are favorable in one's birth chart. The weight recommended for all the gemstones except diamond is between 4.6 to 4.7 carats. The recommended weight for diamond is 1 carat.

The gemstones for the Sun, the Moon, Mars, Mercury, Jupiter, Venus and Saturn are respectively ruby, pearl, red coral, emerald, yellow sapphire/topaz, diamond or white sapphire/topaz and blue sapphire/topaz, respectively. The gemstone used should be flawless, bright and should not contain feathers and silky inclusions. Only the gemstones pertaining to the functional benefic planets are recommended to be used.

RUBY: This gemstone is used to strengthen the Sun in a horoscope. The Sun represents vitality, the heart as life centre, digestive system and circulatory system of the body, bone structure, constitution, blood, brain, bile, digestive fire, right eye for males and left eye in case of females. It also represents one's father, employment, one's social status and one's relationship with the Government.

If the Sun is weak and/or afflicted in the birth chart, it makes the person vulnerable to sufferings on account of weak eyesight, headaches, erratic blood circulation, heart trouble, bone fractures, overheating, fevers, blood pressure, baldness, neuralgia, bone cancer, etc. If the Sun is a functional benefic planet, the use of ruby protects and promotes the foregoing significations. The recommended weight of the ruby is between 4.6 to 4.7 carats.

PEARL: This gemstone is used to strengthen the Moon in a horoscope. The Moon represents fertility, emotional health and functional health as it governs fluids in body, good quality of blood and lymph, glands, tonsils, breasts, stomach, lymphatic system, face, lungs and chest, and is general significator for sleep and emotional peace. It governs the left eye in the case of males, ovaries, menstrual cycle, uterus, generative organs and right eye in the case of females. It also represents mother, mind and wife.

If the Moon is weak and/or afflicted in the birth chart, besides psychic problems it makes the person vulnerable to sleep disorders, lethargy, drowsiness, auto-immune disorders, lung problems, mouth problems (including loss of taste), neurological disorders, epilepsy, digestive complains, water retention, blood disorders, anemia, blood-pressure, enlargement of spleen, diseases of the uterus and ovaries, tuberculosis, menstrual disorders, and the native is vulnerable to frequent cough and cold, fever, lack of appetite, general weakness, etc., and denotes hyper-sensitivity, over-reaction, inability to respond and difficulty getting in touch with feelings. If the Moon is a functional benefic planet, the use of pearl protects and promotes the foregoing significations. The recommended weight of the pearl is between 4.6 to 4.7 carats.

RED CORAL: This gemstone is used to strengthen Mars in a horoscope. Mars represents the chest, bone marrow, blood, bile, digestive fire, intestine, forehead, neck, muscular system, acuity of vision, sinews, nose, external generative organs, physical power and vitality. Mars is also the general significator of younger brothers, which adds to the strength of the native and become a source of strength and courage.

If Mars is weak and/or afflicted in the birth chart, it makes the person vulnerable to inflammations, overheating, inability to tolerate hunger, wounds, burns, accidents, fractures, piles, skin rashes, ulcers, lacerations, operations, all sorts of acute complaints, fevers (particularly eruptive), epilepsy, mental aberration, tumors, cancer in the muscular parts of the body when closely conjunct with Rahu, dysentery, typhoid, cholera, pox and boils, etc., and denotes anger, irritability, haste, impatience, inconstancy, lack of drive and courage, and an 'all-or-nothing' attitude. If Mars is a functional benefic planet, the use of red coral protects and promotes the foregoing significations. The recommended weight of the red coral is between 4.6 to 4.7 carats.

EMERALD: This gemstone is of dark green color and bright and is used to strengthen Mercury in a horoscope. Mercury represents the lower part of abdomen, skin, mind, nervous system, urinary bladder, bronchial tube, gastric juice, digestion, intestines, lungs, tongue, mouth, hands and arms. Mercury rules analytical faculties, speech, sharp intellect, power of discrimination and confidence.

If Mercury is weak and/or afflicted in the birth chart, it makes the person vulnerable to psychic diseases, insomnia, nervous breakdown, epilepsy, skin diseases, leucoderma, impotence, loss of memory or speech, vertigo, deafness, asthma, diseases of respiratory canal, auto-immune disorders, disorders of intestines, dyspepsia, etc. It denotes difficulty in thought and communication, timidity, low self-esteem, aloofness, amorality, expediency, over-intellectualization and poor discrimination. Mercury is weak quite frequently. Whenever its period is in operation in any nativity it creates tensions in life, lack of confidence, situation of indecisiveness, etc., which ultimately leads to faulty decisions. The effect is more if Mercury is weak in the birth chart as well as in transit at the time of operation of its sub-periods. It makes a person a nervous wreck and can even cause paralysis when closely afflicted by Rahu-Ketu axis, if the ascendant and its lord are also weak or the sign Virgo falls in the ascendant. If Mercury is a functional benefic planet, the use of emerald protects and promotes the foregoing significations. The recommended weight of the emerald is between 4.6 to 4.7 carats. The gemstone may contain some silky inclusions but it should not contain feathers and black spots.

YELLOW SAPPHIRE: This gemstone is recommended to strengthen Jupiter in a horoscope. Jupiter represents the hips, the fat tissue, blood, arterial system, glands, liver, gall bladder, pancreas gland, digestion, absorptive power, ears/hearing power, navel, feet, physical development, palate and throat. Jupiter signifies elder brothers, spouse in female nativities, male progeny, wealth, morals, sincerity, friends, divine grace and father and, in fact, all good things in life.

When weak and/or afflicted, it makes the person vulnerable to lymphatic and circulatory congestion, thrombosis, anemia, tumors, jaundice and other liver complaints, ear problems, dyspepsia, flatulence, cough, cold, diabetes and other diseases of pancreas glands, etc. If Jupiter is a functional benefic planet, the use of yellow sapphire protects and promotes the foregoing significations. The recommended weight of the yellow sapphire is between 4.6 to 4.7 carats.

DIAMOND: This gemstone is used to strengthen Venus in a horoscope. Venus represents the pelvis and the sexual organs, desires and yearnings, reproduction, the semen/ovum, private parts, kidneys, face, eyes, neck, throat, chin, cheeks, skin, venous system, etc. Venus is also the general significator of wife.

When weak and/or afflicted, it makes the person vulnerable to venereal diseases, diseases of urinary or reproductive system, diabetes, stones in bladder or kidneys, cataract, weakness of sexual organs, cough, cold, sexual perversions, impotence or inability to have sexual relations, loss of body luster, etc. If Venus is a functional benefic planet, the use of diamond protects and promotes the foregoing significations. The recommended weight of the diamond is 1 carat. The gemstone should be flawless and should not contain silky inclusions.

BLUE SAPPHIRE: This gemstone is of dark blue color and is used to strengthen Saturn in a horoscope. Saturn represents the nerve tissue, tendons, joints, spleen, teeth, knees, shin and part of leg between ankle and knee, gall bladder, phlegm and secretive system, respiratory system and bones.

When weak and/or afflicted, it makes the person vulnerable to constant and painful diseases, all sorts of chronic and degenerative diseases, leg fracture, cancer, diseases of glands, paralysis, arthritis, rheumatism, gout, rickets, consumption, flatulence, deformities, coldness of the body, nerve disorders, insanity, numbness, windy diseases, senility, impotence in men, pain and obstruction in the functions of the body like retention of urine, intestinal obstruction, etc. If Saturn is a functional benefic planet, the use of blue sapphire protects and promotes the foregoing significations. The recommended weight of the blue sapphire is between 4.6 to 4.7 carats. The gemstone should be flawless and should not contain feathers and silky inclusions.

KAVACH

The design and concept of Kavach in the book, "Predictive Techniques and the Application of Astrological Remedial Measures" has been created, tested and popularized by Author and Astrologer Shri V. K. Choudhry.

Kavach Design Copyright (C) 1994 Shri V. K. Choudhry.

Kavach is in the form of a silver/white metal pendant. For some ascending signs the size of Kavach is 4.5 cm x 2 cm approximately while for other ascending signs the size of the Kavach is 3 cm x 2 cm approximately. Kavach can also be created in special designs and in gold.

Kavach also called an amulet or a zodiac pendant is a protective shield in the form of a pendant which is made of silver containing mystical numbers of the functional benefic planets in a nativity and is a strengthening measure, providing protection to the natal and transit afflictions of the weak functional benefic planets. Kavach is energized in an auspiciously elected time. With its use, the weak planets are enabled to protect and promote their significations. The Kavach draws its power from the powerful planetary position in which it is created and it is worn also in a specially elected auspicious time for generating the desired impact. Kavach carries the spiritual blessings of the provider of the Kavach and is used for improving the strength of the planets to enable them to bear the natal and transit afflictions.

Kavach is certainly not a miraculous or magical object. This is part of faith healing and its effectiveness and the amount of help cannot be measured in a scientific manner. The confidence of the Kavach providers is based on the feedback of the users. This is used both for preventive and curative purposes, and dispenses with the necessity of wearing different gems for different planets.

EFFECTIVENESS OF KAVACH

Effectiveness of Kavach and other astral remedies depends on many things including the ascendant and the strength of the natal planets. If the functional malefic planets are more in the natal chart with multiple close afflictions and the functional benefic planets are weak, the person benefits with delay. For example, the people born in the Virgo, Cancer, Pisces, Taurus and Capricorn ascendants after wearing the Kavach need lot of time with simultaneous sincere and faithful performance of propitiatory remedies to get the benefits of the Kavach. Then the further factors to be seen are the strength of the planets, especially of the lord of the operating sub-period, and the transit influences.

Those having the exact afflictions of the most malefic planet or the functional malefic planets amongst themselves or with the functional benefic planets may not appreciate immediately the impact made by the Kavach or a special power Kavach. Such persons need a special purpose Kavach which consists of special power Kavach and the gemstones. But in fact, the Kavach or special power Kavach is believed to provide tremendous support to the planets under stress. For example, the exact affliction in the case of the lords of the sixth and eighth houses makes one vulnerable to paralytic attacks or chronic ailments. The application of an appropriate Kavach here is believed to reduce the vulnerability to a large extent but how much is difficult to show. Such exact afflictions are very difficult to remove.

POWER OF KAVACH:

To generate good healing power, the Kavach provider astrologer should have any one of the following planetary influence in his/her birth chart:

i)   a strong or at least well-placed and unafflicted Jupiter in his/her own natal chart.

ii) a strong fourth or first lord in the ninth house or a strong lord of the ninth house in the fourth or second or first house with an unafflicted Sun.

The Kavach gets power to do well not only due to the engravings being done in an auspicious time but also due to a prescribed way of life followed by the Kavach provider. The astrologer prescribing and providing use of the Kavach should follow these principles:

• Bath in the morning without any bed tea, etc.

• Prayers to Lord.

• Performance of propitiatory remedies as per one's own chart.

• Practice the divine way in life i.e. (1) Be content; (2) Increase utility to humanity; (3) Help poor and needy; (4) Be kind, generous and benevolent; and (5) Avoid deeper involvement in sensual pleasures, anger, pride, greed and envy.

Continuous practice of the above principles helps in generating spiritual power for helping others to ward off evils in life and derive benefits indicated by the functional benefic planets in one's chart.

KAVACH INFORMATION

Kavach is worn in auspiciously elected time. The auspicious time is worked out with reference to the place of stay. Gemstone therapy has limited utility in comparison to the benefits gained by wearing the Kavach. The Kavach acts as a protective shield and at a cost which is far less than the cost of wearing four to six precious gemstones. So, make your life better by strengthening weak birth planets with a Kavach. When used as a preventive therapy it is likely to help in the following matters:-

- Energizes weak birth planets for bringing happiness in life

- Success in studies

- Success in professional career/business

- Develops leadership skills

- Improves memory and analytical skills

- Protects health

- Gives timely marriage

- Gives success in relationships

- Blesses with children

- Blesses with achievements and recognition in life and so on and so forth the list is very long.

The details required for providing a "Kavach" are:

1. Horoscope details - that is date, time and place of birth of the person who desires to have a Kavach.

2. The details of place of stay in the next couple of months for the person to wear the Kavach with longitudes, latitudes and summer time correction, if any.

3. The complete postal address for dispatch of Kavach through registered post (air-mail).

The Kavach can be worn in a thread or a gold/silver chain around the neck and after one starts wearing the Kavach for the first time one should continuously wear it. There is no precaution to be taken by the wearer of the Kavach.

Those who are metal sensitive or have strong aesthetic sense can derive benefits of Kavach by carrying it with them in their wallet or keeping it at the place of worship in the home.

If it is mandatory to take the Kavach off the body, one can do that but should again wear the Kavach as soon as it is possible to derive the impact of the Kavach continuously. The thread of the Kavach can be changed, whenever it requires a change.

For the details of mystical numbers to be engraved on the Kavach for all the twelve ascendants the readers can refer to our book, "Predictive Techniques and Application of Astrological Remedial Measures".

COLOR THERAPY: This is a very potent preventive remedy for epilepsy, mental retardation, psychic problems, etc. and is practiced through the use of favorable colors in the matters of dress and furnishings in one's living room. As each day of the week is ruled by a particular planet, each day we should dress at least one wearable garment of the color indicated for that planet if functional benefic.

These are the days of the week and the colors ruled by each planet:

Sun	Sunday	Orange, Pink, Golden
Moon	Monday	White, Silver
Mars	Tuesday	Burning Red
Mercury	Wednesday	Dark Green
Jupiter	Thursday	Yellow
Venus	Friday	Variegated, Royal Blue
Saturn	Saturday	Black, Dark Brown, Navy Blue

As per the opinion of experts compiled by a Library in Pittsburgh, the grey color of cars was found to be the worst in car safety. As per our color therapy, we had always been suggesting to avoid grey colors by those desirous of happy living and good health.

VASTU: Again this is a preventive as well as a curative therapy for solving the problems in physical and spiritual areas. Wider applications of this therapy are in the field of success of professional ventures. This is practiced through the use of proper outlay of a building to derive geo-magnetic forces for properly energizing the total impact of that building with the help of light, air, space and aura conducive to the main function of the environment.

The minimum vastu to be kept in view is:

1. Place of meditation in north east;

2. Bedrooms in south and south west;

3. Children's study in north;

4. Kitchen in south east;

5. Stairs in south-west;

6. Heavy structures in the house in south-west;

7. One should sleep with one's head in east, or south or south west directions;

8. The central place of the residential unit should be empty;

9. There should be openings in east and west and it would be better if the opening is also in south direction;

10. The opening only in south direction creates conflicts and diseases while the openings only in north direction stops family prosperity and sometimes even continuity. Opening only in the west direction brings poverty.

11. The place should be properly lit and pastel colors of functional benefic planets should be used on the walls;

12. The furnishings should be mostly plain or with very little flowery designs. In any case the patterns and designs on the fabric should not be too imposing.

MANTRAS: As part of the meditation, the recitation of Mantras is prescribed for propitiating the trouble causing planets.

CHARITIES: These are offered for the functional malefic planets causing afflictions/problems in a horoscope. The malefic influences are effectively tackled with the help of one of these propitiatory remedial measures for each planet when acting as a functional malefic:

SUN:

• Serving one's father or helping old age needy persons.

• Give wheat soaked in water with 20 grams of jaggery (Gur) to a cow on Sundays.

• Surya Namaskar at sunrise.

• Observe law of the land meticulously.

MOON:

• Serving one's mother or old age women.

• Keep a fresh water pot for the birds.

• Offering boiled rice with sugar to the birds.

MARS:

• Service or help to younger brother(s).

• Prayers/meditation every morning for at least 10 min.

• Being considerate to one's servant(s).

• Exercising patience.

MERCURY:

- Helping poor students and needy children.

- Donating to orphanages, twice a year.

- Offering green fodder (about 2 Kg) to a cow.

- Donating green pulses.

JUPITER:

- Offering service to one's preceptor/teacher.

- Prayers/meditation every morning.

- Offering banana in small pieces to the birds.

- Offering one bundi laddu (an Indian sweet) or any yellow sweet to the birds.

VENUS:

- Being considerate to one's wife or helping ladies in distress.

- Donating sugar, rice and cooking oil.

- Offering white sweets to the birds.

- Donating silken clothes of bright colors.

SATURN:

- Being considerate to servants.

- Offering simple salty food to the birds.

- Donating black pulses or salt or mustard oil on Saturdays.

- Donate to organizations that help poor people, twice a year.

RAHU:

- Serving one's parents.

- Give part of your breakfast to the birds.

- Donate for old age needy persons or lepers, twice a year.

- Giving away brown colored sweets to the birds.

KETU:

- Offering some food to a street dog.

- Donate for the old age homes, twice a year.

- Prayers to Lord Ganapathi.

- Serving/helping institutions or persons working for spiritualism.

These remedies are to be performed daily in the morning after bath and before breakfast. In case the native is unable to do so as in the case of sickness or out of town or in the case of children, these remedial measures can be performed by parents or spouse. If the offering is not accepted by a dog or cow, another dog/cow should be tried. The remedial measures should be performed regularly and the performance of any one of the suggested measures for a particular planet would suffice.

The weakness of the significator planets, as indicated earlier, is made up with the help of a specially prepared Kavach to be worn by the native in an auspiciously elected time.

ASCENDANT-WISE TESTED HOUSEHOLD JYOTISH/ASTRAL REMEDIES/ PROPITIATORY MEASURES FOR AFFLICTING PLANETS.

Aries Ascendant

1. Offering a sweet parantha (Indian pancake stuffed with sugar and fried) in small pieces to crows daily in the morning for Rahu.

2. Offering breakfast/lunch to lepers on Fridays for Rahu.

3. Offering some slices of bread dipped in milk to street dogs daily in the morning after morning prayers for Ketu.

4. Offering green fodder/vegetables for cows daily for Mercury.

Taurus Ascendant

1. Offering a sweet parantha (Indian pancake stuffed with sugar and fried) in small pieces to crows daily in the morning for Rahu.

2. Offering breakfast/lunch to lepers on Fridays for Rahu.

3. Offering some slices of bread dipped in milk to street dogs daily in the morning for Ketu.

4. Offering morning prayers daily in the morning and prasad in temple on Tuesdays for Mars.

5. Offering Bundi Laddus/yellow colored sweet to crows daily in the morning for Jupiter.

6. Offering white colored sweets like Rasgulla or kheer to crows daily in the morning for Venus.

Gemini Ascendant

1. Offering a sweet parantha (Indian pancake stuffed with sugar and fried) in small pieces to crows daily in the morning for Rahu.

2. Offering breakfast/lunch to lepers on Fridays for Rahu.

3. Offering some slices of bread dipped in milk to street dogs daily in the morning after morning prayers for Ketu.

Cancer Ascendant

1. Offering a sweet parantha (Indian pancake stuffed with sugar and fried) in small pieces to crows daily in the morning for Rahu.

2. Offering breakfast/lunch to lepers on Fridays for Rahu.

3. Offering some slices of bread dipped in milk to street dogs daily in the morning after morning prayers for Ketu.

4. Offering Bundi Laddus/yellow colored sweet to crows daily in the morning for Jupiter.

5. Offering Indian bread (roti) with salt and mustard oil in small pieces to crows daily in the morning for Saturn.

Leo Ascendant

1. Offering a sweet parantha (Indian pancake stuffed with sugar and fried) in small pieces to crows daily in the morning for Rahu.

2. Offering breakfast/lunch to lepers on Fridays for Rahu.

3. Offering some slices of bread dipped in milk to street dogs daily in the morning after morning prayers for Ketu.

4. Keeping a fresh pot of water for the birds daily in the morning for the Moon.

Virgo Ascendant

1. Offering a sweet parantha (Indian pancake stuffed with sugar and fried) in small pieces to crows daily in the morning for Rahu.

2. Offering breakfast/lunch to lepers on Fridays for Rahu.

3. Offering some slices of bread dipped in milk to street dogs daily in the morning after morning prayers for Ketu.

4. Offering morning prayers daily in the morning and prasad in temple on Tuesdays for Mars.

5. Offering sweet food made of wheat, jaggery and in milk to a cow for the Sun daily in the morning or on Sundays depending upon the level of affliction in the chart.

6. Offering roti (Indian bread) with salt and mustard oil in small pieces to crows daily in the morning for Saturn.

Libra Ascendant

1. Offering a sweet parantha (Indian pancake stuffed with sugar and fried) in small pieces to crows daily in the morning for Rahu.

2. Offering breakfast/lunch to lepers on Fridays for Rahu.

3. Offering some slices of bread dipped in milk to street dogs daily in the morning after morning prayers for Ketu.

4. Offering green fodder/vegetables for cows daily for Mercury.

Scorpio Ascendant

1. Offering a sweet parantha (Indian pancake stuffed with sugar and fried) in small pieces to crows daily in the morning for Rahu.

2. Offering breakfast/lunch to lepers on Fridays for Rahu.

3. Offering some slices of bread dipped in milk to street dogs daily in the morning after morning prayers for Ketu.

4. Offering morning prayers daily in the morning and prasad in temple on Tuesdays for Mars.

5. Offering white colored sweets like Rasgulla or Kheer to crows daily in the morning for Venus.

Sagittarius Ascendant

1. Offering a sweet parantha (Indian pancake stuffed with sugar and fried) in small pieces to crows daily in the morning for Rahu.

2. Offering breakfast/lunch to lepers on Fridays for Rahu.

3. Offering some slices of bread dipped in milk to street dogs daily in the morning after morning prayers for Ketu.

4. Keeping a fresh pot of water for the birds daily in the morning for the Moon.

Capricorn Ascendant

1. Offering a sweet parantha (Indian pancake stuffed with sugar and fried) in small pieces to crows daily in the morning for Rahu.

2. Offering breakfast/lunch to lepers on Fridays for Rahu.

3. Offering some slices of bread dipped in milk to street dogs daily in the morning after morning prayers for Ketu.

4. Offering Bundi Laddus/yellow colored sweet to crows daily in the morning for Jupiter.

5. Offering sweet food made of wheat, jaggery and in milk to a cow for the Sun daily in the morning or on Sundays depending upon the level of affliction in the chart.

Aquarius Ascendant

1. Offering a sweet parantha (Indian pancake stuffed with sugar and fried) in small pieces to crows daily in the morning for Rahu.

2. Offering breakfast/lunch to lepers on Fridays for Rahu.

3. Offering some slices of bread dipped in milk to street dogs daily in the morning after morning prayers for Ketu.

4. Keeping a fresh pot of water for the birds daily in the morning for the Moon.

5. Offering green fodder/vegetables for cows daily for Mercury.

Pisces Ascendant

1. Offering a sweet parantha (Indian pancake stuffed with sugar and fried) in small pieces to crows daily in the morning for Rahu.

2. Offering breakfast/lunch to lepers on Fridays for Rahu.

3. Offering some slices of bread dipped in milk to street dogs daily in the morning after morning prayers for Ketu.

4. Offering roti with salt and mustard oil in small pieces to crows daily in the morning for Saturn.

5. Offering sweet food made of wheat, jaggery and in milk to a cow for the Sun daily in the morning or on Sundays depending upon the level of affliction in the chart.

6. Offering white colored sweets like Rasgulla or kheer to crows daily in the morning for Venus.

CHAPTER 10

CASE STUDIES

HEALTH PROBLEMS IN CHILDHOOD

Chart 9

Male born 15th July, 1994, 1030 Hrs. New Delhi, India.

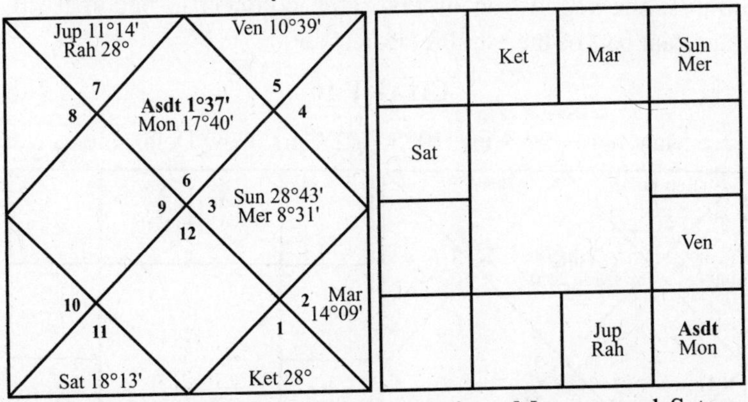

	Ket	Mar	Sun Mer
Sat			
			Ven
		Jup Rah	Asdt Mon

The sign Virgo rises in the ascendant. Mercury and Saturn become the prime determinants of health. Saturn, Mars, the Sun, Rahu and Ketu act as functional malefic planets. Libra rises in the ascendant of the shashthamsa and Venus becomes additional prime determinant for health. No planet is in its sign of debilitation in shashthamsa.

Mercury is strong. The weak Sun is placed in the tenth house and is afflicted by the exact aspect of Rahu from the second house. Jupiter is weak due to debilitation in navamsa and weak dispositor. The native was suffering from jaundice at the time of birth when he was in the sub-period of Saturn in the main period of the Moon.

Saturn is lord of the sixth house and occupies its own mooltrikona sign in the sixth house. Whenever there is an exact affliction in the natal chart, the native suffers ill health at the time of birth. As soon as this conjunction and/or aspect separates, the native recovers from the ill health provided the strong and/or well placed prime significators of health are present in the nativity. In this case the prime significators, Mercury and Saturn are strong in the chart. The parents of the child in this case were advised performance of propitiatory astral remedies for Rahu, who is involved in the single degree afflicting aspect and the performance of the astral remedies helped them relieve of their worry and the child started keeping good health from the beginning of August, 1994. In the case of infants, the suggestion of favorable colors also becomes an important part of the astral remedies.

CHART 10

Male born 12th May, 1995, 1628 Hrs. New Delhi, India.

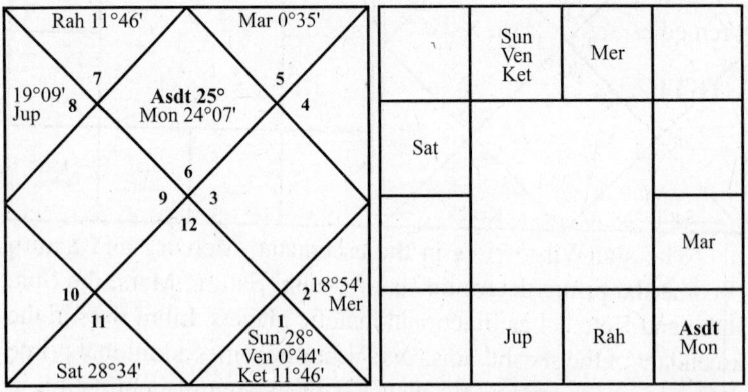

	Rah 11°46'		Mar 0°35'
19°09' Jup	7	8	Asdt 25° Mon 24°07'	5	4
		6	
		9	3
		12	
10			2 18°54' Mer
11		1 Sun 28° Ven 0°44' Ket 11°46'	
	Sat 28°34'		

	Sun Ven Ket	Mer	
Sat			
			Mar
	Jup	Rah	Asdt Mon

The sign Virgo rises in the ascendant. Mercury and Saturn become the prime determinants of health. Saturn, Mars, the Sun, Rahu and Ketu act as functional malefic planets. Pisces rises in the ascendant of the shashthamsa and no planet becomes additional prime determinant for health. Jupiter is in its sign of debilitation in shashthamsa.

This is another case where the child was suffering from jaundice at the time of birth. Mercury is strong and beneficially aspected by weak Jupiter. Jupiter is weak as the most effective point of its house of placement is afflicted by Saturn from the sixth house. The secondary determinant, Saturn, occupies its own mooltrikona sign but it is weak due to old age. The functional malefic Sun afflicts the most effective point of the eighth and second houses. Venus and Mars are weak in this nativity due to infancy and bad placement. At the time of birth the native was running the main period of the most malefic planet, Mars, and the sub-period of Rahu. Rahu was stationary and was moving at a very slow speed. It means that the mutual malefic influence of transit Rahu over natal Rahu continued for a longer duration than the normal. Normally Rahu may travel the longitude of one degree in a period of ten or eleven days. But because of its slow movement in May, 1995, it travelled the longitude of one degree in about a month's time. Whenever we come across the horoscope of an infant, the special consideration of transit is very necessary. The performance of propitiatory astral remedies, in this case too helped relieving the parents of tension.

ASTHMA

CHART 11

Male born 27th October, 1980, 1120 Hrs. New Delhi, India.

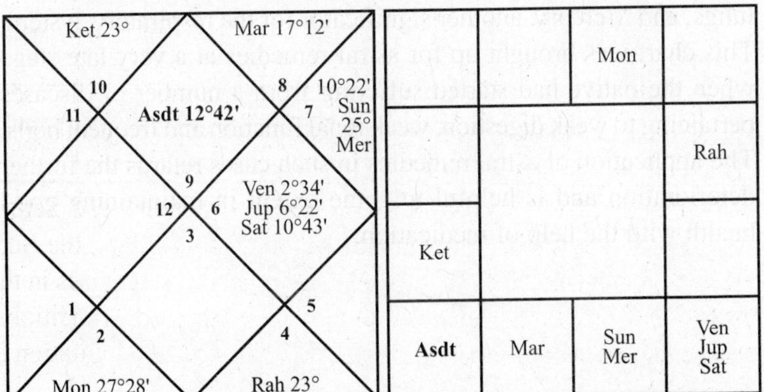

Chart (South Indian and North Indian style):

North Indian chart:
- Ket 23°
- Mar 17°12'
- House 10
- House 11
- Asdt 12°42'
- House 8
- House 7
- 10°22' Sun 25° Mer
- House 9
- House 12
- House 6
- Ven 2°34' Jup 6°22' Sat 10°43'
- House 3
- House 1
- House 2
- House 5
- House 4
- Mon 27°28'
- Rah 23°

South Indian chart:
		Mon	
			Rah
Ket			
Asdt	Mar	Sun Mer	Ven Jup Sat

The sign Sagittarius rises in the ascendant. Jupiter becomes the prime determinant of health. The Moon, Rahu and Ketu act as functional malefic planets. Gemini rises in the ascendant of shashthamsa and no planet becomes the additional prime determinant of health. No planet is in debilitation in shashthamsa.

Jupiter is well placed and unafflicted. There is no close affliction on the most effective point of the ascendant, too. The planets Venus and the Sun are weak in this chart as these planets are in their signs of debilitation. The planets, the Moon, Mars and Rahu are badly placed in this birth chart. The Moon is weak as it is badly placed in the sixth house and is in old age. It becomes additionally weak due to the close aspect of Ketu. The Moon represents the lungs. The weakness of Venus also turns Mercury and the Sun weak. Saturn, Jupiter and Venus are weak due to weakness of dispositor, Mercury. The weakness or bad placement of majority of the planets speak of the weak health of the native. The weakness of the planets like this start giving health problems from a very early stage in life and make the person a chronic patient by the time he turns young. Due to the weak, badly placed and debilitated planets, the ill health started surfacing right from the beginning and from the fourth year of age the child was reported to be a patient of asthma. The planets ruling asthma in this case are Saturn, the lord of the third house, the Moon, the significator of the lungs, and Mercury, another significator for the respiratory system. This chart was brought up for astral remedies at a very late stage when the native had started suffering from a number of diseases pertaining to weak digestion, weak renal function and frequent boils. The application of astral remedies in such cases retards the further deterioration and is helpful to some extent in maintaining good health with the help of medication.

MENINGITIS

Chart 12

Male born 7th July, 1994, 0704 Hrs. Wapi (Gujarat), India.

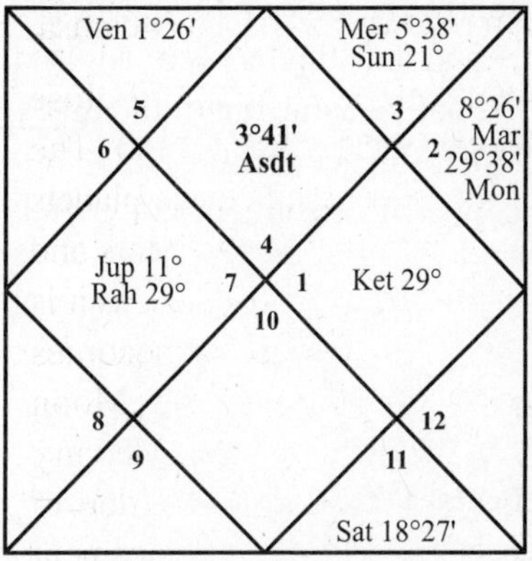

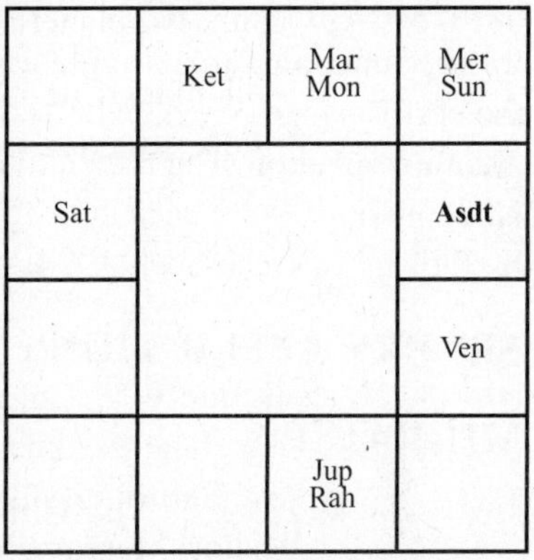

```
Ven 1°26'              Mer 5°38'
                       Sun 21°
    5        3°41'     3    8°26'
  6          Asdt           Mar
                         2  29°38'
                            Mon
                4
  Jup 11°    7    1   Ket 29°
  Rah 29°
             10
  8                        12
    9                  11
               Sat 18°27'
```

Ket	Mar Mon	Mer Sun
Sat		Asdt
		Ven
	Jup Rah	

The sign Cancer rises in the ascendant. The Moon and Jupiter become the prime determinants of health. Jupiter, Saturn, Rahu and Ketu act as functional malefic planets. The sign Libra rises in the ascendant of shashthamsa and Venus becomes the additional prime determinant of health. No planet is placed in its sign of debilitation in shashthamsa.

The Moon is weak due to extreme old age. The other prime determinant of health, Jupiter, is well placed in the chart but is weak due to debilitation in navamsa and weakness of dispositor. Venus is weak as it is in infancy and its dispositor is weak. The functional malefic planets do not cause severe afflictions in the chart. The planets Mercury and the Sun are weak as they are badly placed in the chart. The bad placements, the weakness of planets including the weakness of the prime determinants do not indicate good health though the longevity is not threatened due to the strong placement of the lord of the eighth house, who is the significator for longevity, as well. At the time of the birth the native was in the main period of Mars. In the sub-period of Mercury in the main period of Mars which started from the 13th September, 1994, the native was reported to be suffering from meningitis, when the functional malefic Jupiter exerted its transit influence on natal Saturn and the transit Rahu exerted its influence on the natal Sun. The lord of the sub-period, Mercury, and the transit afflicted Sun are placed in the twelfth house in the natal chart. The propitiatory remedies for the functional malefic planets Rahu and Jupiter were advised, the performance of which helped the native come out of the illness after an operation. The transit malefic influence caused a relapse in November, 1994. The native responded to treatment completely by the end of December, 1994.

SEVERE AFFLICTIONS

MIGRAINE

Chart 13

Female born 27th November, 1954, 1725 Hrs. New Delhi, India.

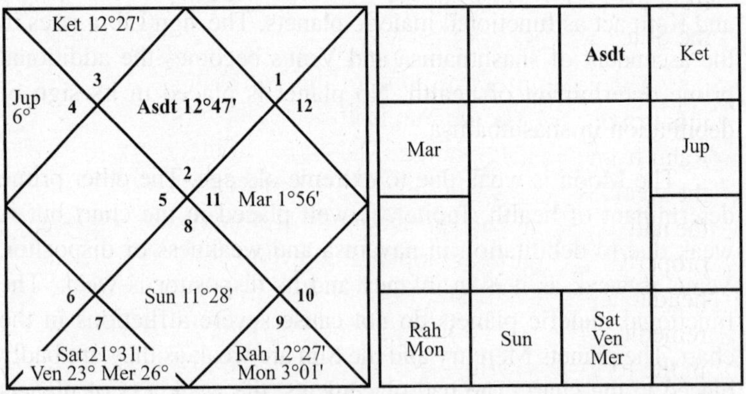

The sign Taurus rises in the ascendant. Venus becomes the prime determinant of health as there is no mooltrikona sign in the ascendant. Venus, Jupiter, Mars, Rahu and Ketu act as functional malefic planets. The sign Sagittarius rises in shashthamsa and Jupiter becomes additional prime determinant of health. No planet is in debilitation in shashthamsa.

All the planets are weak as the Rahu-Ketu axis afflicts the most effective points of their mooltrikona houses and/or houses of placement. Venus though placed in its own mooltrikona sign becomes weak as the most effective point of its house of placement is under the exact affliction of Ketu. Saturn and Mercury are badly placed in the sixth house and closely afflicted as they are in close conjunction with the functional malefic Venus. Mars and the badly placed Moon are weak due to infancy. The Sun is in its sign of debilitation in navamsa. Saturn is also debilitated in navamsa.

The only good point in this chart from the health point of view was that the prime determinant of health, Venus, is in its own mooltrikona sign and is under the benefic influence of Saturn and Mercury. In the conjunction of planets the functional benefic planets suffer while the functional malefic planets gain as the functional malefic planets enjoy good influences on them. The native kept indifferent health and was reported to be suffering from migraine from the 28th year of her life when she was in the main period of the Sun.

The most effective point of the fourth house containing the mooltrikona sign of the Sun is afflicted due to the exact aspect of Rahu from the eighth house. Therefore, during the main period of the weak Sun and the sub-period of Rahu the mental happiness of the native was eluding and her digestive system was not functioning properly. She started complaining acidity followed by persistent headaches. Finally, she became a patient of migraine. Astral remedies were sought in the year 1994, the performance of which in the form of wearing of a Kavach and propitiatory remedies for Rahu, Ketu, Venus, Jupiter and Mars provided a good relief to the native.

BONE TB

Chart 14

Female born 20th April, 1968, 1941 Hrs. Etawah, India.

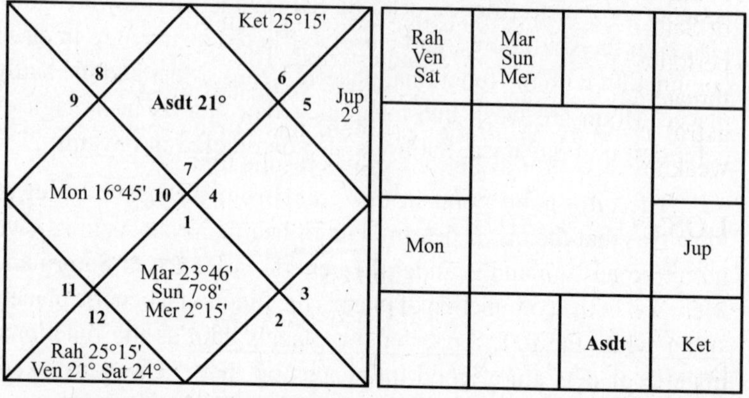

Rah Ven Sat	Mar Sun Mer		
Mon			Jup
		Asdt	Ket

Diamond chart:
- Ket 25°15' (top)
- Asdt 21°, 8, 9, 6, 5, Jup 2°
- 7, Mon 16°45' 10, 4
- 1
- 11, 12, Mar 23°46' Sun 7°8' Mer 2°15', 3, 2
- Rah 25°15' Ven 21° Sat 24° (bottom)

The sign Libra rises in the ascendant. Venus becomes the prime determinant of health. Mercury, Rahu and Ketu act as functional malefic planets. Leo rises in shashthamsa and its lord Sun becomes the additional prime determinant of the health. No planet is in its sign of debilitation in shashthamsa.

Venus is weak as it is badly placed in the sixth house along with Saturn and Rahu. Both Venus and Saturn are under the close affliction of Rahu-Ketu axis. Mercury is weak as it is in infancy and is combust. Mercury has two types of roles. First is its role as a significator for the nervous system and the second is its role as the most malefic planet. Rahu and Ketu are closely placed over the most effective points of the houses occupied. Whenever the natal Rahu-Ketu axis is in the even signs of a nativity, the houses where the signs Virgo and Cancer are placed, suffer more, as these are the two mooltrikona signs in the even signs. The affliction of Rahu-Ketu axis near to the most effective points is more grave when Rahu-Ketu are in the odd signs in a nativity as there are five houses involved in such a case. Coming back to our present case study, the simultaneous affliction of the twelfth/eighth houses, Venus, the lord of the ascendant, and Saturn, the ayushkaraka, with a weak lord of the twelfth house, reduces the longevity of the native. The weakness of Mercury and Saturn and the affliction of Saturn and the lord of the ascendant resulted in the lack of intelligence and nervousness in this child from very early stage in life. The weakness and affliction of Saturn resulted in the native suffering from bone TB in the sub-period of Rahu in its own main period. The severe illness started threatening the longevity. As earlier indicated the application of astral remedies after the problem has surfaced due to natal weaknesses and/or afflictions shows results to a limited extent.

LOSS OF MEMORY

Chart 15

Male born 27th October, 1959, 0655 Hrs. Palwal, India.

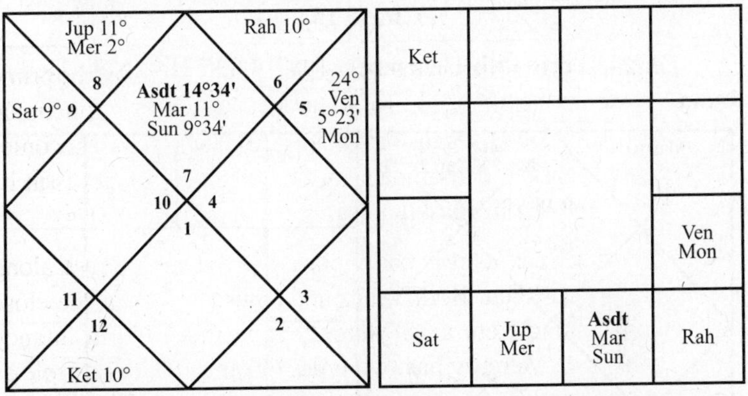

Ket			
			Ven Mon
Sat	Jup Mer	Asdt Mar Sun	Rah

Diamond chart:
- Jup 11° Mer 2° (House 8)
- Rah 10° (House 6)
- Sat 9° (House 9)
- Asdt 14°34' Mar 11° Sun 9°34' (House 7)
- 24° Ven 5°23' Mon (House 5)
- Ket 10° (House 12)

The sign Libra rises in the ascendant. Venus becomes the prime determinant of health. Mercury, Rahu and Ketu act as functional malefic planets. Gemini rises in shashthamsa and no planet becomes the additional prime determinant of the health. No planet is in its sign of debilitation in shashthamsa.

Venus is weak as its dispositor, Sun, is in debilitation. Rahu-Ketu axis exerts malefic influence on the most effective points of the houses occupied/aspected. Jupiter ruling the third house is under the exact affliction of Ketu from the sixth house. Mars is weak due to combustion. Mercury is weak due to infancy. Saturn is weak due to the weakness and affliction of dispositor. The natal affliction of Ketu to Jupiter in the natal chart resulted in lack of initiative and progeny. Jupiter is lord of the third house ruling initiatives and is significator for progeny matters and Saturn is placed in the mooltrikona sign of Jupiter. The weakness of Mercury and affliction to Jupiter exerted constant nervous pressure on the native resulting in the loss of communicative power. The native became an introvert and finally suffered from loss of memory in the sub-period of Jupiter in the main period of the Moon. During the sub-period of an afflicted Jupiter, the transit Rahu exerted its close influence on the weak natal Mercury from March 94 to May 94. Under these circumstances, the native left home and due to loss of memory never came back.

Chart 16

Female born 15th December, 1982, 0835 Hrs. New Delhi, India.

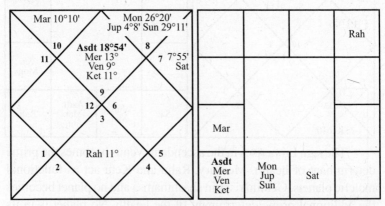

The sign Sagittarius rises in the ascendant. Jupiter becomes the prime determinant of health. The Moon, Rahu and Ketu act as functional malefic planets. The ascendant of the shashthamsa is Cancer and its lord, the Moon, becomes the additional prime determinant of health. No planet is in debilitation in shashthamsa.

Jupiter is weak due to bad placement and infancy. Saturn, Mercury and Venus are closely afflicted by Rahu/Ketu in this nativity. The affliction of Venus adds to the affliction of Saturn as the former is dispositor of the later. The Moon is in its sign of debilitation and being the most malefic planet, it afflicts the old aged and weak Sun by close conjunction. The pressures due to the weakness of Mercury, the Moon and the lord of the third house are indicative of damaging the power of communication of the native. It dampens the native's initiatives and makes one an introvert. In this case too, the native suffered from loss of memory during the main period of Ketu and the sub-period of Mercury. Whenever Rahu-Ketu axis exerts close malefic influence, the sub-period of Rahu in the main period of the afflicted planet or the sub-period of the afflicted planet in the main period of Rahu is always very significant in life as it gives rise to unpleasant happenings/events connected with the significations ruled by the houses/planets involved.

CONVULSIONS

Chart 17

Male born 1st December, 1966, 0523 Hrs. New Delhi, India.

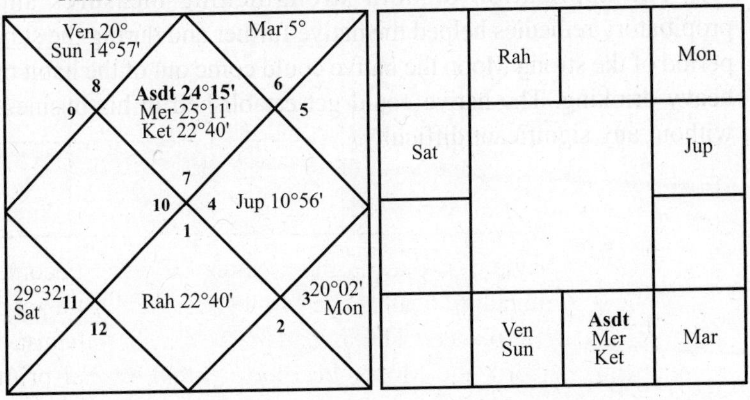

	Rah		Mon
Sat			Jup
	Ven Sun	Asdt Mer Ket	Mar

The sign Libra rises in the ascendant. Venus becomes the prime determinant of health. Mercury, Rahu and Ketu act as functional malefic planets. Leo rises in shashthamsa and its lord, the Sun, becomes the additional prime determinant of health. No planet is in its sign of debilitation in shashthamsa.

Venus is weak due to combustion and its mooltrikona house being under the multiple afflictions of Rahu-Ketu axis and Mercury. Nodal axis exerts its close malefic influence on the most effective points of the houses occupied and aspected and the planet, Mercury. Mars is weak due to close affliction to its mooltrikona sign house and bad placement. Saturn is weak as it is in old age. Mercury, the most malefic planet, afflicts the most effective points of the ascendant and the seventh house. Due to the combined influence of the lord of the twelfth house and Rahu on the most effective point of the ascendant and Rahu's influence over Mercury, the native was involved in the habit of intoxication at the very young age of 14 years besides suffering from convulsions. He was under its influence very badly and continued to remain so up to the sub-period of Ketu in the main period of Saturn. His rehabilitation started from the sub-period of Venus in the main period of Saturn.

The application of both strengthening measures and propitiatory remedies helped the native further and during the sub-period of the strong Moon the native could come out of the habit of heavy drinking. The native could get established in his business without any significant difficulty.

MENTAL RETARDATION

Chart 18

Female born 15th March, 1989, 0859 Hrs. Sirsi (Karnataka), India.

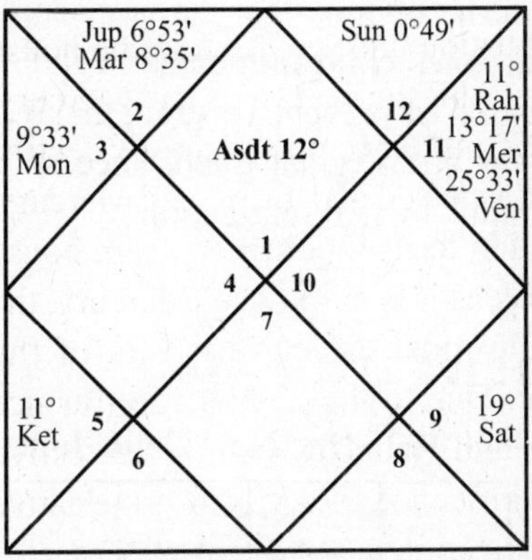

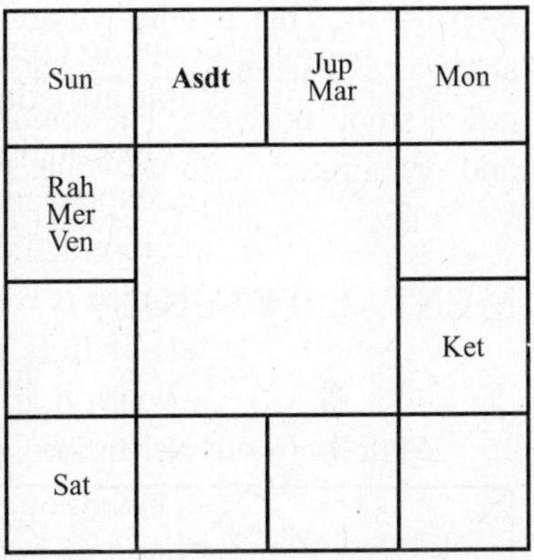

Sun	**Asdt**	Jup Mar	Mon
Rah Mer Ven			
			Ket
Sat			

The sign Aries rises in the ascendant. Mars and Mercury become prime determinants of health. Mercury, Rahu and Ketu act as functional malefic planets. Gemini rises in the ascendant of shashthamsa and the Sun and Venus are in their signs of debilitation in shashthamsa.

Mars, Jupiter, Venus, Saturn and the Sun are weak as their mooltrikona houses are under the exact affliction of the nodes. The Moon and Mercury are weak as their houses of placement are afflicted by Rahu/Ketu. The Rahu-Ketu axis not only afflicts the most effective points of the houses occupied/aspected but also closely afflicts the Moon and Mercury. While Ketu is conjunct with the most effective point of the fifth house, the lord of the fifth house is in infancy and badly placed. The afflictions to the Moon and the most effective points of the third and fifth houses concurrent with the operation of the sub-period of Mercury in the main period of Rahu resulted in the mental retardation of the native. The native also suffered from a weak nervous system and problems in the spinal-cord.

The third house and the planet Mercury rules mental and physical growth while the fifth house governs intelligence and the fourth house rules power of grasp and ability of acquiring education. Weakness and/or affliction of the planets connected with the third, fourth and fifth houses and the Moon and Mercury result in mental retardation. That is why we are of the opinion that the horoscope analysis is as important as having ones child immunized against polio, small pox, etc. The application of preventive strengthening and propitiatory remedial measures are of great importance and, we believe, are able to protect against mental retardation.

MENTAL TENSION

Chart 19

Male born 4th November, 1948, 1937 Hrs. New Delhi, India.

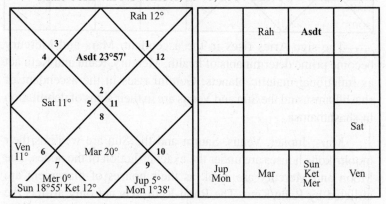

The sign Taurus rises in the ascendant. Venus becomes the prime determinant of health as there is no mooltrikona sign in the ascendant. Venus, Jupiter, Mars, Rahu and Ketu act as functional malefic planets. The sign Aquarius rises in shashthamsa and Saturn becomes additional prime determinant of health. No planet is in debilitation in shashthamsa.

The planets Sun, Ketu, Mercury, Jupiter, Moon and Rahu are badly placed in this chart. Venus is in debilitation and hence weak. Saturn, ruling the tenth house, is weak due to the exact affliction of

Rahu from the twelfth house and a weak dispositor. Mars is weak as the most effective point of its house of placement is afflicted by itself. The most malefic planet, Jupiter, closely afflicts the lord of the third house, the Moon. The afflictions to Saturn and the Moon resulted in injuries and fractures in the legs and the collar bone area. The bad placement of the lord of the fourth house in the house of disputes involved the native in great mental tension due to involvement of the meager assets in disputes. Due to the extreme weakness of Venus for being debilitated with weakly dispositor, the financial position of the native always remained very critical and the inheritance continued to diminish day by day. The native sought astral help in the sub-period of Venus in the main period of Mars, when he was under severe problems both on the health and financial fronts and the performance of the advised astrological remedies resulted in arresting the mounting trends and provided some relief from the existing problems.

THYROID

Chart 20

Female born 6th June, 1957, 0115 Hrs. New Delhi, India.

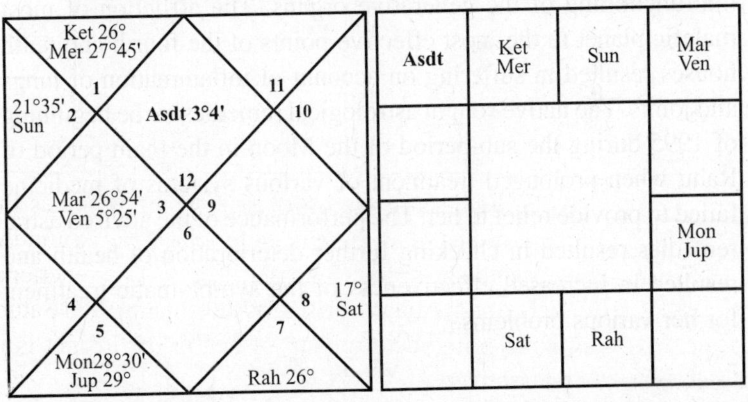

Ket 26° Mer 27°45' **1**		**11**	
21°35' Sun **2**	Asdt 3°4'	**10**	
Mar 26°54' Ven 5°25' **3**	**12** **9** **6**		
4 **5** Mon28°30' Jup 29°		**8** **7** Rah 26°	17° Sat

Asdt	Ket Mer	Sun	Mar Ven
			Mon Jup
	Sat	Rah	

The sign Pisces rises in the ascendant. The Sun becomes the prime determinant of health as there is no mooltrikona sign in the ascendant. The Sun, Venus, Saturn, Rahu and Ketu act as functional malefic planets. Libra rises in the ascendant of the shashthamsa and Venus becomes additional prime determinant of health. No planet is debilitated in shashthamsa.

Mars, the lord of the second house of upper neck and throat and significator of the third house of lower neck and thyroid gland, is under the exact affliction of Rahu from the eighth house. Mercury, the significator of lower neck, is also in close conjunction with Ketu and stands afflicted in addition to the afflicted lord of the second house. The most malefic planet, Venus, significator of generative organs, upper neck and glands, is weak and closely afflicts the most effective points of the fourth and tenth houses. The Moon, the significator of glandular processes, is in old age, placed in the sixth house and closely afflicted by Ketu. Jupiter is in extreme old age, badly placed and is under the close affliction of Ketu. Due to the weakness and/or affliction of Mars, Mercury, Venus and the Moon, the native suffered ill health pertaining to significations of the second, third, fifth, seventh and eighth houses. During the main period of Rahu and the sub-period of Ketu, the native started suffering from thyroid. The bad placement and affliction of the lord of the fifth house denied progeny due to the malfunctioning of the generative organs. The affliction of most malefic planet to the most effective points of the fourth and tenth houses resulted in suffering on account of inflammation of lungs and joints. The native sought astrological remedies in the beginning of 1995 during the sub-period of the Moon in the main period of Rahu when prolonged treatment of various systems of medicine failed to provide relief to her. The performance of the advised astral remedies resulted in checking further deterioration of health and resulted in increased effectiveness of the symptomatic treatment for her various problems.

THYROID & MALFUNCTIONING OF RESPIRATORY SYSTEM

Chart 21

Female born 27th November, 1963, 0526 Hrs. New Delhi, India.

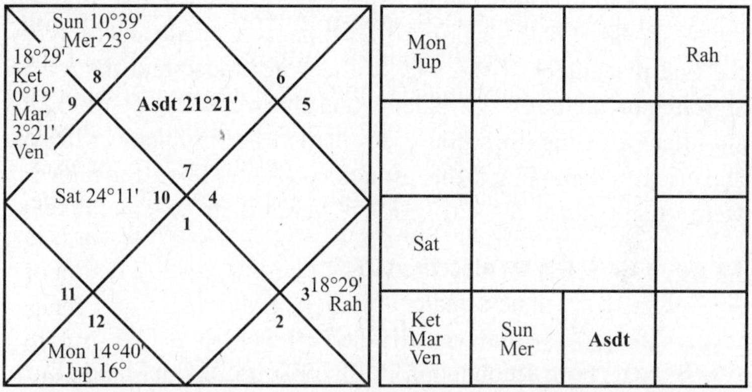

```
Sun 10°39'
  Mer 23°
18°29'
Ket        8              6
0°19'   9     Asdt 21°21'     5
Mar
3°21'
Ven              7
     Sat 24°11' 10    4
                  1
  11                    3 18°29'
    12               2    Rah
  Mon 14°40'
   Jup 16°
```

```
Mon           |     |     | Rah
Jup           |     |     |
--------------|-----|-----|-----
              |     |     |
--------------|     |     |
              | Sat |     |
--------------|-----|-----|-----
Ket   | Sun   | Asdt|
Mar   | Mer   |     |
Ven   |       |     |
```

The sign Libra rises in the ascendant. Venus becomes the prime determinant of health. Mercury, Rahu and Ketu act as functional malefic planets. Leo rises in shashthamsa and its lord, the Sun, becomes the additional prime determinant of health. Jupiter is in its sign of debilitation in shashthamsa.

Venus is weak due to infancy and weakness of dispositor. It becomes additionally weak due to the close affliction of Rahu to its mooltrikona house. Mercury, ruling lungs and being the most malefic planet, is closely conjunct with the most effective point of the second house, becoming weak. Rahu-Ketu axis is near the most effective points of the houses occupied and causes affliction to all the houses occupied and aspected. Mars is weak due to extreme infancy and a weak dispositor. Mars indicates problems related to the muscular system of the body. The Sun is weak due to debilitation in navamsa and close affliction to the most effective point of its house of placement. The Moon and Jupiter are closely conjunct with each other and are placed in the sixth house. This planetary configuration of the Moon and Jupiter in the sixth house make the person of an inflexible or aggressive nature and is indicative of health problems due to one's own actions as the Moon rules the tenth house and Jupiter rules the house of initiatives, the third house. This may be due to lack of proper attention towards maintaining good health. The close affliction of Rahu/Ketu to the most effective point of the third house, ruling respiratory system and thyroid gland, the weakness of both the prime determinants of health and Mercury, the bad placement of the lord of the third house and the Moon, significator of lungs and glands, and the weakness of Mars, the significator of the third house, resulted in the problem of thyroid and diseases pertaining to the respiratory system. The astral remedies were sought during the sub-period of Venus in its own main period.

LOSS OF HEARING POWER

Chart 22

Female born 4th January, 1962, 1550Hrs. Malot Mandi, India.

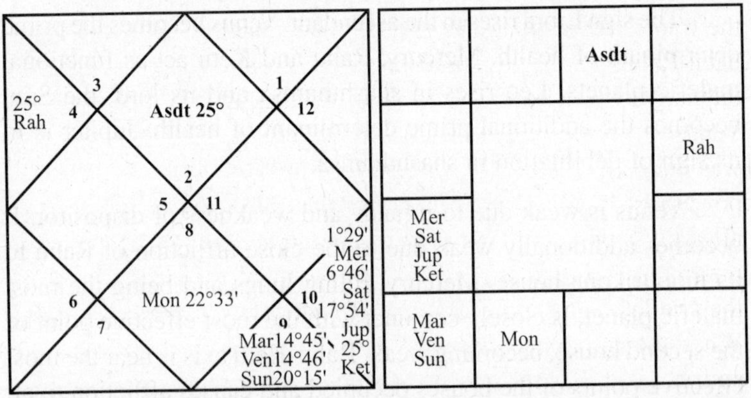

The sign Taurus rises in the ascendant. Venus becomes the prime determinant of health as there is no mooltrikona sign in the ascendant. Venus, Jupiter, Mars, Rahu and Ketu act as functional malefic planets. The sign Pisces rises in shashthamsa. Jupiter is in debilitation in shashthamsa.

Venus, the prime determinant of the health, and the functional malefic Mars are closely conjunct with each other and are badly placed in the eighth house. The affliction of Mars to Venus severely damages health. Rahu-Ketu axis is exactly conjunct with the most effective point of the houses they occupy and afflicts all the houses occupied and aspected, including the third and eleventh houses of right and left ears, respectively. The Sun is weak due to bad placement, debilitation in navamsa and weakness of dispositor. Mercury is extremely weak as it is combust, in infancy and its house of placement and mooltrikona house are both afflicted. Jupiter, ruling ears/hearing power and being the dispositor of Mars, Venus and the Sun, is extremely weak as it is debilitated both in rasi and shashthamsa and its house of placement is exactly afflicted by the Rahu-Ketu axis. Its weakness also makes the position of combust Mars and Venus and the Sun further weak. The affliction to the most effective points of the third house, whose lord the Moon is debilitated and closely aspected by the functional malefic Rahu, resulted in the problem. This problem of deafness occurred when the transit Ketu and Rahu exerted their malefic influence on the natal Rahu and the Moon, respectively, around April, 1996, when the native was in the sub-period of Mercury in the main period of Venus. As the problem had arisen due to the transit affliction, it was indicated that with the help of the astral remedies the hearing power of the native will return after the transit influence was over after June, 1997. The performance of astral remedies did result in return of hearing power. The weakness and affliction of the lord of the twelfth house indicates curtailed longevity and sleeplessness. When the native had problem of deafness in April, 1996, she was so frustrated that she attempted suicide. But improvement started in August, 1996, which brought the native out of depression.

DUMB AT BIRTH

Chart 23

Male born 6th September, 1977, 2242 Hrs. Gurgaon, India.

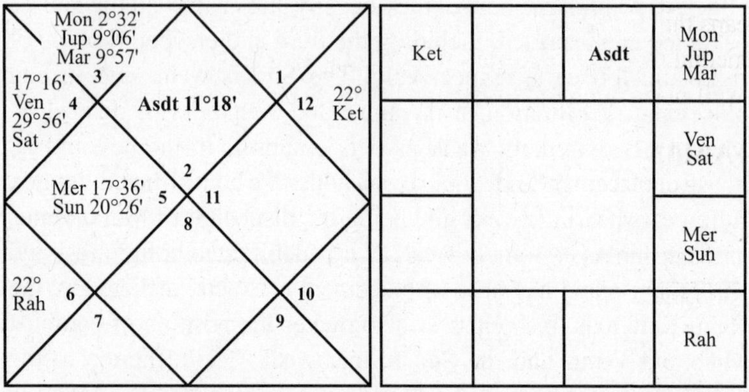

The sign Taurus rises in the ascendant. Venus becomes the prime determinant of health as there is no mooltrikona sign in the ascendant. Venus, Jupiter, Mars, Rahu and Ketu act as functional malefic planets. The sign Sagittarius rises in shashthamsa and Jupiter becomes additional prime determinant of health. No planet is in debilitation in shashthamsa and Jupiter is badly placed in shashthamsa.

The prime determinant of health, Venus, is well placed but becomes weak due to the weakness of dispositor. The Moon is weak in the nativity due to infancy and placement in an afflicted house. The additional prime determinant, Jupiter, and the functional malefic Mars closely afflict each other and the most effective point of the second house. Saturn is weak due to old age and weak dispositor. The Sun and Mercury being functional benefic planets are closely conjunct with each other and are well placed in the fourth house. Mercury is combust and is vulnerable to the malefic transit influences. The Sun is weak due to debilitation in navamsa. The afflictions of two functional malefic planets near the most effective point of the second house resulted in loss of speech at the time of birth as the native was running the dasa of Mars. The native started speaking after the age of 6 years as a result of the persistent performance of astral remedies by the parents of the child. Had the Mercury also been involved in a natal malefic conjunction, the return of speech would not have been possible even at a later stage. This means that for the success of the results of the curative astrological remedial measures it is very important that at least one significator is well placed and/or strong in the nativity.

STAMMERING

Chart 24

Male born 4th February, 1967, 1600 Hrs. New Delhi, India.

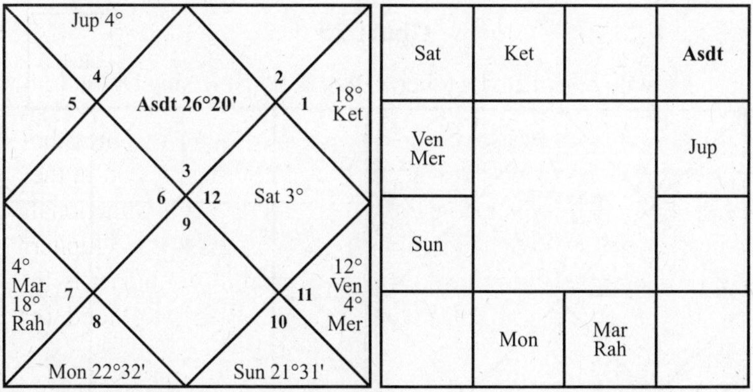

Sat	Ket		Asdt
Ven Mer			Jup
Sun			
	Mon	Mar Rah	

The sign Gemini rises in the ascendant. The Sun becomes the prime determinant of health as there is no mooltrikona sign in the first and sixth houses. Rahu and Ketu act as functional malefic planets. Virgo rises in the ascendant of shashthamsa and Mercury becomes the additional prime determinant of health. No planet is in debilitation in shashthamsa.

The Sun is weak due to bad placement. The lord of the second house is badly placed in the sixth house in debilitation. Jupiter becomes weak due to infancy and bad placement of its dispositor. The lord of the third house, ruling the communicative power, the Sun, is placed in the eighth house. Rahu-Ketu do not cause close afflictions in the chart. Mars and Saturn are weak due to infancy.

Mercury is weak due to combustion, infancy and weakness of dispositor. Venus is weak due to weakness of dispositor. The weakness of most of the planets and the bad placements of the Moon and the Sun resulted in lack of confidence. This created the problem of stammering. The application of the strengthening astral remedies by way of use of a Kavach helped the native with a significant improvement in his stammering habits. The native was advised both propitiatory astral remedies for the functional malefic planets and wearing of a Kavach for strengthening the weak functional benefic planets in an auspiciously elected time.

EAR PROBLEM

Chart 25

Female born 12th October, 1988, 0805 Hrs. New Delhi, India.

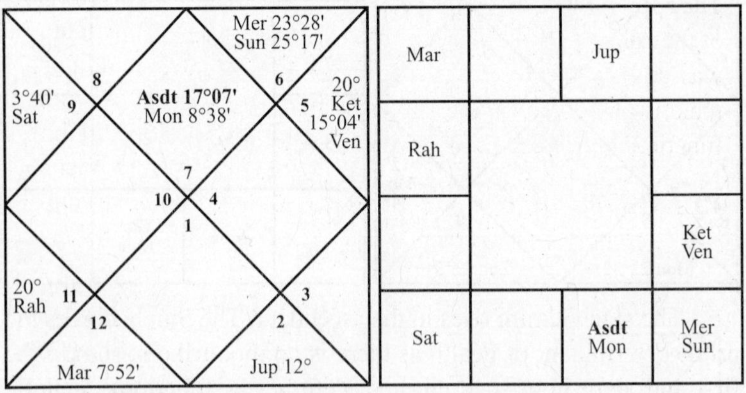

North Indian chart:
- Mer 23°28', Sun 25°17' (house 6, top)
- 20° Ket 15°04' Ven (house 5)
- 3°40' Sat (house 9), 8
- Asdt 17°07' Mon 8°38'
- 7, 10, 4, 1
- 20° Rah (house 11), 12, 2, 3
- Mar 7°52'
- Jup 12°

South Indian chart:

	Mar	Jup	
Rah			
			Ket Ven
Sat	Asdt Mon	Mer Sun	

The sign Libra rises in the ascendant. Venus becomes the prime determinant of health. Mercury, Rahu and Ketu act as functional malefic planets. Cancer rises in the ascendant of shashthamsa and the Moon becomes the additional prime determinant of health. Saturn is in debilitation in shashthamsa.

Venus is weak due to weakness of dispositor and placement in an afflicted house. The most malefic planet, Mercury, closely afflicts the weak Sun placed in the twelfth house. Ketu is conjunct with the most effective point of the eleventh house and also aspects the most effective point of the third house besides the Rahu-Ketu axis afflicting the other houses occupied/aspected by them. The Moon is weak due to the weakness of its dispositor and becomes additionally weak as it is placed in an afflicted house. Mars is badly placed in the sixth house. The concentration of affliction is more on the third and eleventh houses and the lords of these houses are badly placed. These afflictions resulted in ear problems. During the main period of Rahu and sub-period of Ketu, the problem increased in the form of pus formation and swelling in both the ears and the native was advised an operation for treatment. It is at this stage that the parents of the native sought astrological help for assessing the chances of a successful surgical operation and sought astral remedies so that the operation would be a positive success. The application of astral remedies was able to meet the expectations of the parents and the surgical operation was successful. The native was advised both propitiatory astral remedies for the functional malefic planets and wearing of a Kavach for strengthening the weak functional benefic planets in an auspiciously elected time.

PLEURISY

Chart 26

Male born 24th October, 1976, 0535 Hrs. New Delhi, India.

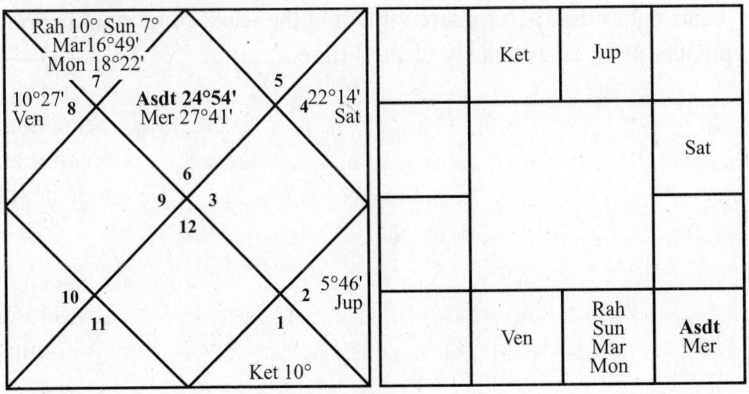

Rah 10° Sun 7° Mar16°49' Mon 18°22'			

Chart diagram:

North Indian chart:
- House 7: Rah 10° Sun 7° Mar 16°49' Mon 18°22'
- House 8: 10°27' Ven
- Asdt 24°54' Mer 27°41'
- House 5
- House 4: 22°14' Sat
- House 6
- House 9, 3, 12
- House 10, 11
- House 1, 2: 5°46' Jup
- Ket 10°

South Indian chart:

	Ket	Jup	
			Sat
Ven	Rah Sun Mar Mon	Asdt Mer	

The sign Virgo rises in the ascendant. Mercury and Saturn become the prime determinants of health. Saturn, Mars, the Sun, Rahu and Ketu act as functional malefic planets. Aquarius rises in the ascendant of shashthamsa and Saturn becomes the additional prime determinant of health. Mars and Mercury are in debilitation in shashthamsa.

Mercury is well placed in the chart but is weak due to combustion, placement in an afflicted house and old age. Its placement in its sign of exaltation is helpful to some extent. The functional malefic Saturn occupies the sign Cancer in the eleventh house and closely afflicts the most effective points of the eleventh house, ascendant, fifth and eighth houses. Saturn is weak due to combustion, placement in an afflicted house and close affliction to its dispositor, the Moon. The Sun is weak due to debilitation and stands afflicted due to the close affliction of Rahu-Ketu axis. The most malefic planet exerts its close influence on the Moon. The affliction of the sign Cancer, the ascendant and the Moon resulted in pleurisy. Jupiter and Venus are strong. The astral remedies were sought when medical treatment failed to give permanent satisfactory relief.

The application of astral remedies increases the power of symptomatic treatment to do well. The native was advised both propitiatory astral remedies for the functional malefic planets and wearing of a Kavach for strengthening the weak functional benefic planets in an auspiciously elected time.

CONGENITAL LUNGS PROBLEM
Chart 27
Female born 20th February, 1993, 1211 Hrs. New Delhi, India.

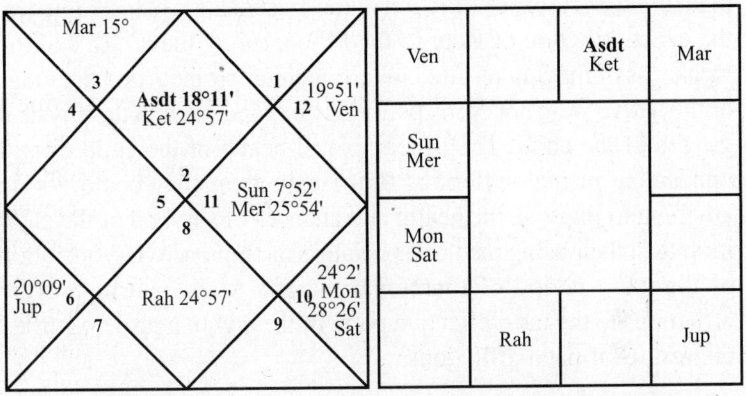

Ven		**Asdt** Ket	Mar
Sun Mer			
Mon Sat			
	Rah		Jup

Diamond chart:
- Mar 15°
- House 3, 4
- Asdt 18°11' Ket 24°57'
- House 1, 12: 19°51' Ven
- House 2, 5, 11: Sun 7°52' Mer 25°54'
- House 8
- 20°09' Jup, House 6, 7
- Rah 24°57'
- House 9, 10: 24°2' Mon 28°26' Sat

The sign Taurus rises in the ascendant. Venus becomes the prime determinant of health as there is no mooltrikona sign in the ascendant. Venus, Jupiter, Mars, Rahu and Ketu act as functional malefic planets. Capricorn rises in the ascendant of shashthamsa. Mars is in debilitation in shashthamsa.

The most malefic planet, Jupiter, is mutually involved in exact affliction with the prime determinant of health, weak Venus, and exactly afflicts the houses aspected and occupied in the natal chart. The Moon is very weak as it is exactly afflicted by Ketu, closely afflicted by afflicted Jupiter, and its house of placement is closely afflicted by Jupiter and Mars. Besides being also placed in the afflicted ninth house, old aged and combust Saturn is suffering from the close affliction of Ketu. The Sun is well placed in the chart but weak due to the weakness and affliction of its dispositor. Mercury is very weak due to old age, weak dispositor and multiple afflictions of its mooltrikona sign house. The mutual aspect of Jupiter and Venus, exactly afflicting each other and the most effective points of their houses of placement, not only endangers health but also endangers longevity. Mars is weak as the most effective point of its house of placement is afflicted by itself. The functional malefic

Mars closely afflicts the most effective points of the houses aspected and occupied in the natal chart.

The child was born in the main period of the functional malefic planet Mars. The exact affliction of the most malefic planet to Venus; the exact affliction of Ketu to the Moon, ruling the lungs, and the weakness of the Sun resulted in a congenital problem and the lungs of the native were not correspondingly expanding with the physical growth of the child. The irreparable ill health of the child caused unbearable mental sufferings to the parents as they could not do anything to improve the health and chances of survival of the child in spite of their being medical specialists of eminence. The operation of the main period of functional malefic Mars, causing severe afflictions to the most effective point of the eighth house magnified the results of natal afflictions.

TUBERCULOSIS

Chart 28

Female born 22nd February, 1957, 0300 Hrs. Srinagar, India.

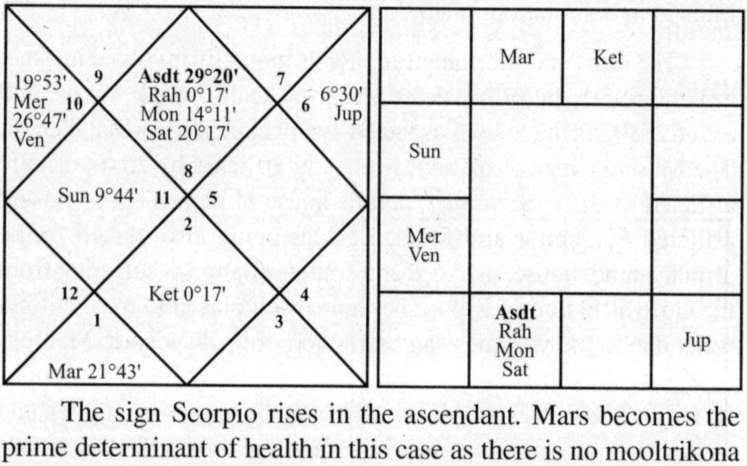

	Mar	Ket	
Sun			
Mer Ven			
	Asdt Rah Mon Sat	Jup	

North Indian chart:
- House 9: 19°53' Mer 26°47' Ven; House 10
- Asdt 29°20' Rah 0°17' Mon 14°11' Sat 20°17'
- House 7; House 6: 6°30' Jup
- Sun 9°44' (House 11); House 8; House 5; House 2
- House 12; House 1; Ket 0°17'; House 3; House 4
- Mar 21°43'

The sign Scorpio rises in the ascendant. Mars becomes the prime determinant of health in this case as there is no mooltrikona sign in the ascendant. Mars, Venus, Rahu and Ketu act as functional malefic planets. Pisces rises in the ascendant of shashthamsa. No planet is in debilitation in shashthamsa.

The Moon is weak as it is in its sign of debilitation. Mercury is placed in an afflicted house. The most malefic planet, Venus, afflicts the most effective point of the third house and the sign Cancer placed in the ninth house. The functional malefic Mars closely afflicts the lord of the fourth house by way of an aspect. Rahu-Ketu axis is exactly over the most effective points of the twelfth and sixth houses and afflicts the second, fourth, eighth and tenth houses by exact aspects, as well. The Sun is weak due to weakness of dispositor, placement in an afflicted house and exact affliction of its mooltrikona sign house.

The affliction to the most effective point of the third house, the lord of the fourth house and the most effective point of the fourth house resulted in problems of health pertaining to the lungs manifesting in the form of tuberculosis. It started in the sub-period of Venus in the main period of Venus and continued to trouble the native. During the sub-period of Jupiter in the main period of Venus, the native sought astrological remedies which were prescribed in the form of wearing of a Kavach for the functional benefic planets besides the use of a pearl. The propitiatory remedial measures for the afflicting planets Venus, Mars, Rahu and Ketu were also advised.

BREATHING PROBLEMS

Chart 29

Male born 9th January, 1944, 0920 Hrs. Palivel (A.P.), India.

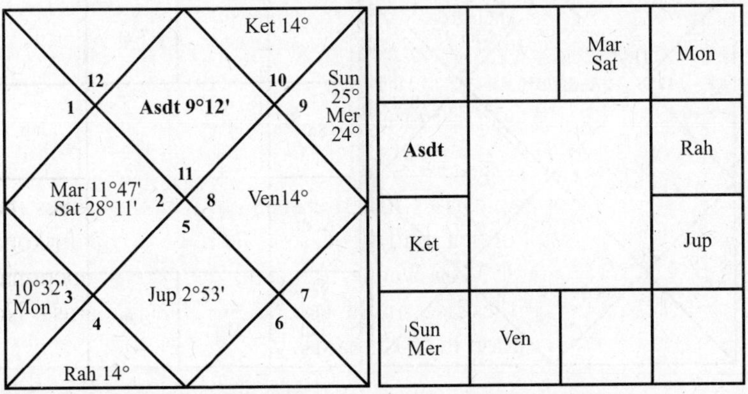

Left chart (diamond):
- Ket 14°
- 12, 1, Asdt 9°12'
- 10, 9, Sun 25° Mer 24°
- 11
- Mar 11°47' Sat 28°11', 2
- 8, Ven 14°
- 5
- 10°32' Mon, 3
- 4, Jup 2°53'
- 7
- 6
- Rah 14°

Right chart (square):

		Mar Sat	Mon
Asdt			Rah
Ket			Jup
Sun Mer	Ven		

The sign Aquarius rises in the ascendant. Saturn and the Moon become the prime determinants of health. The Moon, Mercury, Rahu and Ketu act as functional malefic planets. Taurus rises in the ascendant of shashthamsa. No planet is in debilitation in shashthamsa.

Saturn and Jupiter are weak as they are in old age and infancy, respectively. There are a number of close afflictions in this chart. The most malefic planet, Mercury, afflicts the Sun by way of an exact conjunction. The Moon afflicts the most effective points of the fifth and eleventh houses. The Moon is weak due to placement in an afflicted house. Ketu afflicts Mars by way of a close aspect and Rahu afflicts Venus by way of an exact aspect from the sixth house ruling diseases. Mercury is weak due to combustion and weak dispositor, and is placed in an afflicted house.

The native never kept good health and suffered from breathing problems and the problem of acidity which is one of the major causes of breathing problems. The onset of the main period of Mercury resulted in an acute dust allergy. The native was advised both propitiatory astral remedies for the functional malefic planets and wearing of a Kavach for strengthening the weak functional benefic planets in an auspiciously elected time.

Chart 30

Male born 8th January, 1994, 0904 Hrs. New Delhi, India.

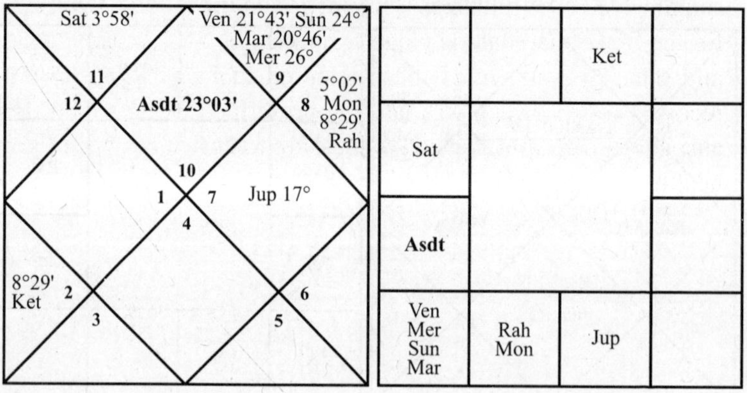

The sign Capricorn rises in the ascendant. The Sun becomes the prime determinant of health as there is no mooltrikona sign in both first and sixth houses. The Sun, Jupiter, Rahu and Ketu act as functional malefic planets. Aquarius rises in the ascendant of the shashthamsa and Saturn becomes the additional prime determinant of health. The Moon, Saturn and Rahu are placed in debilitation in shashthamsa.

Mars, Mercury and Venus are all weak due to bad placement, combustion, and exact affliction of the Sun to the most effective point of their house of placement. They become additionally weak due to the close affliction of the Sun. The Sun is weak due to bad placement, weak dispositor, and placement in an afflicted house. The weak Moon and Rahu are closely conjunct with each other and are in their signs of debilitation. The functional malefic Jupiter is weak due to the weakness of its dispositor, and the exact affliction of its mooltrikona house. Saturn is well placed and unafflicted and is fairly strong. When the child was just one month old, the functional malefic Jupiter started exerting malefic transit influence on the most effective point of the fourth house, whose lord is also badly placed and afflicted in the nativity and the malefic Rahu formed exact conjunction with the natal Moon. The transit influences resulted in serious breathing problems to the native (infant). The parents were under acute mental tension and the child was admitted to an intensive care unit when astral remedies were sought. The astral remedies were suggested in the form of charities for the functional malefic planets, Jupiter, the Sun, Rahu and Ketu and the performance of these resulted in fast and miraculous recovery. The Kavach was later on prescribed for the child in an auspicious time as a preventive measure to ensure continued good health.

HYPERTENSION AT YOUNG AGE

Chart 31

Female born 17th October, 1960, 0400 Hrs. Deolali, India.

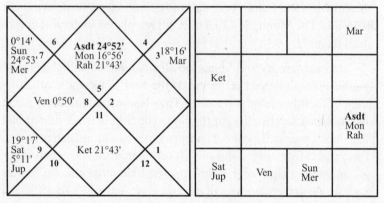

The sign Leo rises in the ascendant. The Sun becomes the prime determinant of the health. The Moon, Rahu and Ketu act as functional malefic planets. Leo rises in the ascendant of the shashthamsa and the Sun becomes also the additional prime determinant of health. Mars is placed in debilitation in shashthamsa.

The Sun is weak due to infancy, debilitation and weak dispositor. The most malefic planet, the Moon, occupies the ascendant and is weak due to weak dispositor and placement in an afflicted house. Venus, the dispositor of the Sun and Mercury, is weak due to infancy, and becomes additionally weak due to the close affliction to its mooltrikona house. Mars is placed in an afflicted house. Ketu afflicts and causes malefic influence to the most effective point of the third house and Mercury placed therein. Saturn and Jupiter are strong in this case.

The weakness of the lord of the ascendant of the natal chart and the affliction of the most malefic planet in the ascendant caused illness in the form of high blood pressure to the native at a young age from the ending part of the main period of the Moon. It was detected in the sub period of Mars in it own main period.

The weakness and/or affliction of the Sun and/or Mars give health problems pertaining to malfunctioning of heart and hypertension. The native was advised both propitiatory astral remedies for the functional malefic planets and wearing of a Kavach for strengthening the weak functional benefic planets in an auspiciously elected time which benefited the native.

Chart 32

Male born 19th July, 1966, 0725 Hrs. New Delhi, India.

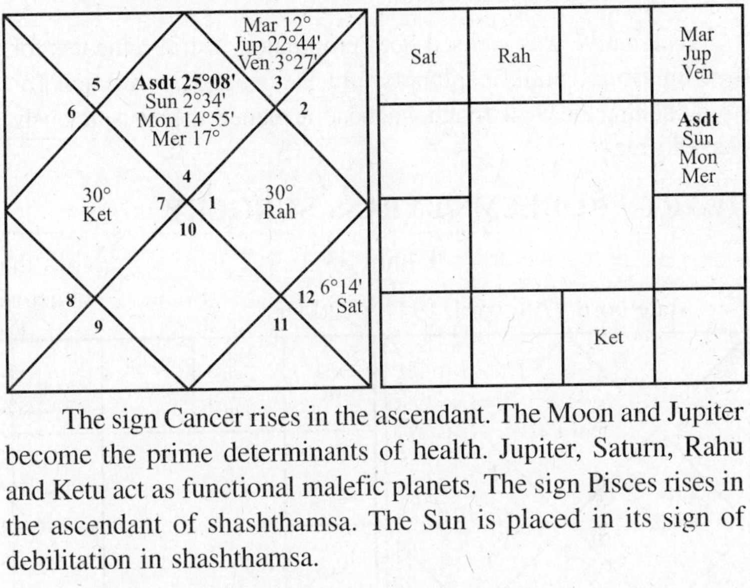

The sign Cancer rises in the ascendant. The Moon and Jupiter become the prime determinants of health. Jupiter, Saturn, Rahu and Ketu act as functional malefic planets. The sign Pisces rises in the ascendant of shashthamsa. The Sun is placed in its sign of debilitation in shashthamsa.

The Moon is weak due to debilitation in navamsa. Jupiter is weak as it is combust and badly placed. Jupiter closely afflicts the most effective points of the twelfth, fourth and eighth houses. The influence of Jupiter on the sixth house is protective as the sixth house contains its mooltrikona sign. But the close influence of Jupiter on the fourth house is indicative of coronary diseases and the influence on the most effective point of the eighth and twelfth houses curtails longevity. Mars and the fourth lord Venus are badly placed in an afflicted house and weak. The weak Sun suffers from the close afflicting aspect of Ketu. The native suffered from heart problem and hypertension from the beginning of the dasa of Ketu at a very young age. Mercury is weak due to the weakness of dispositor. The good placement of Mercury and the operation of the main period of Mercury in the young age helped the native in acquiring good education in the analytical field of software engineering signified by the planet Mercury. The ill health given by the main period of Ketu followed by the dasa of badly placed Venus, however, checked the progress in his professional career primarily because of bad health.

The native was advised both propitiatory astral remedies for the functional malefic planets and wearing of a Kavach for strengthening the weak functional benefic planets in an auspiciously elected time.

HEART PROBLEMS/BYPASS SURGERY

Chart 33

Male born 17th April, 1941, 0920 Hrs.

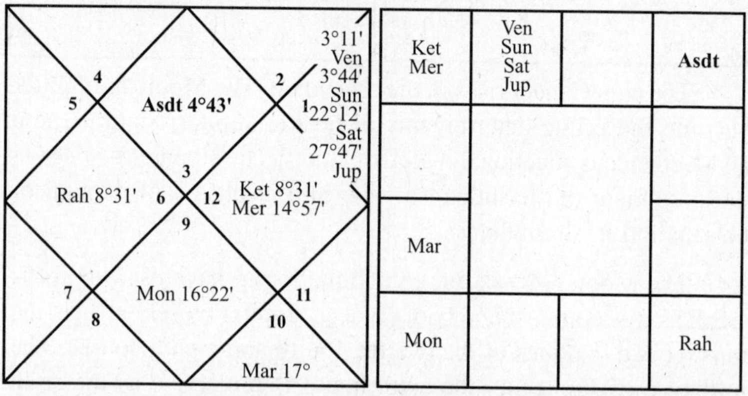

Ket Mer	Ven Sun Sat Jup		Asdt
Mar			
Mon			Rah

The sign Gemini rises in the ascendant. The Sun becomes the prime determinant of health as there is no mooltrikona sign in the first and sixth house. Rahu and Ketu act as functional malefic planets. Aries rises in the ascendant of shashthamsa and Mars becomes the additional prime determinant of health. Rahu is in debilitation in shashthamsa.

Mercury as lord of the fourth house is weak due to debilitation and placement in an afflicted house. Rahu and Ketu afflict the houses occupied and aspected closely. The Moon is weak due to the weakness of dispositor and due to close affliction to its mooltrikona sign house. The Sun significator of the heart is weak due to weakness of dispositor. Venus is weak due to combustion and due to weak dispositor. Mars is weak due to bad placement. Saturn is weak due to debilitation and weak dispositor.

The exact afflictions to the fourth and sixth houses and to the significators of heart, the Sun and the weakness of the Moon, Mercury and Mars resulted in persisting multiple health problems including hypertension. Later the native suffered from heart problem during the sub-period of Mars in the main period of Rahu.

Chart 34

Male born 9th July, 1939, 1635 Hrs. Churu, India.

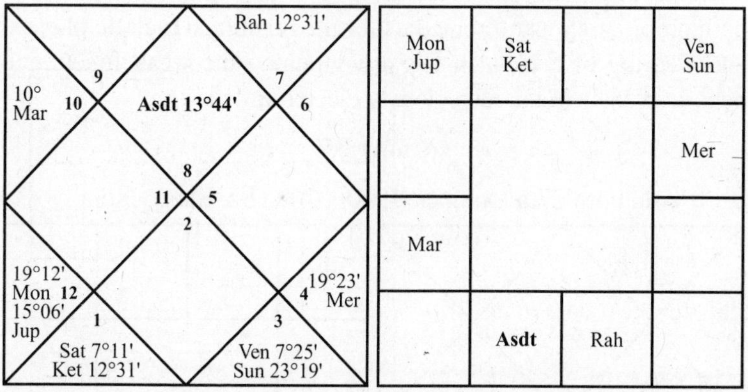

The sign Scorpio rises in the ascendant. Mars becomes the prime determinant of health in this case as there is no mooltrikona sign in the ascendant. Mars, Venus, Rahu and Ketu act as functional malefic planets. Sagittarius rises in the ascendant of the shashthamsa and Jupiter becomes the additional prime determinant of health. Jupiter is in debilitation in shashthamsa.

Badly placed Rahu-Ketu axis causes close afflictions to the houses occupied and aspected and makes the planets Jupiter, Saturn, Mars, Sun and Venus weak. The functional malefic Mars closely aspects and afflicts Saturn. Mars afflicts the most effective points of the houses occupied and aspected. The planets Saturn, the Sun and Venus are badly placed and weak. Saturn is in its sign of debilitation.

The bad placement and weakness of the lord of the fourth house and the afflicting aspects of Rahu to the most effective point of the fourth house and of Mars to the weak lord of the fourth house resulted in hypertension and persistent health problems to the native. The good placement of the prime determinant of health, however, helped the native in bearing the health problems manifested through heart attacks. The Moon and Mercury are strong.

The native had to undergo bypass surgery in the sub-period of Venus and main period of the Moon. The native was advised both propitiatory astral remedies for the functional malefic planets and wearing of a Kavach for strengthening the weak functional benefic planets in an auspiciously elected time.

Chart 35

Male born 27th October, 1940, 0209 Hrs. Eluru, India.

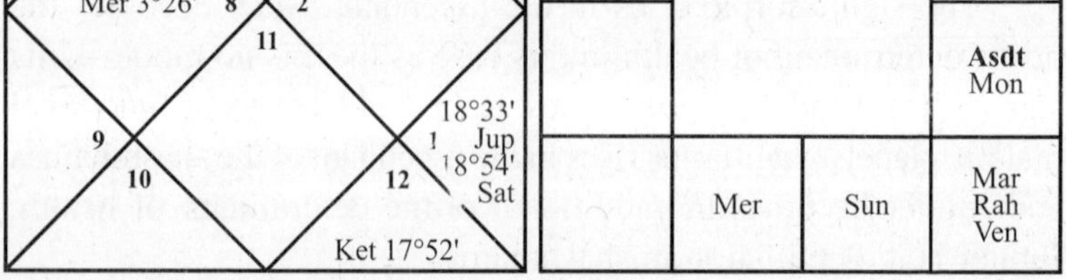

Mar 20°43' Rah 17°52' Ven 0° **6** / 10°15' **7** Sun	Asdt 14° Mon 13°48'	**4** **3**	
Mer 3°26' **8**	**5** **2** **11**		
9 **10**		**12** 18°33' **1** Jup 18°54' Sat	
	Ket 17°52'		

Ket	Jup Sat		
			Asdt Mon
	Mer	Sun	Mar Rah Ven

The sign Leo rises in the ascendant. The Sun becomes the prime determinant of the health. The Moon, Rahu and Ketu act as functional malefic planets. Gemini rises in the ascendant of shashthamsa. No planet is in its sign of debilitation in shashthamsa.

The Sun is weak due to debilitation, weak dispositor and exact affliction to its mooltrikona house. The Moon is weak due to weak dispositor and it exactly afflicts its house of placement. Rahu-Ketu axis closely afflicts Mars and the most effective points of the houses occupied and aspected, having a weakening effect over the planets Moon and Mercury. Ketu aspects and severely afflicts the most effective point of the fourth house. Venus, the dispositor of the Sun, is weak due to debilitation and extreme infancy. This renders the Sun very weak. Saturn is debilitated in the chart. Jupiter is weak due to the weakness and affliction to its dispositor. The impact of the most malefic planet, the Moon, on the most effective point of the ascendant when the lord of the ascendant is quite weak, is indicative of fatal disease.

The Sun indicates diseases pertaining to the functioning of heart. The native suffered from heart attack and had to undergo bypass surgery of heart in the main period of Rahu and the sub-period of Jupiter. The native was advised both propitiatory astral remedies for the functional malefic planets and wearing of a Kavach for strengthening the weak functional benefic planets in an auspiciously elected time.

Chart 36

Male born 3rd April, 1964, 0750 Hrs. Ferozepur, India.

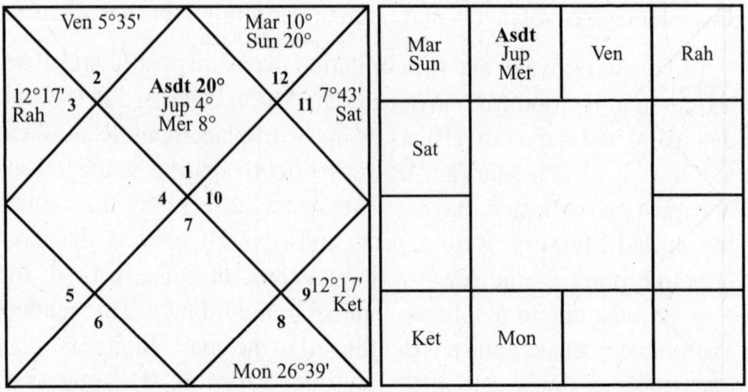

Mar Sun	Asdt Jup Mer	Ven	Rah
Sat			
Ket	Mon		

The sign Aries rises in the ascendant. Mars and Mercury become prime determinants of health. Mercury, Rahu and Ketu act as functional malefic planets. Cancer rises in the ascendant of shashthamsa and the Moon becomes the additional prime determinant of health. No planet is in its sign of debilitation in shashthamsa.

Mars is combust and badly placed. Mercury is placed in the ascendant and is under the close affliction of Ketu. The Moon being lord of the fourth house and additional prime determinant of health and ruling heart is weak due to old age, debilitation and bad placement. The Sun is weak due to bad placement. Mercury and Jupiter become weak due to weakness of dispositor. The weak Jupiter is under the close affliction of Mercury. Venus and Saturn are strong in the nativity.

The native suffered from heart problem at a very young age of 26 years and had to undergo bypass surgery in middle of 1991. The native was advised both propitiatory astrological remedial measures and wearing of a Kavach in an auspiciously elected time for strengthening the weak functional benefic planets.

Chart 37

Female born 11th November, 1976, 1630 Hrs. Gurgaon, India.

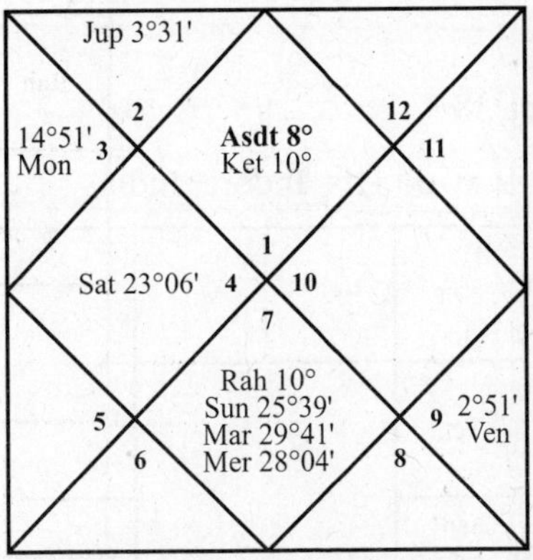

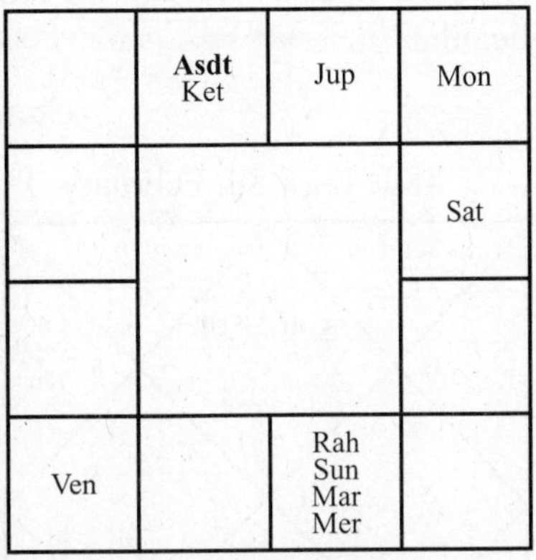

Asdt Ket	Jup	Mon
		Sat
Ven	Rah Sun Mar Mer	

The sign Aries rises in the ascendant. Mars and Mercury become prime determinants of health. Mercury, Rahu and Ketu act as functional malefic planets. Taurus rises in the ascendant of shashthamsa. Ketu is in its sign of debilitation in shashthamsa.

Mars, the lord of the ascendant, is quite weak as it is combust, in extreme old age, its house of placement and its mooltrikona house are afflicted and its dispositor, Venus, is weak due to infancy. Mercury is quite weak as it is combust, in old age, its house of placement is afflicted and its dispositor, Venus, is weak due to infancy. The functional malefic Mercury closely afflicts Mars and the Sun. Jupiter is also weak as it is in infancy and its mooltrikona house is afflicted by the most malefic planet, Ketu. Rahu and Ketu closely afflict the houses occupied and aspected and make the planets Saturn, the Sun, Venus, Mars and Jupiter weak by afflicting their mooltrikona houses.

The planetary configuration shows that the ascendant, the prime determinants of health and the significator of vitality are quite weak and afflicted. Due to the afflictions and weaknesses, the native did not keep sound health from the very beginning and was suffering from increased heartbeat and pain in legs persistently.

With the wearing of Kavach for the weak functional benefic planets and performing charities for the functional malefic planets, Ketu, Rahu and Mercury, the native found an improvement in her health.

Chart 38

Male born 8th February, 1959, 0700 Hrs. Indore, India.

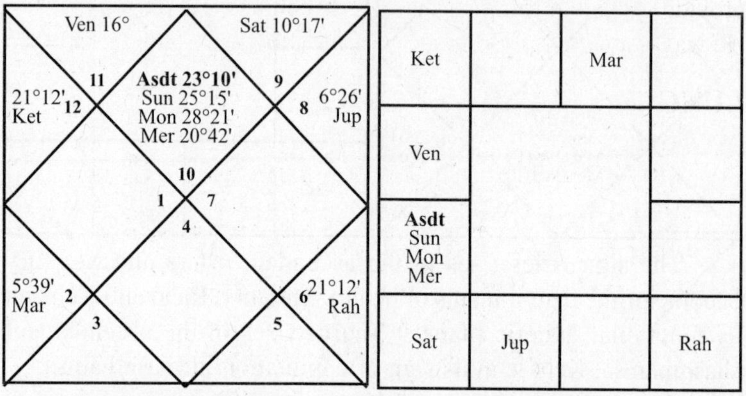

```
            Ven 16°              Sat 10°17'

      11        Asdt 23°10'        9
21°12' 12       Sun 25°15'            8   6°26'
Ket             Mon 28°21'               Jup
                Mer 20°42'
                   10
              1        7
                  4
5°39'                            21°12'
Mar   2                       6   Rah
        3              5
```

Ket		Mar	
Ven			
Asdt Sun Mon Mer			
Sat	Jup		Rah

The sign Capricorn rises in the ascendant. The Sun becomes the prime determinant of health as there is no mooltrikona sign in both first and sixth houses. The Sun, Jupiter, Rahu and Ketu act as functional malefic planets. Aquarius rises in the ascendant of the shashthamsa and Saturn becomes the additional prime determinant of health. No planet is placed in its sign of debilitation in shashthamsa. Functional malefic planets Mercury, Rahu and Ketu of the shashthamsa occupy the ascendant of shashthamsa.

The Sun is the most malefic planet and its location near the most effective point of the ascendant is a major health hazard in itself. Jupiter is weak as the most effective point of its house of placement is afflicted by the Ketu. Rahu-Ketu axis is close to the most effective points of the houses occupied and aspected and closely afflicts them besides severely afflicting the Sun and Mercury. The functional malefic Jupiter closely aspects and afflicts the secondary significator for vitality, Mars, ruling the fourth house.

The Moon is weak due to combustion and old age. Venus becomes weak due to the bad placement of its dispositor, Saturn.

The severe afflictions to the ascendant, the Sun and Mars, caused severe health problems to the native at a very young age. The involvement of the Sun resulted in the problem of hypertension and heart trouble. The native was advised to wear a Kavach to provide strength to the weak and afflicted functional benefic planets. He was also advised propitiation of the functional malefic planets.

LUNG DISORDER

Chart 39

Male born 6th December, 1953, 1515 Hrs. Rajgarh, India.

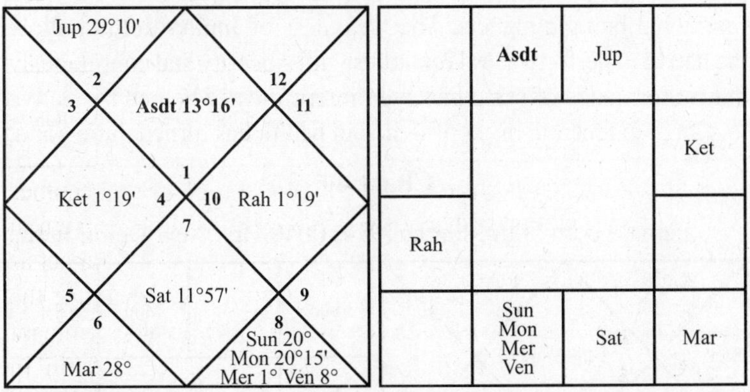

		Asdt	Jup
			Ket
Rah			
	Sun Mon Mer Ven	Sat	Mar

Chart (left, diamond format):
- Jup 29°10' (house 2)
- Asdt 13°16' (house 1)
- Ket 1°19' (house 4)
- Rah 1°19' (house 10)
- Sat 11°57' (house 7)
- Mar 28° (house 6)
- Sun 20°, Mon 20°15', Mer 1° Ven 8° (house 8)

The sign Aries rises in the ascendant. Mars and Mercury become prime determinants of health. Mercury, Rahu and Ketu act as functional malefic planets. Gemini rises in the ascendant of shashthamsa and there is no planet in its sign of debilitation in shashthamsa.

Mars is weak due to bad placement in the sixth house, old age and weak dispositor. The other prime determinant of health, Mercury, is badly placed in the eighth house, in infancy and exactly afflicted by Ketu. The lord of the fourth house, the Moon, is badly placed in the eighth house, debilitated and combust. The lord of the seventh house, Venus, is badly placed in the eighth house and is in its sign of debilitation in navamsa. Jupiter is weak as it is in the extreme old age. The well placed exalted Saturn becomes weak due to the weakness of its dispositor.

The weaknesses and afflictions in the chart inflicted severe illness on the native. The native suffered from acute problems of lungs and respiratory system. The severe affliction of Ketu to Mercury in the sub-period of Ketu, in the main period of Venus, resulted in such severity that the native seriously thought of resigning his job in the year 1994 at the very young age of 41 years. He was advised propitiatory astral remedies for Ketu, Rahu and Mercury for warding of the afflictions of the functional malefic planets and wearing of a Kavach for providing strength to the weak functional benefic planets. The weakness of Jupiter did not allow the native to perform astral remedies with sincerity and continuously but performance of remedies even intermittently helped the native to a large extent and his confidence in health has turned quite good.

Chart 40

Female born 30th March, 1974, 0040 Hrs. New Delhi, India.

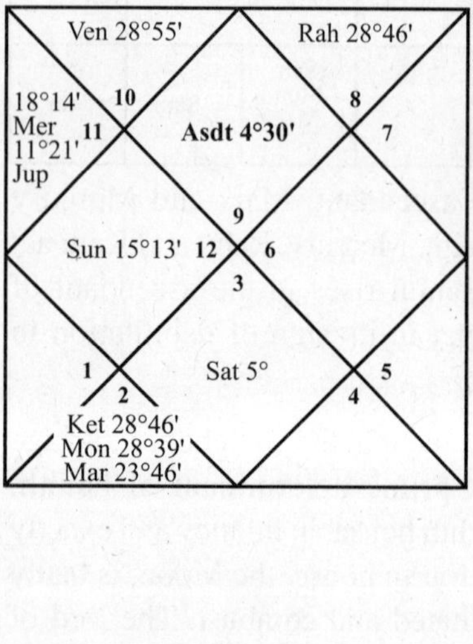

Sun		Ket Mon Mar	Sat
Mer Jup			
Ven			
Asdt	Rah		

Chart details (diamond chart):
- Ven 28°55'
- Rah 28°46'
- 18°14' 10
- Mer 11 11°21'
- Jup
- Asdt 4°30'
- 8
- 7
- 9
- Sun 15°13' 12
- 6
- 3
- 1
- Sat 5°
- 5
- 2
- 4
- Ket 28°46'
- Mon 28°39'
- Mar 23°46'

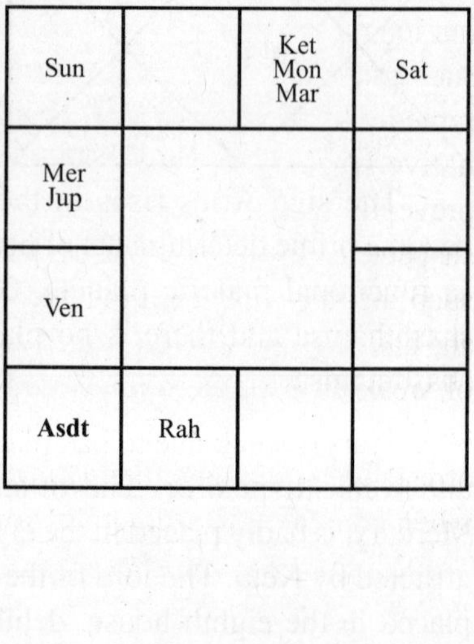

The sign Sagittarius rises in the ascendant. Jupiter becomes the prime determinant of health. The Moon, Rahu and Ketu act as functional malefic planets. The ascendant of the shashthamsa is Aries and Mars becomes the additional prime determinant of the health. No planet is in debilitation in shashthamsa.

The prime determinant of health, Jupiter, is well placed in the nativity but becomes weak as it is in its sign of debilitation in navamsa. The lord of the eighth house, ruling longevity, is badly placed in the sixth house and is in exact conjunction with the functional malefic, Ketu. Ketu also afflicts the weak Venus with an exact aspect. Mars is badly placed in the sixth house. Mercury is weak as it is debilitated in navamsa. Whenever any weak planet is under the severe affliction of Rahu-Ketu axis and is badly placed, it gives growth of a cancerous disease. Venus is weak due to old age and debilitation in navamsa.

The diseases manifest in the sub-periods of either afflicting planet or in the sub-period of the afflicted planet. The close affliction of the nodes to weak planets makes one vulnerable to cancerous diseases. Ever since the author, V.K.Choudhry identified this planetary configuration giving cancerous results in the year 1989, our team had been very particular in watching the horoscopes with such planetary configuration for administering preventive astral remedies and we are very proud to say that in cases where the native had not started suffering from such a fatal disease, the preventive astral remedies proved to be of great help and the natives suspected for cancerous disease did not suffer in the sub-periods of such afflicting/afflicted planets. This native approached us when she had already suffered from a cancerous disease in the sub-period of weak and afflicted Venus and the main period of badly placed and afflicting Rahu. Though the astral remedies are suggested to arrest the fast malignant growth yet these remedies are not so helpful when compared to the application of preventive remedies.

Chart 41

Female born 30th August, 1972, 2145 Hrs. New Delhi, India.

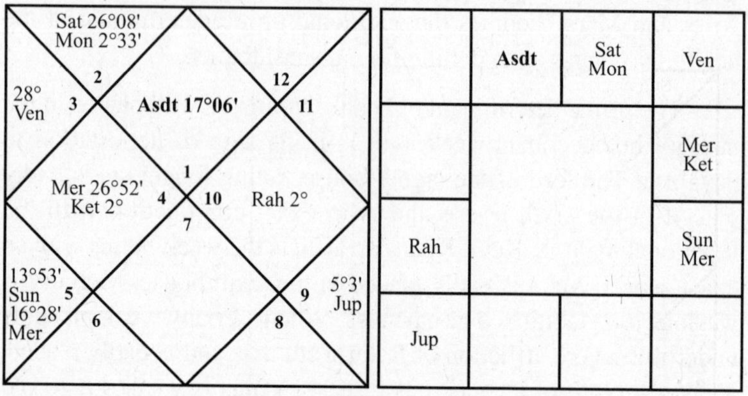

	Asdt	Sat Mon	Ven
			Mer Ket
Rah			Sun Mer
Jup			

The sign Aries rises in the ascendant. Mars and Mercury become prime determinants of health. Mercury, Rahu and Ketu act as functional malefic planets. Cancer rises in the ascendant of shashthamsa and the Moon becomes the additional prime determinant of health. Mars, Mercury and Venus are in debilitation in shashthamsa.

The prime determinant of health, Mars, is well placed in conjunction with the functional benefic Sun but is weak due to combustion. Mercury is weak due to old age, debilitation in navamsa and weak dispositor. The Moon is weak due to infancy and exact affliction. The malefic Rahu closely afflicts the Moon by an exact aspect. Venus, is weak and afflicted due to old age and close conjunction with the most malefic planet, Ketu. The house ruled by the weak and afflicted Moon is occupied by the functional malefic Mercury.

At the time of birth, Rahu-Ketu axis was stationary at two degrees from July, 1972 to August, 1972 and caused irreparable loss to the native's health. The native suffered from polio since birth. This problem was also the result of the exact aspect of Rahu to the Moon.

AIDS

Chart 42

Male born 11th May, 1962, 0400 Hrs.

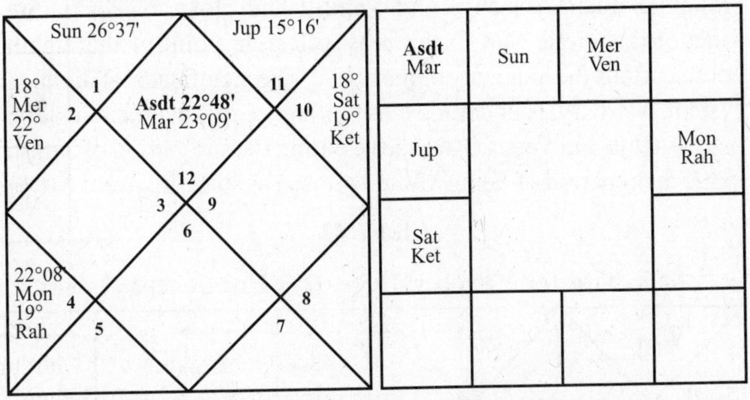

Sun 26°37'	Jup 15°16'		

North Indian chart:
- Sun 26°37' (top center left)
- Jup 15°16' (top center right)
- 18° Mer 22° Ven — house 1, 2
- Asdt 22°48' Mar 23°09' — center
- 11, 10
- 18° Sat 19° Ket — house 10
- 12
- 3, 9
- 6
- 22°08 Mon 19° Rah — house 4, 5
- 8, 7

South Indian chart:

Asdt Mar	Sun	Mer Ven	
Jup			Mon Rah
Sat Ket			

The sign Pisces rises in the ascendant. The Sun becomes the prime determinant of health as there is no mooltrikona sign in the ascendant. The Sun, Venus, Saturn, Rahu and Ketu act as functional malefic planets. Aquarius rises in the ascendant of shashthamsa and Saturn becomes the additional prime determinant of health. No planet is in debilitation in shashthamsa. Saturn is badly placed in Shashthamsa alongwith three functional malefics of Shashthamsa.

The Sun closely influences the most effective points of the second and eighth houses. The Sun is weak due to old age. The most malefic planet Venus closely afflicts the lord of the seventh house, Mercury, and the most effective points of the third and ninth houses. Jupiter is weak due to bad placement and weak dispositor.

The close influence of the lord of the eighth house or Rahu or the lord of the twelfth house on the lord of the seventh house and/ or the most effective point of the seventh house and/or Venus and the influence of Rahu on the lord of the eighth house gives indulgence out of marital bond for excessive sensual pleasures and endangers the native with sexually transmitted diseases.

In this nativity, the lord of the seventh house is under the close influence of the lord of the eighth house. Rahu-Ketu are on the most effective points of the houses of their location and closely afflicts all the houses occupied and aspected besides afflicting the planets Saturn, Mercury and Venus. The close aspect of the functional malefic Sun to the most effective point of the eighth house curtails the longevity of the native. The significator of immune system, Mercury, is under the close influence of functional malefic planets Ketu and Venus. This native during the sub-period of Saturn in the main period of Venus was diagnosed as suffering from AIDS.

Chart 43

Male born 16th October, 1956, 0127 Hrs. Sonepat, India.

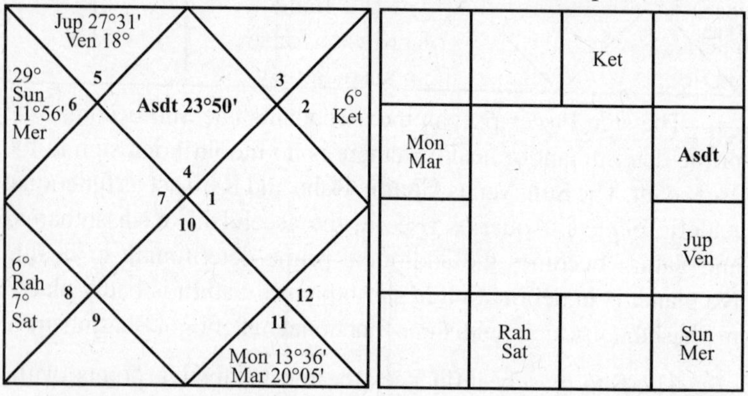

		Ket	
Mon Mar			Asdt
			Jup Ven
	Rah Sat		Sun Mer

South Indian chart data:
Jup 27°31' Ven 18° / 29° Sun 11°56' Mer (house 5, 6) / Asdt 23°50' (house 3) / 6° Ket (house 2) / 6° Rah 7° Sat (house 8) / Mon 13°36' Mar 20°05' (house 11) / houses 4, 7, 1, 10, 9, 12

The sign Cancer rises in the ascendant. The Moon and Jupiter become the prime determinants of health. Jupiter, Saturn, Rahu and Ketu act as functional malefic planets. Aquarius rises in the ascendant of shashthamsa and Saturn becomes the additional prime determinant of health. Saturn is under close influence of Rahu and Ketu in Shashthamsa.

The Moon is badly placed and weak in this nativity and its dispositor, Saturn, is under the severe affliction of Rahu-Ketu axis. Jupiter is weak due to old age and weak dispositor. The significator for vitality, the Sun, is in extreme old age. Venus is weak due to debilitation in navamsa and weak dispositor. Mars is weak as it is badly placed and its dispositor is severely afflicted. Jupiter closely afflicts the most effective points of the second, eighth and tenth houses.

During the sub-period of Rahu in the main period of Saturn, the most malefic planet, the native was suspected to be a patient of AIDS. He was already suffering from piles, which is indicated by the affliction of the lord of the eighth house in the nativity and affliction to the most effective point of the eighth house. He had practically all types of vices due to the close conjunction of debilitated Rahu with Saturn in the fifth house. The operation of main period of Saturn played the complimentary role. The native was advised both propitiatory astral remedies for the functional malefic planets and wearing of a Kavach for strengthening the weak functional benefic planets in an auspiciously elected time.

INTESTINAL CANCER

Chart 44

Female born 29th October, 1968, 2215 Hrs. Ambala, India.

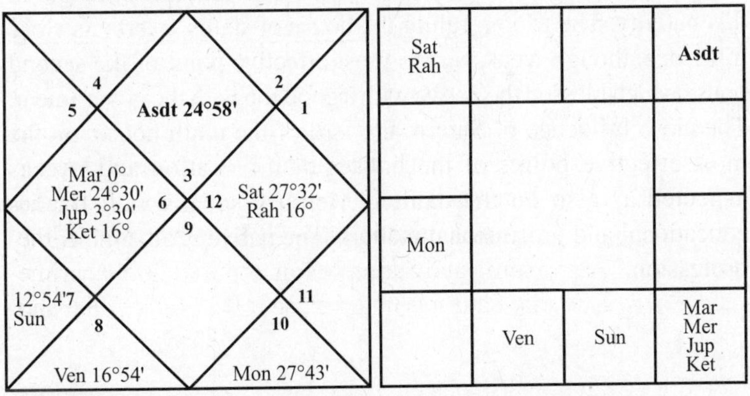

5 / 4	Asdt 24°58' / 2		1
Mar 0° Mer 24°30' Jup 3°30' Ket 16°	3 6 / 12 9	Sat 27°32' Rah 16°	
12°54'7 Sun 8	10 / 11		
Ven 16°54'	Mon 27°43'		

Sat Rah			Asdt
Mon			
	Ven	Sun	Mar Mer Jup Ket

The sign Gemini rises in the ascendant. The Sun becomes the prime determinant of health as there is no mooltrikona sign in the first and sixth houses. Rahu and Ketu act as functional malefic planets. Leo rises in the ascendant of shashthamsa and the Sun becomes also the additional prime determinant of health. No planet is in debilitation in shashthamsa.

The Sun is weak due to debilitation and weakness of dispositor. Venus ruling the fifth house is badly placed in the sixth house and is under the exact afflicting aspect of Rahu. Mars is weak due to extreme infancy. Jupiter is in infancy but fairly strong. Saturn is weak due to old age. The Moon is weak due to bad placement and old age. Exalted Mercury being lord of the fourth house is exactly on the most effective point of the fourth house and promotes both the fourth and tenth houses.

The exact aspect of Rahu, as explained earlier, is indicative of a cancerous disease. In this case, as Venus is placed in the house of diseases ruling intestines, the native suffered from intestinal cancer. The intensity increased in June, 1996, when the transit Ketu was also exerting its malefic influence on both the natal and transit Venus. The native was advised performance of propitiatory remedies for Ketu and wearing of a Kavach for strengthening the weak functional benefic planets and the prime determinants of health in this nativity. The Moon, ruling the house of status, exerts its close influence, though weak, on the most effective point of the second house which blessed the native with a good job with the government. The close influence of Saturn, the lord of the ninth house, on the most effective points of the houses of its location and houses aspected as also on the exalted Mercury speaks well for his educational and professional matters. The native is an engineer by profession.

TUMOR IN STOMACH

Chart 45

Female born 14th May, 1967, 1725 Hrs. Srinagar, India.

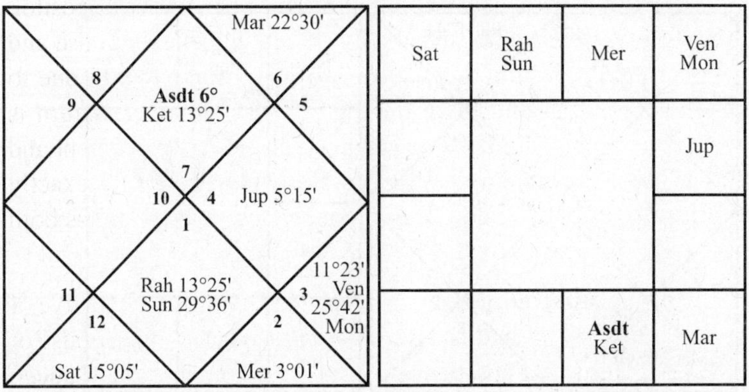

Sat	Rah Sun	Mer	Ven Mon
			Jup
		Asdt Ket	Mar

The sign Libra rises in the ascendant. Venus becomes the prime determinant of health. Mercury, Rahu and Ketu act as functional malefic planets. Taurus rises in the ascendant of shashthamsa. No planet is in debilitation in shashthamsa.

The most malefic planet, Mercury, afflicts the most effective point of the eighth house indicating a curtailed life span for the native. The lord of the fifth house is badly placed in the sixth house and the significator for stomach, the Sun, is weak as it is in extreme old age. Mars is badly placed in the twelfth house, debilitated in the navamsa and has a weak dispositor.

As the lord of fifth house is placed in the sixth house and the significator of the fifth house, the Sun, is weak, the native suffered from severe illness due to a tumour in the stomach when transit Rahu was stationary and was closely conjunct with Mars during the sub-period of Mercury in its own main period. Though the astral remedies were sought and were prescribed, the curative remedies are always of little help when a particular disease has already manifested. This is more so when the chart indicates curtailed longevity.

BRAIN CANCER

Chart 46

Female born 3rd October, 1987, 1911 Hrs. Gurgaon, India.

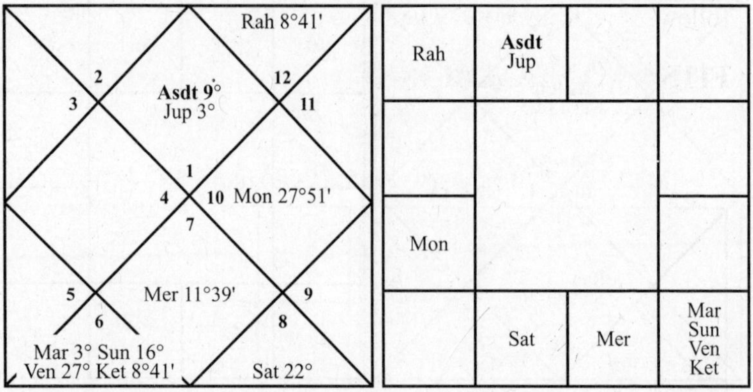

Rah	Asdt Jup	
Mon		
Sat	Mer	Mar Sun Ven Ket

The sign Aries rises in the ascendant. Mars and Mercury become the prime determinants of health. Mercury, Rahu and Ketu act as functional malefic planets. Taurus rises in the ascendant of shashthamsa. Rahu is in debilitation in shashthamsa.

Mars is weak due to combustion, bad placement, infancy, weak dispositor and its house of placement is afflicted. The functional malefic Mercury closely afflicts the most effective points of the seventh and first houses. Mercury is weak due to the weakness of dispositor and afflicted mooltrikona house. The Moon is weak due to old age, afflicted house of placement and afflicted mooltrikona house. Jupiter is weak due to infancy and weak dispositor.

The lord of the seventh house is weak due to bad placement, debilitation, old age, debilitated navamsa, weak dispositor and afflicted house of placement. Rahu-Ketu axis is exactly on the most effective points of the houses of their location and afflicts all the houses occupied and aspected including the houses sixth and eighth, ruling health and longevity, respectively. The Sun and Saturn are also weak due to bad placement and being placed in the afflicted houses in the chart.

The weakness of the Moon and Jupiter and absence of their close beneficial influence in this nativity failed to reduce the impact of afflictions in the chart. During the sub-period of Rahu in its own main period, the native suffered from brain cancer and turned blind followed by death at the young age of 7 years.

FITS AND STAMMERING

Chart 47

Male born 7th January, 1985, 2048 Hrs. New Delhi, India.

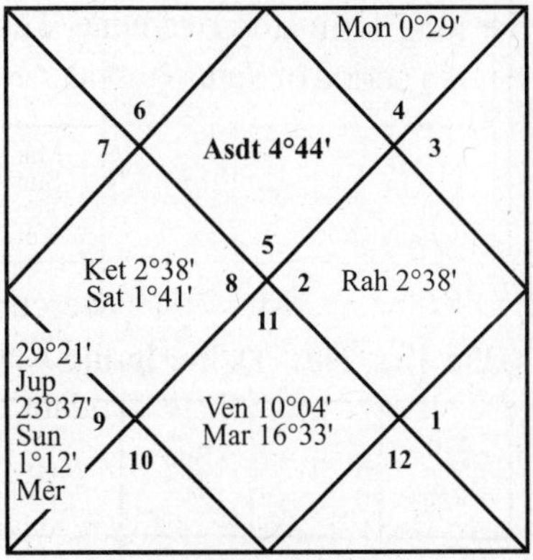

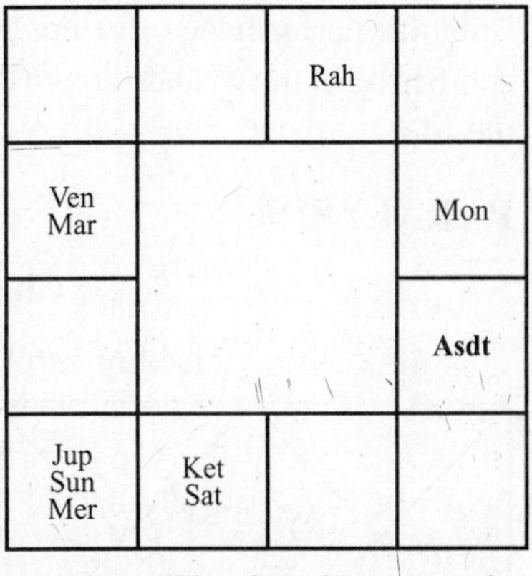

		Rah	
Ven Mar			Mon
			Asdt
Jup Sun Mer	Ket Sat		

Chart North Indian style with:
Mon 0°29', Asdt 4°44', Rah 2°38', Ket 2°38', Sat 1°41', 29°21' Jup 23°37' Sun 1°12' Mer, Ven 10°04' Mar 16°33'. Houses numbered 6, 7, 4, 3, 5, 8, 2, 11, 9, 10, 1, 12.

The sign Leo rises in the ascendant. The Sun becomes the prime determinant of health. The Moon, Rahu and Ketu act as functional malefic planets. Aries rises in the ascendant of the shashthamsa and Mars becomes additional prime determinant for health. Mars is in its sign of debilitation in shashthamsa.

The Sun is weak as it is placed in the sign of a combust, extremely old aged and afflicted Jupiter. Rahu and Ketu closely aspect and afflict the most effective points of the houses occupied and aspected and the planets Saturn and the Moon. The Moon is weak due to infancy. Mercury is weak due to infancy and weak dispositor. Venus and Mars become weak as their dispositor, Saturn, is in infancy and afflicted. The weakness of all the planets and severe afflictions indicate major health problems in life from a very early stage.

The afflictions to the most effective point of the fourth house and the Moon caused sufferings from fits during the sub-period of Rahu in the main period of Jupiter. He lost his father. The weakness of the lord of the second house and close affliction to the second house gave the problem of stammering. Health became very weak. The child could not support his body and could not balance while walking. Successive further sub-periods of Saturn, Mercury, Ketu and Venus in the main period of Saturn could not show any improvement in health. During the sub-period of Venus some improvement was there with the help of astral remedies but their irregular performance did not give long term improvement. The sub-period of the weak Moon in the main period of Saturn threatened the life.

PARALYSIS

Chart 48

Male born 19th May 1969, 0335 Hrs. New Delhi, India.

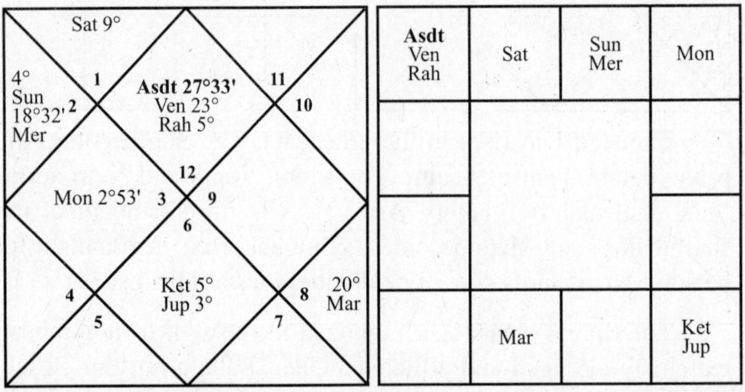

The sign Pisces rises in the ascendant. The Sun becomes the prime determinant of health as there is no mooltrikona sign in the ascendant. The Sun, Venus, Saturn, Rahu and Ketu act as functional malefic planets. Pisces rises in the ascendant of shashthamsa. The Sun is in debilitation in shashthamsa.

The fairly strong Sun turns weak as it is exactly afflicted by Ketu. The most malefic planet, Venus, closely afflicts the ascendant and the seventh house containing the mooltrikona sign of Mercury. The affliction of the eighth lord to the ascendant gives severe health problems and accidents. Jupiter is weak due to infancy, close affliction by Rahu-Ketu axis and debilitation in navamsa. The Moon is weak due to infancy. Mars and Mercury are strong in the chart.

During the main period of Rahu occupying the severely afflicted ascendant and in the sub-period of Ketu occupying the severely afflicted seventh house, ruled by Mercury, the native suffered from a paralytic stroke involving the whole body below the arms and shoulders.

Chart 49

Male born 9th June 1959, 0500 Hrs. Ludhiana, India.

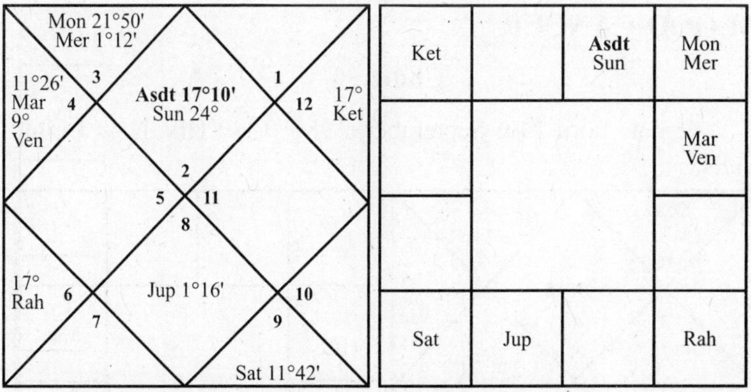

The sign Taurus rises in the ascendant. Venus becomes the prime determinant of health as there is no mooltrikona sign in the ascendant. Venus, Jupiter, Mars, Rahu and Ketu act as functional malefic planets. Capricorn rises in shashthamsa. No planet is in debilitation in shashthamsa. Rahu and Ketu influence the ascendant of shashthamsa.

Venus is placed in the afflicted third house, is debilitated in navamsa, has a weak dispositor, and is under the close malefic influence of Mars. Mercury is weak as it is combust, in infancy, and its mooltrikona sign house is exactly afflicted by the Rahu-Ketu axis. Jupiter is weak as it is in infancy and its house of placement is exactly afflicted by Ketu. Rahu and Ketu exactly afflict the most effective points of the houses occupied and aspected. With this affliction the planets the Moon and Mercury become weak due to afflicted mooltrikona houses. The impact of the affliction of Rahu and Ketu becomes much more severe on the fifth house containing the mooltrikona sign of weak Mercury. Saturn is weak due to bad placement and weak dispositor.

During the sub-period of Mercury in its own main period, the health of the person was badly damaged. He suffered from nervous disorders, paralysis of the lower limbs and multiple cirrhosis.

BLOOD CANCER

Chart 50

Female born 24th September, 1981, 1340 Hrs. New Delhi, India.

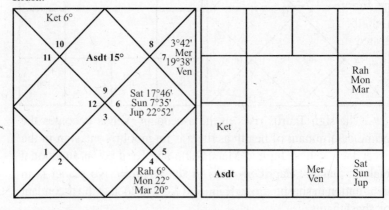

The sign Sagittarius rises in the ascendant. Jupiter becomes the prime determinant of health. The Moon, Rahu and Ketu act as functional malefic planets. Gemini rises in the ascendant of shashthamsa.

The most malefic planet, the Moon, closely afflicts Mars. The functional malefic Ketu closely afflicts the weak Sun by way of an aspect. Mercury, the dispositor of the Sun, Saturn and Jupiter is fairly strong. The well placed Saturn is in combustion but is unafflicted.

During the sub-period of Rahu and the main period of Ketu the native suffered from blood cancer.

Due to the well placed Jupiter and Moon in its own mooltrikona sign house, early detection of the disease resulted in successful symptomatic treatment. The main period of Ketu was to be followed by the main period of strong Venus. The application of astral remedies and the operation of the main period of a strong functional benefic planet, Venus, were expected to protect longevity in its main period.

The native was advised both propitiatory astral remedies for the functional malefic planets and wearing of a Kavach for strengthening the weak functional benefic planets in an auspiciously elected time.

BREAST CANCER

Chart 51

Female born 8th September, 1946, 1256 Hrs. Farrukhabad, India.

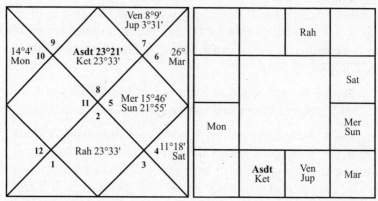

The sign Scorpio rises in the ascendant. Mars becomes the prime determinant of health in this case as there is no mooltrikona sign in the ascendant. Mars, Venus, Rahu and Ketu act as functional malefic planets. Aquarius rises in the ascendant of shashthamsa and Saturn becomes additional prime determinant of health. No planet is in its sign of debilitation in shashthamsa.

Rahu-Ketu axis is exactly on the most effective points of the houses of its location and severely afflicts the houses occupied and aspected besides afflicting Mars, the prime determinant of health in this case. The functional malefic Mars also closely afflicts the eleventh, second and fifth houses. Saturn is weak due to placement in an afflicted house and weak dispositor. The Moon is weak due to placement in an afflicted house and afflicted mooltrikona house. Saturn is lord of the fourth house and the Moon is the significator for the fourth house and the body parts ruled by the fourth house. The Sun is in its sign of debilitation in navamsa. Jupiter is weak due to bad placement and infancy, and becomes additionally weak due to close affliction to its mooltrikona house. The close affliction of Rahu to Mars indicates malignant growth in the muscular parts of the body.

The native suffered from breast cancer during the sub-period of Rahu in the main period of badly placed Jupiter. This resulted in the removal of the infected part of the body.

Chart 52

Female born 2nd March, 1953, 1336 Hrs. New Delhi, India.

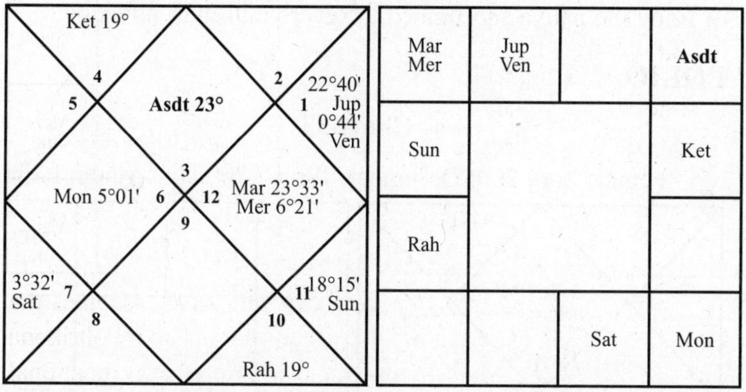

Mar Mer	Jup Ven		Asdt
Sun			Ket
Rah			
		Sat	Mon

North Indian chart:
- Ket 19°
- House 4, 5
- House 2, 1: 22°40', Jup 0°44', Ven
- Asdt 23°
- House 3
- Mon 5°01' 6
- House 12: Mar 23°33', Mer 6°21'
- House 9
- 3°32' Sat 7
- House 8
- House 10
- 11: 18°15' Sun
- Rah 19°

The sign Gemini rises in the ascendant. The Sun becomes the prime determinant of health as there is no mooltrikona sign in the first and sixth houses. Rahu and Ketu act as functional malefic planets. Cancer rises in the ascendant of shashthamsa and the Moon becomes the additional prime determinant of health. The Moon and Saturn are in debilitation in shashthamsa.

Rahu-Ketu axis is on the most effective points of the houses occupied and closely afflicts the houses occupied and aspected besides making the Moon and Mercury weak by afflicting their mooltrikona houses. Besides, the lord of the fourth house is placed in an afflicted house and in debilitation. The lord of the fifth house is weak as it is in infancy and its dispositor is weak. Mars is weak due to placement in an afflicted house. The Sun, Jupiter and Saturn become weak due to weakness of their dispositors.

The placement of Rahu on the most effective point of the eighth house as also its influence on the most effective point of the fourth house whose lord is debilitated resulted in the disease of breast cancer during the sub-period of Mercury and the main period of Rahu. When the sub-period of a planet is in operation its general significations and the significations of the house containing its mooltrikona sign are spoiled if the most effective point of the house involved is afflicted. During the sub-period of Mars and main period of Rahu the native succumbed to severe muscular infection.

POLIO

Chart 53

Female born 20th December, 1965, 1800 Hrs. Ajmer, India.

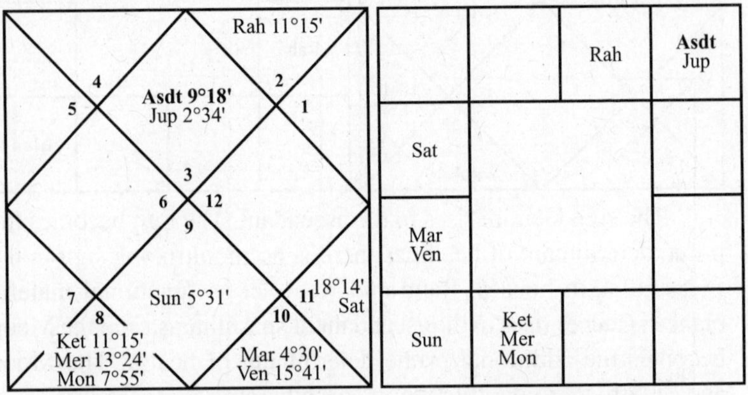

		Rah	Asdt Jup
Sat			
Mar Ven			
Sun	Ket Mer Mon		

(Left chart, North Indian style):
Rah 11°15' (house 2/1)
Asdt 9°18' Jup 2°34' (houses 4, 5)
3, 6, 12, 9
Sun 5°31' (house 10/11) 18°14' Sat
Ket 11°15' Mer 13°24' Mon 7°55' (houses 7, 8)
Mar 4°30' Ven 15°41' (house 10)

The sign Gemini rises in the ascendant. The Sun becomes the prime determinant of health as there is no mooltrikona sign in the first and sixth houses. Rahu and Ketu act as functional malefic planets. Taurus rises in the ascendant of shashthamsa. The Moon is in debilitation in shashthamsa.

Rahu-Ketu axis is on the most effective point of the houses of its location and afflicts all the houses occupied and aspected besides afflicting the badly placed planets, Mercury, the debilitated Moon and Venus. Mars, though exalted, is weak as it is badly placed in the afflicted eighth house. The Sun is weak as its dispositor, Jupiter, is weak due to infancy. At the time of birth, the native was running the sub-period of Ketu in the main period of Saturn.

The close affliction of Ketu to the debilitated Moon and Mercury and the operation of the sub-period of Ketu at the time of birth resulted in a polio attack. Afterwards there was a partial recovery in the sub-period of Venus and the Sun. The extent of affliction to Venus was only 10% while the Sun is well placed and unafflicted. The recovery in the sub-period of the Moon and afterwards was negligible. In 1995, astral remedies were suggested to the native for strengthening the weak functional benefic planets for protection against further health problems.

BRAIN TUMOUR

Chart 54

Male born 20th November, 1985, 0847 Hrs. Calcutta, India.

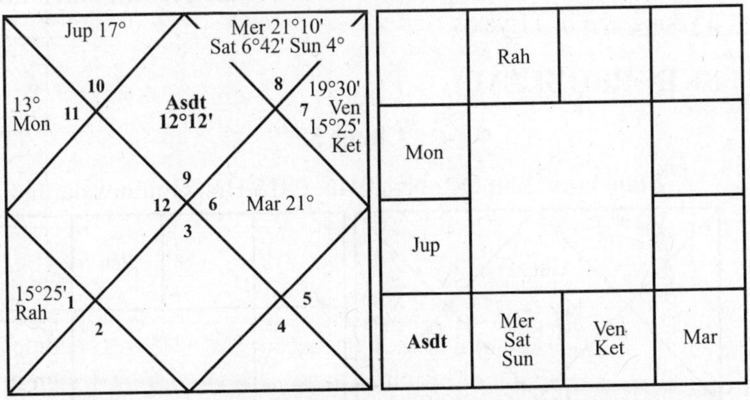

		Rah	
Mon			
Jup			
Asdt	Mer Sat Sun	Ven Ket	Mar

The sign Sagittarius rises in the ascendant. Jupiter becomes the prime determinant of health. The Moon, Rahu and Ketu act as functional malefic planets. Gemini rises in the ascendant of the shashthamsa. The Sun and Jupiter are in debilitation in shashthamsa.

Jupiter is in debilitation. The most effective points of the houses occupied and aspected by Rahu-Ketu axis are severely afflicted. This affliction increases the weakness of the Sun, Mars,

Jupiter and Saturn. The most malefic planet, the Moon, occupies the most effective point of the third house and is under the close affliction of Ketu. Saturn, the lord of the third house ruling development, has its mooltrikona house exactly afflicted and is badly placed in combustion in the twelfth house. The Sun is badly placed and has its mooltrikona house exactly afflicted by the most malefic planet. Mercury is also badly placed,

The close afflictions of Rahu to the most effective point of the ascendant and of Ketu to the Moon resulted in a brain tumor in the sub-period of the Moon and the main period of Rahu. During the sub-period of Jupiter in its own main period the intensity increased when the stationary malefic influence of Ketu was exerted on natal Mercury and subsequently on the most effective point of various houses in August and September, 1996. The stationary malefic impact of Rahu-Ketu axis on the most effective point of various houses in October, 1996 resulted in the death of the child at a young age of 11 years.

SKIN PROBLEM

Chart 55

Male born 20th October, 1946, 0816 Hrs. Gujranwala, India.

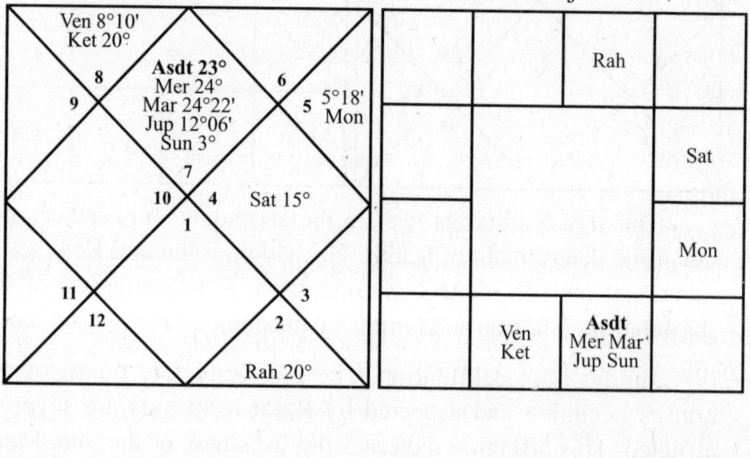

Ven 8°10' Ket 20°	Asdt 23° Mer 24° Mar 24°22' Jup 12°06' Sun 3°		
			5°18' Mon
		Sat 15°	
		Rah 20°	

		Rah	
			Sat
			Mon
	Ven Ket	Asdt Mer Mar Jup Sun	

The sign Libra rises in the ascendant. Venus becomes the prime determinant of health. Mercury, Rahu and Ketu act as functional malefic planets. Leo rises in shashthamsa and the Sun becomes the additional prime determinant of health. No planet is in its sign of debilitation in shashthamsa.

Rahu-Ketu axis is close to the most effective point of the eighth and second houses and afflicts the houses occupied and aspected, thereby adding to the weakness of the Moon and Mercury by afflicting their mooltrikona houses and to the weakness of Venus and Saturn by afflicting their houses of placement. The most malefic planet, Mercury, afflicts the most effective point of the ascendant and the seventh house besides afflicting the lord of the seventh house. The lord of the ascendant is well placed but in an afflicted house and is weak due to an afflicted mooltrikona house and debilitated navamsa. The Sun is weak as it is debilitated in rasi and navamsa, is in infancy, has a weak dispositor and is placed in an afflicted house. The Moon becomes weak due to the weakness of its dispositor. Jupiter is well placed in the main chart but is weak due to combustion, debilitation in navamsa and placement in an afflicted house.

The influence of the lord of the twelfth house on the seventh house and its lord Mars and the influence of Rahu on the eighth house gave extra marital relations and inflicted skin disease on the native. The affliction of Ketu on the most effective point of the second house resulted in the death of a male child. The native also suffered on account of persisting nose bleeding. The placement of the most malefic planet on the most effective point of ascendant causes nose bleeding and endangers the health and physical appearance of the native. The placement of the functional benefic planet, Saturn, in the tenth house and the lord of the tenth house, the Moon, in the house of income gave good financial gains to the native from a hotel project.

Chart 56

Male born 4th May, 1963, 1851 Hrs. New Delhi, India.

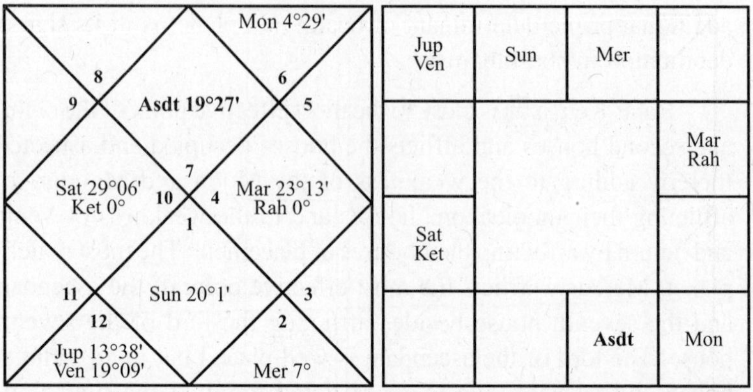

Jup Ven	Sun	Mer	
			Mar Rah
Sat Ket			
		Asdt	Mon

North Indian chart:
- Mon 4°29'
- 8, 6
- 9, Asdt 19°27', 5
- 7
- Sat 29°06' Ket 0°, 10, 4, Mar 23°13' Rah 0°
- 1
- 11, Sun 20°1', 3
- 12, 2
- Jup 13°38' Ven 19°09', Mer 7°

The sign Libra rises in the ascendant. Venus becomes the prime determinant of health. Mercury, Rahu and Ketu act as functional malefic planets. Cancer rises in the ascendant of shashthamsa and the Moon becomes the additional prime determinant of health. No planet is in its sign of debilitation in shashthamsa.

Venus is badly placed in the chart. Besides Venus, the planets Jupiter, Mercury and the Moon are also badly placed. Mercury does not cause close afflictions in the chart. Saturn is extremely weak as it is in the thirtieth degree of the sign. The Sun and Mercury are in their signs of debilitation in navamsa. Mars is weak due to debilitation and weak dispositor. The weak Moon is afflicted by Ketu. The weakness of the significator of skin and the bad placement of Venus resulted in skin cirrhosis.

When Venus is the lord of the ascendant and is weak, it makes the personality less charming and the weakness of the significator of the skin results in a skin disease. The native developed this disease in the sub-period of Venus in the main period of Rahu.

Chart 57

Female born 19th June, 1963, 1935 Hrs. Bombay, India.

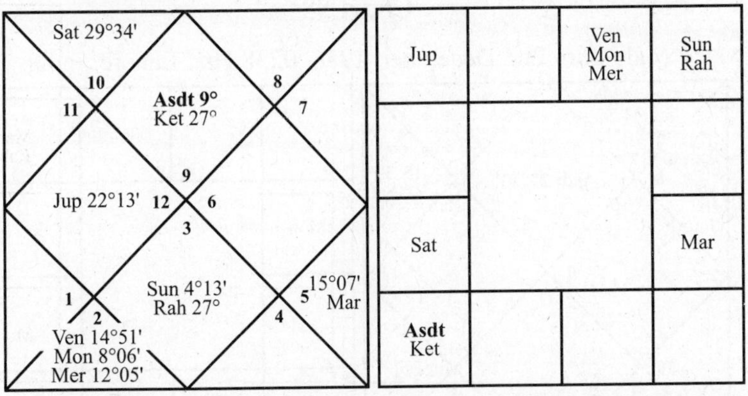

Sat 29°34' 10 11	Asdt 9° Ket 27° 9	8 7	
Jup 22°13' 12	6 3		
1 2 Ven 14°51' Mon 8°06' Mer 12°05'	Sun 4°13' Rah 27°	4	15°07' 5 Mar

Jup		Ven Mon Mer	Sun Rah
Sat			Mar
Asdt Ket			

The sign Sagittarius rises in the ascendant. Jupiter becomes the prime determinant of health. The Moon, Rahu and Ketu act as functional malefic planets. Taurus rises in the ascendant of shashthamsa. The Moon and Mars are in their signs of debilitation in shashthamsa.

Jupiter is well placed in the nativity but is weak due to debilitation in navamsa. The planets Venus, the Moon and Mercury are all placed in the sixth house and these become very weak due to bad placement in an afflicted house. The most malefic planet, the Moon, is on the most effective point of the sixth house and afflicts both the sixth and twelfth house with an exact conjunction/aspect besides afflicting the planet, Mercury.

As both Venus and Mercury are badly placed, the native during the sub-period of Mercury in the main period of Rahu suffered from leuco-derma, a skin disease resulting in white patches on the body. Whenever Mercury, the planet ruling skin, and Venus, the planet ruling beauty, are both weak, the person is vulnerable to a skin disease. The weakness of Mercury results in the person acting in a confused manner without giving proper attention to one's personal hygiene. This finally results in some sort of a skin problem making the presentation of the person in a group of people embarrassing.

Chart 58

Male born 2nd December, 1946, 0238 Hrs. Lahore, India.

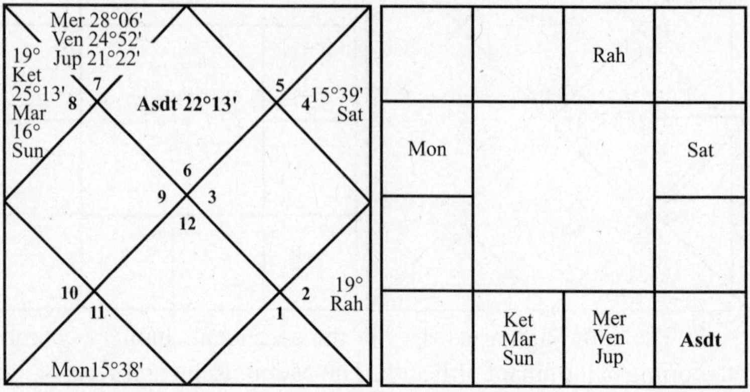

		Rah	
Mon			Sat
	Ket Mar Sun	Mer Ven Jup	**Asdt**

The sign Virgo rises in the ascendant. Mercury and Saturn become the prime determinants of health. Saturn, Mars, the Sun, Rahu and Ketu act as functional malefic planets. Aquarius rises in the ascendant of the shashthamsa and Saturn becomes additional prime determinant of health. No planet is in debilitation in shashthamsa. Saturn is placed in the twelfth house of shashthamsa in conjunction with Rahu and Ketu.

Mercury is well placed in this nativity but is weak as it is in old age, and becomes additionally weak as its mooltrikona sign house is afflicted by Rahu. Saturn is weak due to the weakness of its dispositor Moon, which is badly placed, and becomes additionally weak as it is placed in an afflicted house and is closely afflicted by Ketu. Rahu-Ketu axis causes affliction to the Sun. The most malefic planet, Mars, closely afflicts the third, sixth, ninth and tenth houses. Mars is weak due to combustion, but becomes additionally weak due to placement in an afflicted house. Jupiter and Venus are strong.

The affliction to the sixth house and the lord of the sixth house, Saturn, resulted in serious ailments. During the main period of Saturn and the sub-period of Ketu causing serious afflictions, explained above, the native started suffering from a number of diseases like arthritis, diabetes and the skin problems.

Chart 59

Female born 20th January, 1978, 2250 Hrs. New Delhi, India.

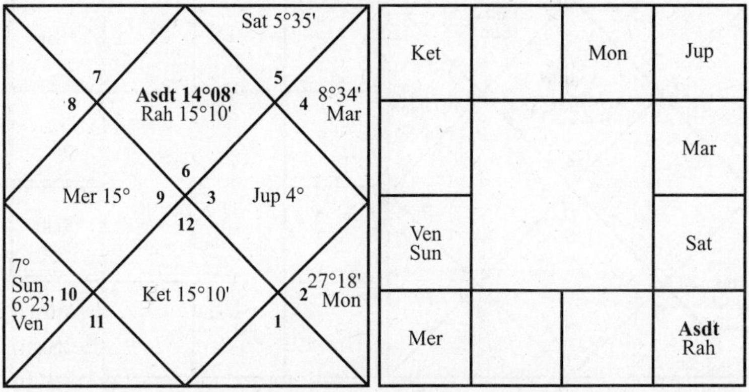

Ket		Mon	Jup
			Mar
Ven Sun			Sat
Mer			Asdt Rah

(Diagram: South Indian style chart with the following entries —
Sat 5°35'; 7; 8; Asdt 14°08' Rah 15°10'; 5; 4; 8°34' Mar; 6; Mer 15°; 9; 3; Jup 4°; 12; 7° Sun 6°23' Ven; 10; 11; Ket 15°10'; 1; 2; 27°18' Mon)

The sign Virgo rises in the ascendant. Mercury and Saturn become the prime determinants of health. Saturn, Mars, the Sun, Rahu and Ketu act as functional malefic planets. Sagittarius rises in the ascendant of shashthamsa and Jupiter becomes additional prime determinant of health. No planet is in its sign of debilitation in shashthamsa.

Mercury is weak due to the close affliction to its mooltrikona house. Rahu-Ketu axis afflicts the most effective point of the houses occupied and aspected. The Sun, being a functional malefic planet, closely afflicts Venus and both the Sun and combust Venus are under the close afflicting aspect of the most malefic planet, Mars. The Moon is weak as it is in the old age and its mooltrikona house is afflicted. The second prime determinant of health, Saturn, is badly placed in the twelfth house and its dispositor is afflicted.

The severe affliction of Rahu to the most effective point of the ascendant and of Mars and the Sun to Venus gave a skin problem from the sub-period of Venus in the main period of Mars when the native was only of three years of age.

Chart 60

Female born 7th September, 1961, 0735 Hrs. Nangal Dev, India.

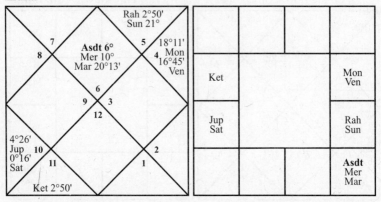

The sign Virgo rises in the ascendant. Mercury and Saturn become the prime determinants of health. Saturn, Mars, the Sun, Rahu and Ketu act as functional malefic planets. Scorpio rises in the ascendant of the shashthamsa. No planet is in its sign of debilitation in shashthamsa.

The most malefic planet, Mars, occupies the ascendant but it does not afflict the most effective point. Rahu-Ketu axis is on the most effective points of the houses occupied and closely afflicts the houses occupied and aspected besides making Mars, the Sun, Venus, Jupiter and Saturn weak by afflicting their mooltrikona houses.

The lord of the ascendant, Mercury, is strong in the ascendant. Mercury rules intestines, skin and nervous system in our body. However, the other prime determinant, Saturn, is extremely weak as it is in infancy and its mooltrikona house is simultaneously afflicted by Ketu and Rahu. Jupiter is weak due to debilitation, infancy, and afflicted mooltrikona house, and is afflicted by Saturn. The Sun and Mars are in their signs of debilitation in navamsa.

Virgos are prone to nervous pressures, skin problems and intestinal problems. In this case, the close afflictions caused by Rahu-Ketu axis, utter weakness of Saturn and the presence of the most malefic planet in the ascendant caused sufferings to the native on all these accounts including skin problem in the form of leuco-derma.

Chart 61

Male born 4th August, 1962, 0043 Hrs. New Delhi, India.

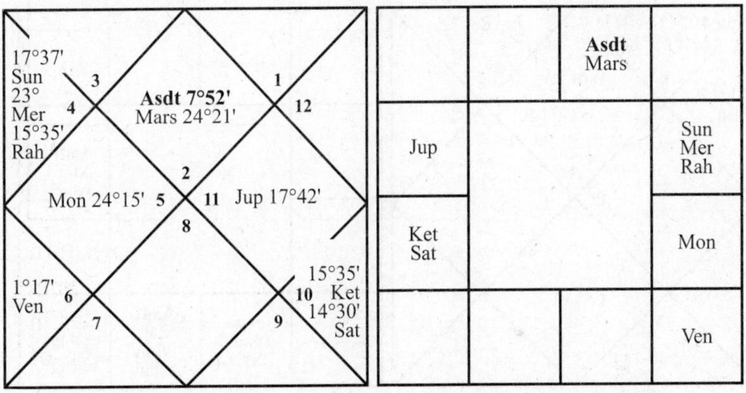

			Asdt Mars
	Jup		Sun Mer Rah
	Ket Sat		Mon
			Ven

The sign Taurus rises in the ascendant. Venus becomes the prime determinant of health as there is no mooltrikona sign in the ascendant. Venus, Jupiter, Mars, Rahu and Ketu act as functional malefic planets. Scorpio rises in the ascendant of shashthamsa. No planet is in its sign of debilitation in shashthamsa.

Venus is weak in this nativity due to infancy and debilitation. Mars exactly aspects and afflicts the weak Moon. Saturn is weak as it is exactly afflicted by the Rahu-Ketu axis. The Sun is weak due to weak dispositor and is also afflicted by the Rahu-Ketu axis. Mercury is placed in the house ruled by the afflicted Moon and is weak due to combustion. The most malefic planet, Jupiter, does not form a close affliction in this chart but is weak due to its weak dispositor. The Moon is in debilitation in navamsa.

During the sub-period of Mercury in the main period of Rahu, the native developed the skin problem in the form of leucoderma. The skin infections are also due to severe affliction of Rahu to the significators of blood. In this nativity, besides the weakness of Venus and close affliction of the Moon by Mars acting as Rahu, Rahu closely afflicts the significator of blood, the Sun.

Chart 62

Female born 20th November, 1957, 0600 Hrs. New Delhi, India.

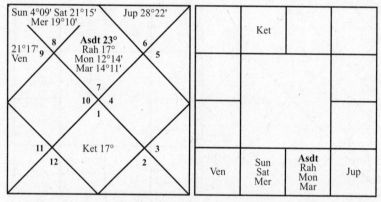

The sign Libra rises in the ascendant. Venus becomes the prime determinant of health. Mercury, Rahu and Ketu act as functional malefic planets. Leo rises in shashthamsa and its lord, the Sun, becomes the additional prime determinant of health. The Sun is in its sign of debilitation in shashthamsa.

Venus is weak due to the weakness of its dispositor, Jupiter. Ketu closely afflicts the weak Venus. Jupiter is weak as it is in old age and badly placed. The most malefic planet, Mercury, acting as Rahu closely afflicts the most effective points of the second and eighth houses. Rahu-Ketu axis closely afflicts weak Mars which is weak due to weakness of its dispositor. The Sun is placed in an afflicted house. Saturn is also placed in an afflicted house.

During the sub-period of Venus and the main period of Saturn, the native developed skin rashes. The severe affliction of the most malefic planet to the second house and the lord of the fifth house placed in the afflicted second house not only resulted in lack of a male child but also resulted in weak digestion power and peptic ulcer.

Chart 63

Female born 11th July, 1989, 1258 Hrs. New Delhi, India.

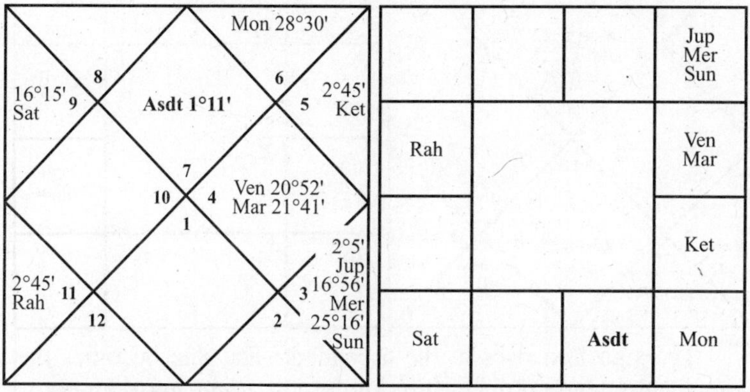

The sign Libra rises in the ascendant. Venus becomes the prime determinant of health. Mercury, Rahu and Ketu act as functional malefic planets. Aries rises in shashthamsa and its lord, Mars, becomes the additional prime determinant of health. No planet is in its sign of debilitation in shashthamsa.

Venus and Mars are weak due to the weakness of the dispositor Moon which is badly placed and is in old age. Mars is debilitated. Rahu-Ketu axis is on the most effective points of the houses occupied and closely afflicts the houses occupied and aspected besides making Mars, the Sun, Venus, Jupiter and Saturn weak by afflicting their mooltrikona houses. Rahu afflicts the weak Jupiter by an exact aspect. The most malefic planet, Mercury, causes an exact aspect to Saturn and afflicts the same. Mercury is in its sign of debilitation in navamsa.

The native started suffering from skin infection to her hands at a very young age of 4 years in the beginning of the main period of Rahu. Rahu closely afflicts the ascendant, the Moon and Jupiter while the lord of the ascendant is weak.

Chart 64

Female born 17th February, 1992, 1755 Hrs. Hisar, India.

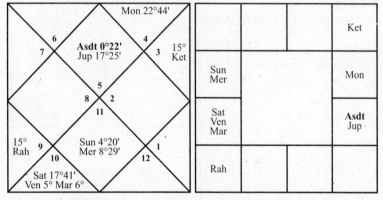

The sign Leo rises in the ascendant. The Sun becomes the prime determinant of the health. The Moon, Rahu and Ketu act as functional malefic planets. Aries rises in the ascendant of shashthamsa and Mars becomes the additional prime determinant of health. No planet is in its sign of debilitation in shashthamsa.

The Sun is weak due to infancy and weakness of dispositor. Rahu closely aspects Jupiter and afflicts the same. Saturn, Venus and Mars are badly placed in the sixth house and are weak. Mercury is weak due to combustion and is vulnerable to transit afflictions. The planets placed in the sixth house indicate problems relating to losses through theft, fire, cheating, ill-health and tight financial position during the sub-periods of these planets.

During the sub-period of Rahu in the main period of Mercury, the native suffered from stomach disorders and blood infections which resulted in skin problems, as well. The parents of the native were advised both propitiatory astral remedies for the functional malefic planets and the use of a Kavach for strengthening the weak functional benefic planets in an auspiciously elected time. Although during the sub-period of Jupiter the indications would have remained same as Jupiter is afflicted by Rahu yet the performance of astral remedies provided the protecting cover and the native was not suffering from stomach disorders in the sub-period of Jupiter.

PEPTIC ULCER

Chart 65

Male born 27th September, 1950, 2102 Hrs. New Delhi, India.

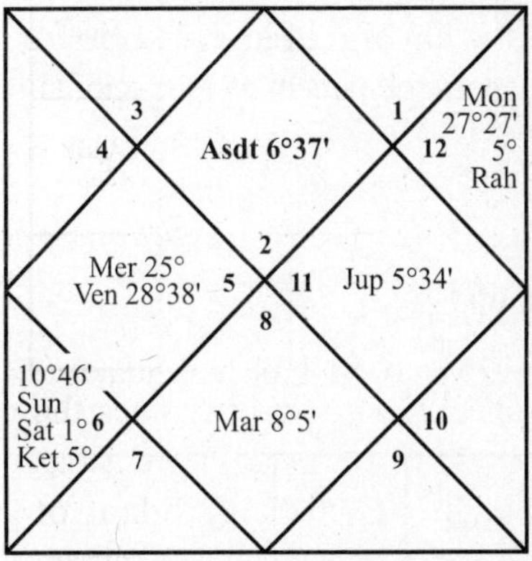

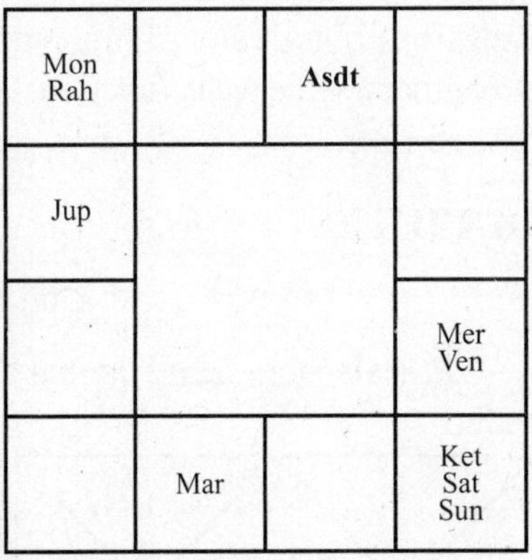

The sign Taurus rises in the ascendant. Venus becomes the prime determinant of health as there is no mooltrikona sign in the ascendant. Venus, Jupiter, Mars, Rahu and Ketu act as functional malefic planets. Scorpio rises in shashthamsa. Rahu and Venus are in debilitation in shashthamsa.

Rahu-Ketu axis is near the most effective points of the houses and afflicts all the houses occupied and aspected besides afflicting the planets Saturn and Mars. Jupiter and Mars, also afflict the most effective points of the houses occupied and aspected. Venus afflicts Mercury.

The close affliction of Rahu-Ketu axis to the ascendant and Saturn, the afflictions of Mars and Jupiter to the most effective point of the second house and affliction of the functional malefic planet, Mars, to the most malefic planet, Jupiter, resulted in number of problems to the native. The native suffered from problems of the eyes and peptic ulcer. Afflictions to the second house result in eye problem. The problem of peptic ulcer arises due to afflictions to the fifth house, planets placed therein and the planets, the Sun and Jupiter. In this case, the native suffered from the problem of peptic ulcer in the sub-period of weak and afflicted Saturn posited in the fifth house and the main period of the lord of the sixth house, Venus, which closely afflicts the weak lord of the fifth house. The native was advised both propitiatory astral remedies for the functional malefic planets and wearing of a Kavach for strengthening the weak functional benefic planets in an auspiciously elected time.

DIABETES

Chart 66

Female born 22nd January, 1951, 1054 Hrs. Kumbakona, India.

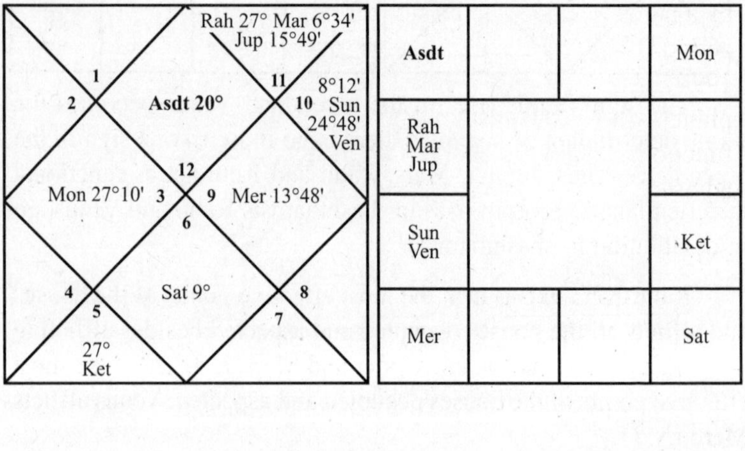

The sign Pisces rises in the ascendant. The Sun becomes the prime determinant of health as there is no mooltrikona sign in the ascendant. The Sun, Venus, Saturn, Rahu and Ketu act as functional malefic planets. Aquarius rises in the ascendant of the shashthamsa and Saturn becomes the additional prime determinant of health. No planet is debilitated in shashthamsa.

The old aged weak lord of the fifth house is under the exact affliction of Rahu from the twelfth house. Whenever the functional malefic planets cause afflictions by way of aspects from the malefic houses, the intensity of affliction is increased. The functional benefic planets, Mars and Jupiter, are weak as they are badly placed and their dispositor is weak. Mercury and Saturn are weak due to the weakness of their dispositors. The weakness of Jupiter and the fifth lord and affliction to the Moon resulted in the disease of diabetes to the native from her teens in the sub-period of the most malefic planet Venus in the main period of the functional malefic planet, Saturn. It was detected in her 25th year causing a lot of damage due to delay in diagnosis and the treatment. The affliction to the Moon in the fourth house gave a heart attack to the native followed by a paralytic attack in the sub-period of Mercury in its own main period. The relations of the native sought astral help in later part of 1994 and both propitiatory astral remedies for the functional malefic planets and wearing of a Kavach for strengthening the weak functional benefic planets in an auspiciously elected time were advised.

WEAK DIGESTION

Chart 67

Male born 31st May, 1990, 0337 Hrs. New Delhi, India.

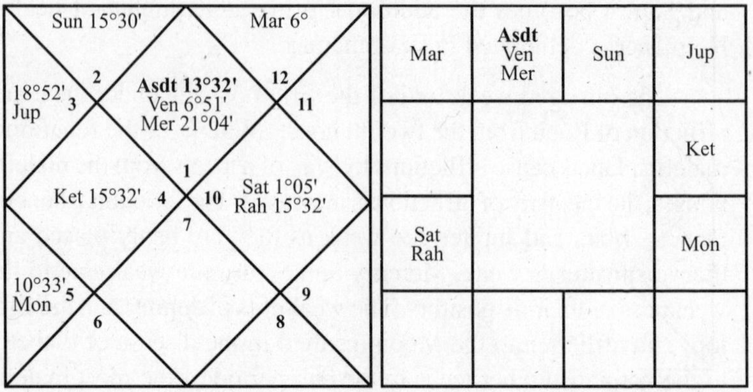

Mar	Asdt Ven Mer	Sun	Jup
			Ket
Sat Rah			Mon

North Indian chart (left):
- Sun 15°30'
- Mar 6°
- 2 — 18°52' Jup 3
- Asdt 13°32' / Ven 6°51' / Mer 21°04'
- 12 / 11
- 1
- Ket 15°32' 4 / 10 Sat 1°05' Rah 15°32'
- 7
- 10°33' Mon 5
- 6 / 8 / 9

The sign Aries rises in the ascendant. Mars and Mercury become prime determinants of health. Mercury, Rahu and Ketu act as functional malefic planets. Gemini rises in the ascendant of shashthamsa. No planet is in debilitation in shashthamsa.

Mars is weak as it is badly placed and Mercury becomes weak due to the weakness of dispositor. Rahu casts an exact aspect to the Sun and afflicts it. Rahu-Ketu axis is near the most effective points of the houses and afflicts all the houses occupied and aspected, weakening the Moon and Mercury. Saturn is weak as it is in infancy and placed in an afflicted house.

The severely afflicted Sun governs the digestive system and the circulatory system. As immediately after the birth, the native saw the sub-periods of Mercury in the main period of Ketu, the health of the native started showing deterioration. From the sub-period of the Sun in the dasa of Venus, the digestive system started causing concern in a chronic way spoiling the overall health of the native and astral remedies were sought. Both propitiatory astral remedies for the functional malefic planets and wearing of a Kavach for strengthening the weak functional benefic planets in an auspiciously elected time were advised.

FITS AND APPENDICITIS

Chart 68

Female born 11th November, 1982, 0237 Hrs. Gurgaon, India.

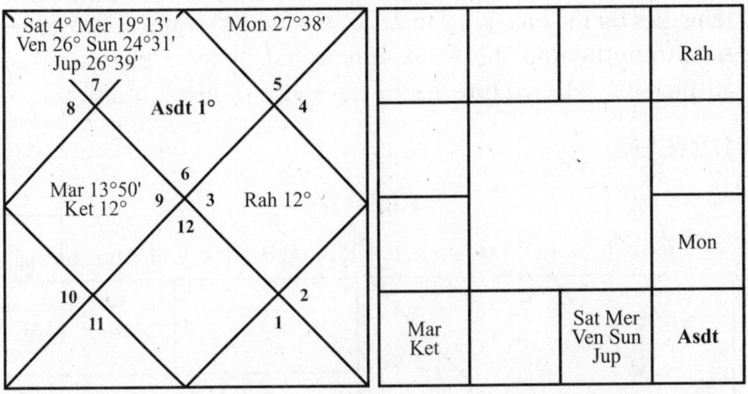

The sign Virgo rises in the ascendant. Mercury and Saturn become the prime determinants of health. Saturn, Mars, the Sun, Rahu and Ketu act as functional malefic planets. Libra rises in the ascendant of the shashthamsa and Venus becomes additional prime determinant for health. Venus and Saturn are in their signs of debilitation in shashthamsa.

Mercury is combust, debilitated in navamsa and its dispositor is weak. Saturn is weak due to infancy and weakness of dispositor. Saturn is weak due to weakness of its dispositor. The Moon is weak due to bad placement, old age and weakness of dispositor. The most malefic planet, Mars, is closely conjunct with Ketu in the fourth house indicating curtailed longevity. The functional malefic Sun is closely conjunct with the functional benefic planets, Jupiter and Venus, and severely afflicts these combust planets. There are severe afflictions in the chart. The native suffered from a number of ailments at a very young age before astral remedies were sought. Her intelligence was low due to the afflictions to both Venus and Jupiter and she suffered from fits in the sub-period of Mercury and in the main period of the badly placed Moon. During the sub-period of the sixth lord, she was operated for appendicitis. The severe affliction of Mars and affliction to the most effective point of the second house resulted in loss of one younger brother and one younger sister. The astral remedies were sought in the end of the year 1994 and the native was advised both propitiatory astral remedies for the functional malefic planets and wearing of a Kavach for strengthening the weak functional benefic planets in an auspiciously elected time for maintenance of better health.

HERNIA

Chart 69

Female born 21st August, 1953, 0419 Hrs. Calcutta, India.

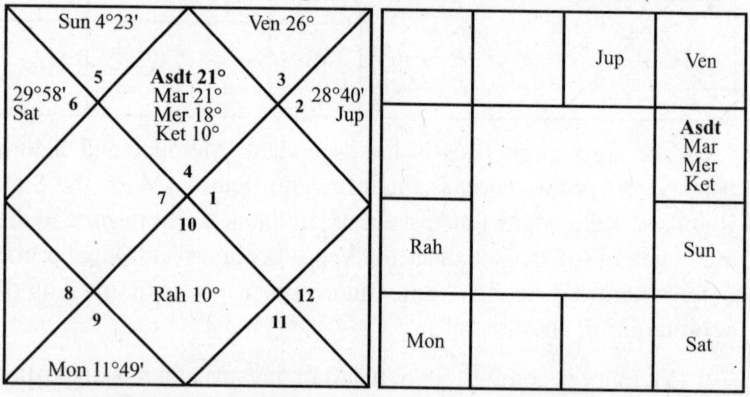

<table>
<tr><td colspan="2">Sun 4°23'</td><td colspan="2">Ven 26°</td></tr>
<tr><td>29°58' 6
Sat</td><td>5
Asdt 21°
Mar 21°
Mer 18°
Ket 10°</td><td>3
4</td><td>28°40'
Jup 2</td></tr>
<tr><td colspan="2">7 / 1
10</td><td colspan="2"></td></tr>
<tr><td>8
9</td><td>Rah 10°</td><td>11</td><td>12</td></tr>
<tr><td colspan="2">Mon 11°49'</td><td colspan="2"></td></tr>
</table>

<table>
<tr><td></td><td></td><td>Jup</td><td>Ven</td></tr>
<tr><td></td><td></td><td></td><td>Asdt
Mar
Mer
Ket</td></tr>
<tr><td>Rah</td><td></td><td></td><td>Sun</td></tr>
<tr><td>Mon</td><td></td><td></td><td>Sat</td></tr>
</table>

The sign Cancer rises in the ascendant. The Moon and Jupiter become the prime determinants of health. Jupiter, Saturn, Rahu and Ketu act as functional malefic planets. Aquarius rises in the ascendant of shashthamsa and Saturn becomes additional prime determinant of health. Rahu and Venus are in their signs of debilitation in shashthamsa.

The Moon is weak due to bad placement and weakness of its dispositor, Jupiter, due to old age. Venus is weak due to bad placement and old age and is closely afflicted by the aspect of Saturn. Jupiter closely aspects and afflicts the most malefic planet, Saturn, in the third house. Rahu and Ketu do not cause close afflictions in the chart. Mars is weak as it is in debilitation and combustion. Jupiter and Saturn are weak as they are in old age. The bad placement of the Moon in the main chart gave many health problems to the native. During the sub-period of the badly placed and afflicted Venus in the main period of Mars, the native was operated for hernia. The native was advised both propitiatory astral remedies for the functional malefic planets and wearing of a Kavach for strengthening the weak functional benefic planets in an auspiciously elected time. The performance of the astral remedies has resulted in maintenance of good health by the native.

HYPERTENSION AND APPENDICITIS

Chart 70

Female born 5th June, 1965, 2325 Hrs. New Delhi, India.

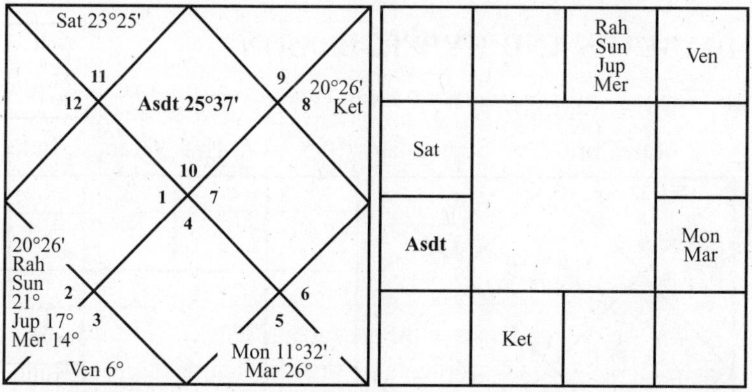

```
Sat 23°25'
        11              9     20°26'
   12       Asdt 25°37'    8   Ket
           10
        1      7
          4
20°26'
Rah
Sun
21°    2            6
Jup 17°  3        5
Mer 14°
      Ven 6°      Mon 11°32'
                  Mar 26°
```

		Rah Sun Jup Mer	Ven
Sat			
Asdt			Mon Mar
	Ket		

The sign Capricorn rises in the ascendant. The Sun becomes the prime determinant of health as there is no mooltrikona sign in both first and sixth houses. The Sun, Jupiter, Rahu and Ketu act as functional malefic planets. Pisces rises in the ascendant of the shashthamsa. Jupiter is in its sign of debilitation in shashthamsa.

The Moon, Mars and Venus are badly placed in the nativity. The functional malefic Rahu-Ketu axis severely afflicts combust Jupiter and the Sun. The most malefic planet, the Sun, is also afflicting combust Jupiter. The functional malefic planet, Jupiter, is involved in afflicting combust Mercury placed in the fifth house.

The severe afflictions in the fifth house resulted in serious infections in the generative organs for three months after the delivery and the native almost took a second birth. The affliction of the Sun resulted in the problem of hypertension at a very early stage in life with the onset of the main period of the Sun in the year 1986. During the sub-period of Jupiter in the main period of the Sun, the native was operated upon for appendicitis. The native sought astral remedies in the year 1993 for better health and the birth of a male child. The native was advised both propitiatory astral remedies for the functional malefic planets and wearing of a Kavach for strengthening the weak functional benefic planets in an auspiciously elected time. The performance of the advised astral remedies helped the native in enjoying comparatively good health and the birth of a male child.

DIABETES AND HYPERTENSION

Chart 71

Male born 22nd September, 1955, 0140 Hrs. Varanasi, India.

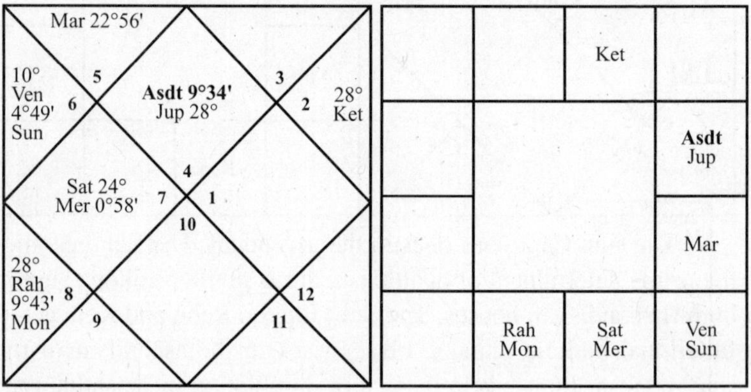

		Ket	
			Asdt Jup
			Mar
Rah Mon	Sat Mer	Ven Sun	

The sign Cancer rises in the ascendant. The Moon and Jupiter become the prime determinants of health. Jupiter, Saturn, Rahu and Ketu act as functional malefic planets. Scorpio rises in the ascendant of shashthamsa. The Sun and the Moon are in their signs of debilitation in shashthamsa.

The Moon is weak due to debilitation. The Sun is weak due to weakness of dispositor. Mercury is weak due to infancy and weakness of its dispositor. Venus is weak due to debilitation and combustion. Jupiter, though exalted, is weak due to old age, weak dispositor and exact affliction by Rahu.

The most malefic planet Saturn also closely aspects and afflicts Jupiter, the significator of the liver, pancreas, etc. The weakness of Jupiter and the close afflictions in the chart resulted in jaundice, diabetes, hypertension and malfunctioning of the heart. The weakness of Mercury resulted in damages to three of his arteries. Despite so many health problems, due to the weakness of and affliction to Jupiter, the native does not follow good advice and has turned into a drunkard endangering his life very badly during the sub-period of Rahu in the main period of Venus. The native was advised both propitiatory astral remedies for the functional malefic planets and wearing of a Kavach for strengthening the weak functional benefic planets in an auspiciously elected time. However, the position of Jupiter in the chart does not allow the sincere performance of the astral remedies for good relief.

INFLAMMATION OF PANCREAS
Chart 72

Male born 10th October, 1957, 0345 Hrs. Amritsar, India.

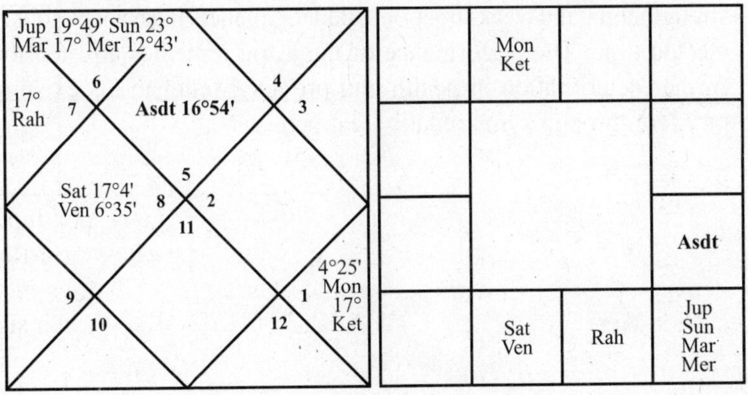

The sign Leo rises in the ascendant. The Sun becomes the prime determinant of health. The Moon, Rahu and Ketu act as functional malefic planets. Cancer rises in the ascendant of shashthamsa and the Moon becomes the additional prime determinant of health. Jupiter is in debilitation in shashthamsa. The functional malefic planets in shashthamsa influence the ascendant of shashthamsa.

The Sun is weak due to weak dispositor and affliction of its mooltrikona house. Rahu-Ketu axis is on the most effective points of the houses occupied and exactly afflicts the houses occupied and aspected besides making Mars, the Sun, Venus, Jupiter and Saturn weak by afflicting their mooltrikona houses. Mercury, Mars and Jupiter are additionally weak due to combustion. Mercury is exalted as lord of the second house and is placed therein. The exalted Mercury provided good status to the native. The influence of the Sun, Jupiter and Mars in the second house resulted in his becoming a physician.

The weakness of Jupiter and affliction to the most effective point of the fifth house resulted in physical problems related to the parts governed by the fifth house and the native suffered from the inflammation of the head of pancreas when he sought astral remedies. The native was advised both propitiatory astral remedies for the functional malefic planets and wearing of a Kavach for strengthening the weak functional benefic planets in an auspiciously elected time. The performance of the astral remedies arrested the further deterioration in health and provided relief to his existing problem through symptomatic treatment.

WEAK LIVER

Chart 73

Female born 10th September, 1961, 0600 Hrs. New Delhi, India.

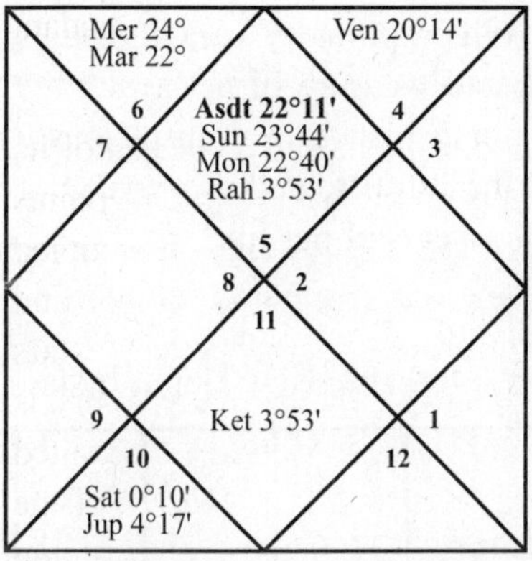

Ket			Ven
Sat Jup			**Asdt** Sun Mon Rah
			Mer Mar

North Indian chart:
- Mer 24° Mar 22° (top left)
- Ven 20°14' (top)
- Asdt 22°11', Sun 23°44', Mon 22°40', Rah 3°53'
- Houses marked 6, 7, 4, 3, 5, 8, 2, 11, 9, Ket 3°53', 1, 10, 12
- Sat 0°10', Jup 4°17' (bottom left)

The sign Leo rises in the ascendant. The Sun becomes the prime determinant of the health. The Moon, Rahu and Ketu act as functional malefic planets. Leo rises in the ascendant of shashthamsa and the Sun also becomes additional prime determinant of health. No planet is in debilitation in shashthamsa.

The most malefic planet, the Moon, is combust and extremely weak as it is exactly conjunct with the most effective point of the ascendant and the lord of the ascendant, the Sun, placed in the ascendant. The Sun, dispositor of the Moon, is extremely weak and severely afflicted. Venus, Saturn and Jupiter are badly placed in the nativity and weak. Jupiter is additionally weak due to debilitation and infancy. Saturn is additionally weak due to infancy and affliction to its mooltrikona house. The affliction of the most effective point of ascendant and the lord of the ascendant makes the native vulnerable to serious health problems related to the Sun, Saturn, Jupiter and Venus. The native has a weak liver and suffered from problems related to it in the sub-period of Rahu in its own main period. The native also suffered from jaundice. The weakness of the lord of the seventh house and severe affliction of the most malefic planet to the most effective point of the seventh house resulted in severe health problems to the husband of the native and also makes the kidney of the native vulnerable to serious illness. In the beginning of the main period of Rahu, the native sought astral remedies. The native was advised both propitiatory astral remedies for the functional malefic planets and wearing of a Kavach for strengthening the weak functional benefic planets in an auspiciously elected time. The performance of the astral remedies provided a protective cover to the native in all aspects of her life.

Chart 74

Male born 15th January, 1955, 1400 Hrs. New Delhi, India.

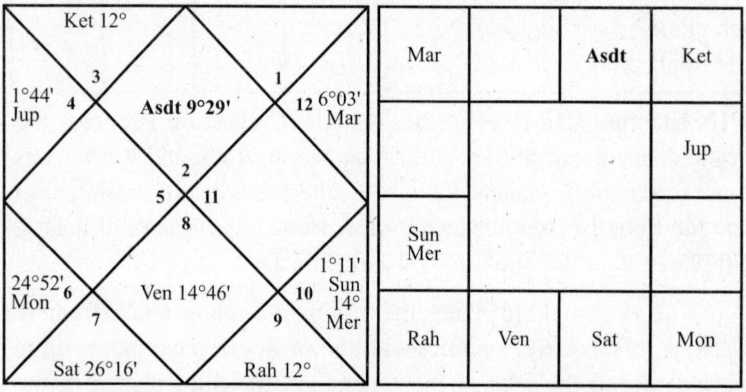

Mar		**Asdt**	Ket
			Jup
Sun Mer			
Rah	Ven	Sat	Mon

The sign Taurus rises in the ascendant. Venus becomes the prime determinant of health as there is no mooltrikona sign in the ascendant. Venus, Jupiter, Mars, Rahu and Ketu act as functional malefic planets. Scorpio rises in shashthamsa. The Sun is in debilitation in shashthamsa.

Venus is weak due to affliction of its mooltrikona house by the combined effect of Mars and Ketu. Saturn and Rahu are badly placed. Mars is weak as the most effective point of its house of placement is afflicted by itself. Rahu-Ketu axis and the functional malefic planet, Mars, are near the most effective points of the houses and afflict all the houses occupied and aspected. The Sun and Jupiter are weak as they are in infancy. The exact aspect of the most malefic planet, Jupiter, badly damages the significations of the Sun.

The weakness of Venus, the close afflictions to the most effective point of the sixth house and the weakness and affliction of the Sun in the main chart resulted in severe stomach disorders and problems of malfunctioning of liver. When medical treatment failed to give relief to the native, he sought astral remedies. The native was advised both propitiatory astral remedies for the functional malefic planets and wearing of a Kavach for strengthening the weak functional benefic planets in an auspiciously elected time. But, here also the weakness of Jupiter denies performance of astral remedies religiously for good relief. Under such planetary configurations, medical treatment is always of very little relief and for a short duration.

SPINAL PROBLEMS AND ACCIDENTS

Chart 75

Male born 23rd November, 1952, 0702 Hrs. Lucknow, India.

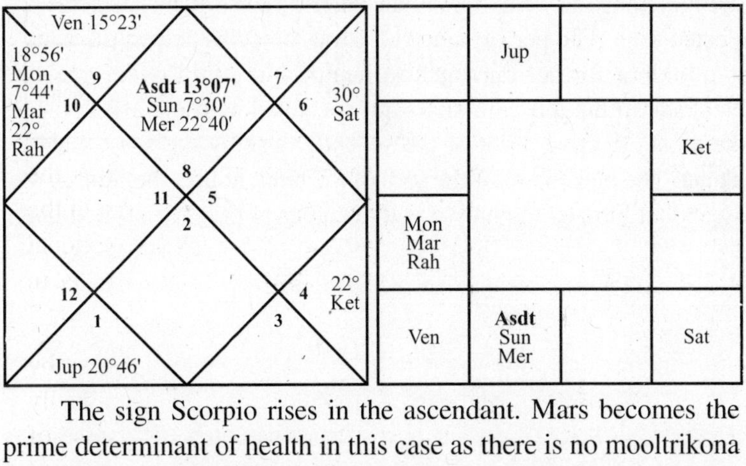

The sign Scorpio rises in the ascendant. Mars becomes the prime determinant of health in this case as there is no mooltrikona sign in the ascendant. Mars, Venus, Rahu and Ketu act as functional malefic planets. Sagittarius rises in the ascendant of the shashthamsa and Jupiter becomes the additional prime determinant of health. No planet is in its sign of debilitation in shashthamsa.

Venus is near the most effective point of the second house and afflicts the houses occupied and aspected. Jupiter is badly placed and weak in the chart. Jupiter is additionally weak due to affliction of its mooltrikona house. Saturn is weak due to extreme old age and weak dispositor. Ketu afflicts Mercury by an exact aspect. The Sun and the Moon are strong in the chart.

The weakness of Saturn, affliction of Mercury in the ascendant and close affliction to the most effective point of the second house caused nervousness and spine problems to the native in the main period of Jupiter and the sub-period of the most malefic planet, Venus, afflicting the most effective point of the second and eighth houses. The close aspect of the most malefic planet to the most effective point of eighth house also caused three accidents to the native in the sub-period of Venus. The native sought astral remedies in the sub-period of the Sun in the main period of Jupiter. The native was advised both propitiatory astral remedies for the functional malefic planets and wearing of a Kavach for strengthening the weak functional benefic planets in an auspiciously elected time. The performance of astral remedies helped the native in avoiding further damages to health and could overcome the blockade in his job-cum-status prospectus due to the affliction of the most effective point of the second house by the most malefic planet. The placement of the lord of the tenth house, the Sun, in the ascendant blessed the native with a career of practice of medicine.

Chart 76

Female born 10th November, 1964, 1645 Hrs. Rohtak, India.

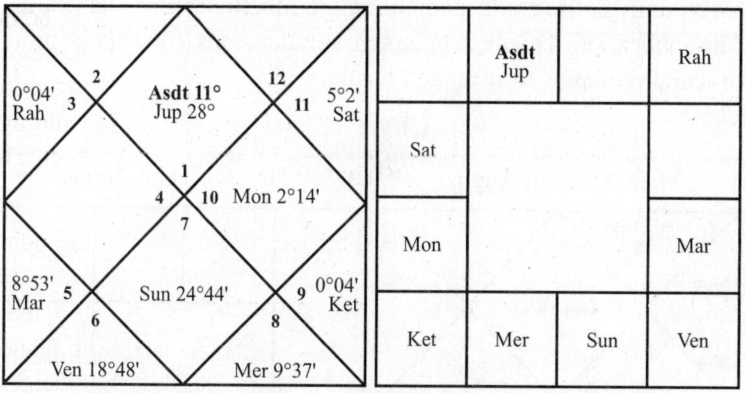

	2	Asdt 11°	12	11 5°2'
0°04' 3 Rah		Jup 28°		Sat
	1			
	4 10	Mon 2°14'		
	7			
8°53' 5 Mar		Sun 24°44'	9	0°04' Ket
6			8	
	Ven 18°48'		Mer 9°37'	

	Asdt Jup		Rah
Sat			
Mon			Mar
Ket	Mer	Sun	Ven

The sign Aries rises in the ascendant. Mars and Mercury become prime determinants of health. Mercury, Rahu and Ketu act as functional malefic planets. Gemini rises in the ascendant of the shashthamsa. No planet is in its sign of debilitation in shashthamsa.

Mars, Sun and Venus are weak due to the weakness of their dispositors. The Sun and Venus are additionally weak due to debilitation. Mercury is badly placed and weak. Bad placement of the sixth lord in the eighth house gives chronic health problems including accidents. Mercury is closely afflicting the most effective points of the second and eighth houses. Jupiter is weak due to old age and weakness of dispositor. The Moon is weak due to infancy. Saturn is strong in the chart and helps Mars and Mercury to some extent. The close affliction of Mercury resulted into a number of accidents to the native.

During the sub-period of Mercury in the main period of Rahu the native met with a severe accident and she was not in a position to move her legs and hands. There were multiple fractures in the spine and the surgeons attending had not shown any hope of relief. The Kavach for the native, who had sought an astral consultation earlier, was lying ready for wearing in an auspicious time. When no relief was indicated by the medical science, the wearing of the

Kavach in the intensive care unit of the hospital gave spontaneous movement to the body of the native and the native who was feared for a paralytic life could attain an active functional physical health. The application of medical treatment simultaneous to the application of astral remedies shows good results.

Chart 77

Male born 6th August, 1959, 0330 Hrs. Gurgaon, India.

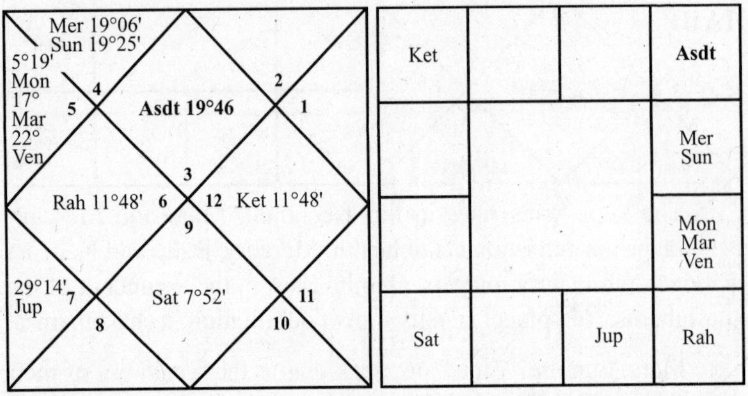

Ket			Asdt
			Mer Sun
			Mon Mar /Ven
Sat		Jup	Rah

(North Indian chart: Mer 19°06', Sun 19°25', Mon 17°, Mar 22°, Ven 5°19' in house 5; Asdt 19°46'; Rah 11°48' house 6; Ket 11°48' house 12; Jup 29°14' house 7; Sat 7°52'.)

The sign Gemini rises in the ascendant. The Sun becomes the prime determinant of health as there is no mooltrikona sign in the first and sixth houses. Rahu and Ketu act as functional malefic planets. Cancer rises in the ascendant of shashthamsa and the Moon becomes the additional prime determinant of health. Mars is in debilitation in shashthamsa.

The planets Sun, Moon, Mars and Venus are strong. Mercury is in conjunction with the Sun and turns weak due to combustion. Jupiter is weak as it is in old age. Both weak Mercury and Jupiter expose themselves to the transit afflictions of the functional malefic planets. Saturn becomes weak due to weakness of its dispositor. The Moon is prime determinant of the status / job. The transit strength of the Moon is always volatile. The native suffers from acute mental tension on account of the time demanded by his job. The native suffered from the problem of slip disc in the sub-period of Mercury in the main period of the Moon when the transit Rahu-

Ketu exerted their stationary influence on their own natal position. The native sought astral remedies for recovery and relief. The native was advised both propitiatory astral remedies for the functional malefic planets and wearing of a Kavach for strengthening the weak functional benefic planets in an auspiciously elected time. However, the weak Jupiter does not allow the native the performance of remedies on a regular basis. The native has come out of the problem but his carelessness continues.

DIABETES AT YOUNG AGE

Chart 78

Male born 10th November, 1975, 0200 Hrs. New Delhi, India.

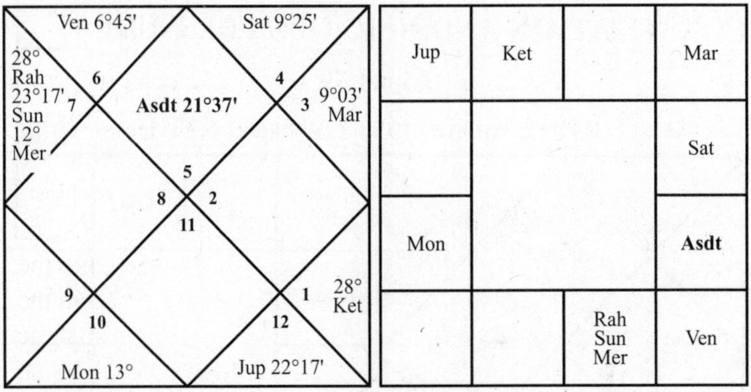

The sign Leo rises in the ascendant. The Sun becomes the prime determinant of health. The Moon, Rahu and Ketu act as functional malefic planets. Leo rises in the ascendant of shashthamsa and the Sun becomes the additional prime determinant of health. No planet is in debilitation in shashthamsa.

The Sun is weak as it is in debilitation. The planets, the Moon, Saturn and Jupiter are badly placed and weak. Jupiter is additionally weak as it is in debilitation in navamsa. Venus is weak due to debilitation. Mercury is weak due to combustion. The weakness of the lords of the first, second, third, fifth and seventh houses and placement of the lord of the house of losses in the sixth house indicating loss of good health resulted in the native suffering from the chronic disease of diabetes at the very young age of 13 years. The weakness of the fifth house also resulted in low level of intelligence, mental pressures and the native could not pursue his studies brilliantly. The native was advised both propitiatory astral remedies for the functional malefic planets and wearing of a Kavach for strengthening the weak functional benefic planets in an auspiciously elected time. The regular performance of astral remedies due to the weakness of Jupiter, in this case, too, posed problems and the native used to become careless again and again as soon as there is some improvement in his health and mental peace.

CONSTIPATION AND NERVOUS PRESSURE

Chart 79

Male born 31st August, 1950, 0005 Hrs. New Delhi, India.

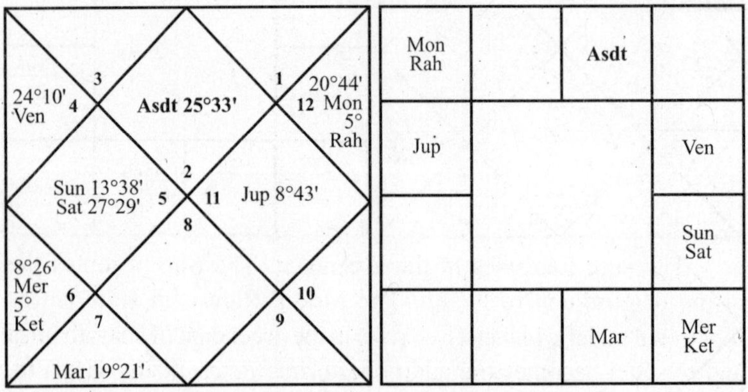

Mon Rah		Asdt	
Jup			Ven
			Sun Sat
		Mar	Mer Ket

The sign Taurus rises in the ascendant. Venus becomes the prime determinant of health as there is no mooltrikona sign in the ascendant. Venus, Jupiter, Mars, Rahu and Ketu act as functional malefic planets. Pisces rises in the ascendant of shashthamsa. Mars and Rahu are in debilitation in shashthamsa.

Rahu and Ketu exercise their close malefic influence on Mercury, which is weak due to debilitation in the navamsa. The functional malefic Venus closely afflicts the most effective point of the third and ninth houses in the main chart. The planet Mars ruling the house of losses is placed in the sixth house indicating loss of good health. **The weakness of Mercury indicates nervous pressure and weak and erratic intestinal function. Such people suffer from acute and persistent complaints of constipation.** In this case the native had to take enema twice or thrice every week. The involvement of Mercury gave nervous pressures because of losses incurred by the native in speculative investments. **Whenever, the lord of the first, third, fifth or tenth house is under the close affliction of Rahu, the native is tempted by gambling and speculative opportunities and incurs losses.** The placement of the lord of the house of injuries on the most effective point of the third house caused severe injury to his right hand. **The affliction of the third house by the lord of the sixth house causes sufferings through involvement in disputes and makes the native of inflexible/aggressive temperament.**

Chart 80

Female born 8th October, 1971, 0316 Hrs. New Delhi, India..

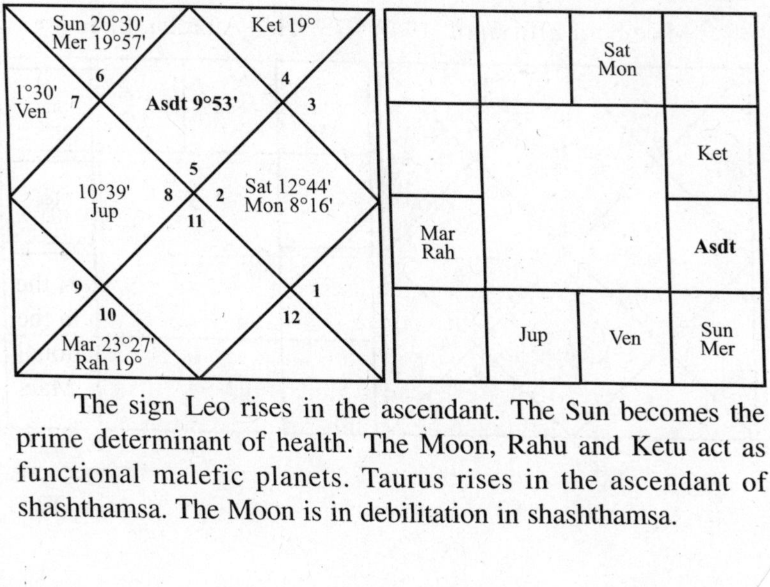

		Sat Mon	
			Ket
Mar Rah			Asdt
Jup	Ven	Sun Mer	

North Indian chart: Sun 20°30' Mer 19°57' (house 6); Ket 19° (house 4); 1°30' Ven (house 7); Asdt 9°53'; (house 3); (house 5); 10°39' Jup (house 8); Sat 12°44' Mon 8°16' (house 2); (house 11); (house 9); (house 10); (house 1); (house 12); Mar 23°27' Rah 19°

The sign Leo rises in the ascendant. The Sun becomes the prime determinant of health. The Moon, Rahu and Ketu act as functional malefic planets. Taurus rises in the ascendant of shashthamsa. The Moon is in debilitation in shashthamsa.

Rahu afflicts combust Mercury and the Sun. Though Mercury is exalted, its weakness due to combustion exposes it to transit malefic influences and makes the natal Sun weak. Venus is weak as it is in infancy. The most malefic planet, the Moon, closely afflicts Jupiter, Saturn and the most effective points of the tenth and fourth houses. Saturn is weak as it is in its sign of debilitation in navamsa and is placed in an afflicted house. The affliction of Jupiter, the fifth lord, the Sun and Mercury resulted in weak intestinal functioning and persistent stomach-ache to the native. These afflictions also exerted lot of mental pressure on the native on account of constant bad health and cheating in marriage resulting in an immediate divorce. Because of acute mental pressure, the native is suffering from depression and trembling of her hands. The astral remedies were sought in the sub-period of Venus in the dasa / main period of Rahu. The native was advised both propitiatory astral remedies for the functional malefic planets and wearing of a Kavach for strengthening the weak functional benefic planets in an auspiciously elected time.

Chart 81

Male born 27th April, 1947, 0737 Hrs. Amroha, India..

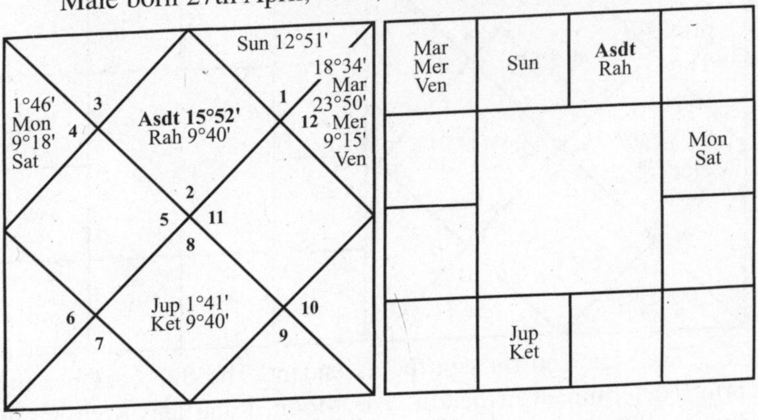

Mar Mer Ven	Sun	**Asdt** Rah	-
			Mon Sat
	Jup Ket		

North Indian chart:
- Sun 12°51'
- 18°34' Mar 23°50'
- Mer 9°15' Ven
- Asdt 15°52' Rah 9°40'
- 1°46' Mon 9°18' Sat
- Jup 1°41' Ket 9°40'

Houses: 1, 12, 3, 4, 2, 5, 11, 8, 6, 7, 9, 10

The sign Taurus rises in the ascendant. Venus becomes the prime determinant of health as there is no mooltrikona sign in the ascendant. Venus, Jupiter, Mars, Rahu and Ketu act as functional malefic planets. Capricorn rises in shashthamsa. Rahu is in debilitation in shashthamsa.

Venus is weak due to debilitation in navamsa and exact affliction from the aspect of Ketu, and is placed in an afflicted house. Saturn is weak due to exact affliction from the aspect of Ketu and weakness of dispositor. The Moon is weak due to infancy and exact afflicting aspect of Jupiter. Jupiter is weak due to infancy. The exalted Sun is weak due to bad placement. Mercury is weak due to debilitation and as it is placed in an afflicted house. Mars is weak as the most effective point of its house of placement is afflicted by itself. The functional malefic Mars is near the most effective point of the eleventh house and afflicts all the houses occupied and aspected.

The afflicting aspect of Mars to the fifth and sixth houses and the weakness of the lords of the fifth and sixth houses resulted in intestinal malfunctioning and the native had to undergo intestinal surgery in the sub-period of severely afflicted Venus in the main period of Mercury. Afterwards, the astral remedies were sought for preventive purposes to arrest the further deterioration of health. The native was advised both propitiatory astral remedies for the functional malefic planets and wearing of a Kavach for strengthening the weak functional benefic planets in an auspiciously elected time.

KIDNEY PROBLEM / TRANSPLANT

Chart 82

Male born 10th December, 1959, 0120 Hrs. Taranagar, India.

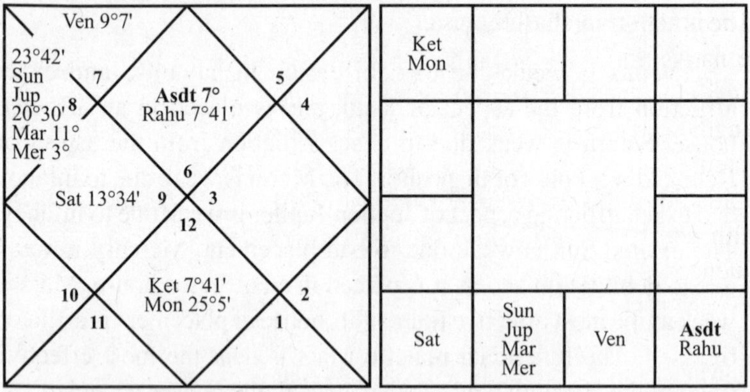

Ket Mon			
Sat	Sun Jup Mar Mer	Ven	Asdt Rahu

North Indian chart (left):
- Ven 9°7'
- 23°42' Sun, Jup 20°30', Mar 11°, Mer 3° (house 8)
- Asdt 7°, Rahu 7°41'
- Sat 13°34' (house 9)
- Ket 7°41', Mon 25°5' (house 1)
- House numbers: 7, 8, 5, 4, 6, 9, 3, 12, 10, 11, 1, 2

The sign Virgo rises in the ascendant. Mercury and Saturn become the prime determinants of health. Saturn, Mars, the Sun, Rahu and Ketu act as functional malefic planets. Scorpio rises in shashthamsa. Rahu is in debilitation in shashthamsa and occupies the ascendant.

Rahu-Ketu axis is placed exactly over the most effective points of houses containing even signs and afflicts the houses occupied and aspected. This nodal affliction turns the planets the Moon and Mercury weak by afflicting their mooltrikona houses besides afflicting weak Mercury and Mars. Mercury is additionally weak as it is in infancy. Jupiter is weak as it is placed in an afflicted house, combust, in debilitation in navamsa, and is afflicted due to the close conjunction with the Sun. The most malefic planet, Mars, also mildly afflicts the third, sixth, ninth and tenth houses to the extent of 20%. Saturn is weak due to the weakness of dispositor. The chart shows extreme health problems spoiling the health in general. The involvement of afflictions to seventh and sixth houses, Mercury and Jupiter resulted in acute health problems related to renal function and hypertension. The native had to undergo kidney transplant during the main period of Venus and the sub-period of

Mercury. The astral remedies were sought for protecting further deterioration in health as the native had serious concern for his young wife and an infant female child. However, the good placement of the lord of the second house bestowed good status on the native and he is in a position to get good treatment for his health problems. The native was advised both propitiatory astral remedies for the functional malefic planets and wearing of a Kavach for strengthening the weak functional benefic planets in an auspiciously elected time. The wearing of the Kavach and performance of propitiatory remedies resulted in arresting further deterioration of health except some tension during short lived transit malefic influences.

Chart 83

Male born 12th October, 1965, 1942 Hrs. New Delhi, India.

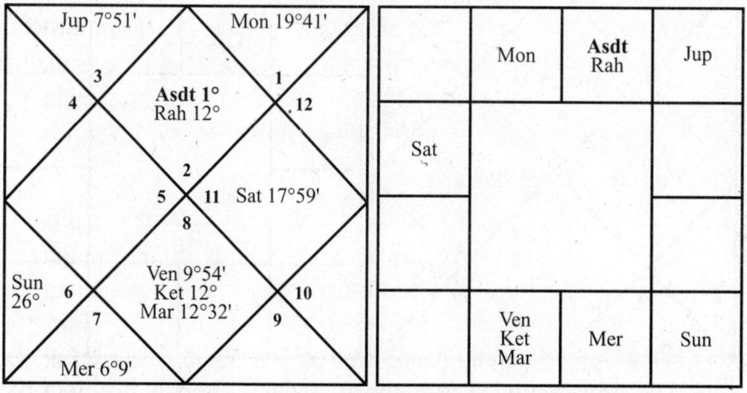

		Mon	Asdt Rah	Jup
	Sat			
		Ven Ket Mar	Mer	Sun

```
Jup 7°51'            Mon 19°41'
       3          1
    4      Asdt 1°      12
           Rah 12°
              2
           5  11  Sat 17°59'
              8
 Sun      Ven 9°54'
 26°  6   Ket 12°      10
      7   Mar 12°32'  9
   Mer 6°9'
```

The sign Taurus rises in the ascendant. Venus becomes the prime determinant of health as there is no mooltrikona sign in the ascendant. Venus, Jupiter, Mars, Rahu and Ketu act as functional malefic planets. Libra rises in the ascendant of shashthamsa and Venus also becomes the additional prime determinant of health. No planet is in debilitation in shashthamsa.

Venus is weak due to debilitation in navamsa and is closely afflicted by Mars, Rahu and Ketu. The Moon and Mercury are badly placed and weak. Rahu and Ketu closely afflict Mars. Mars and

Venus are in conjunction and mutually afflict each other in the seventh house. The most malefic planet, Jupiter, closely aspects and afflicts the badly placed weak Mercury. The close afflictions to Venus, Mars, and Mercury in the chart resulted in severe health problems endangering the life of the native. The native suffered from severe renal problems and loss of protein weakening his vitality. The astral remedies were sought as no significant permanent cure was seen in the health problem of the native. The native was advised both propitiatory astral remedies for the functional malefic planets and wearing of a Kavach for strengthening the weak functional benefic planets in an auspiciously elected time.

Chart 84

Male born 19th April, 1969, 1055 Hrs. New Delhi, India.

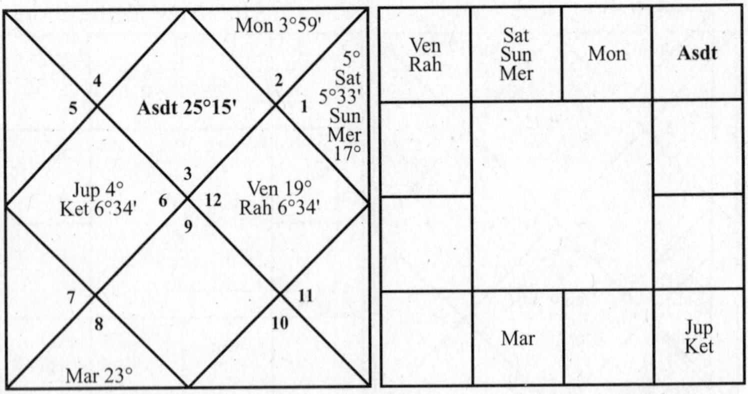

Ven Rah	Sat Sun Mer	Mon	Asdt
	Mar		Jup Ket

The sign Gemini rises in the ascendant. The Sun becomes the prime determinant of health as there is no mooltrikona sign in the first and sixth houses. Rahu and Ketu act as functional malefic planets. Virgo rises in the ascendant of shashthamsa and Mercury becomes the additional prime determinant of health. Rahu is in debilitation in shashthamsa.

Mars is badly placed and weak indicating weak muscular system and infections in the muscular parts. The Sun is weak due to the weakness of dispositor. Rahu and Ketu exert malefic influence over weak Jupiter, and Ketu afflicts the badly placed weak Moon.

Mercury and debilitated Saturn are combust and they are weak due to the weakness of dispositor. The weakness and affliction of the lord of the seventh house resulted in acute renal problems. The native had to undergo a kidney transplant in the sub-period of Rahu in the main period of Rahu. Again in the sub-period of Saturn the native was admitted to Apollo Hospital for his renal problem when his father sought astral remedies. In September, 1994, when everything was set for a second operation and all the tests, etc., had been conducted, just one day before the operation he was discharged by the hospital authorities as per the prediction and the impact of the performance of the astral remedies.

Chart 85

Male born 17th November, 1968, 0730 Hrs. Rohtak, India.

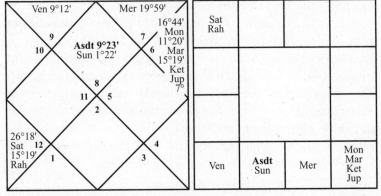

The sign Scorpio rises in the ascendant. Mars becomes the prime determinant of health in this case as there is no mooltrikona sign in the ascendant. Mars, Venus, Rahu and Ketu act as functional malefic planets. Scorpio rises in the ascendant of shashthamsa. The Sun is in debilitation in shashthamsa.

Mars is weak as its dispositor is badly placed and combust, and it is afflicted by Rahu and Ketu. The Sun is weak as it is in infancy. Rahu-Ketu exert severe affliction on the weak Moon whose dispositor is badly placed. The functional malefic Mars is near the most effective point of the eleventh house and closely afflicts the eleventh, second and fifth houses besides closely afflicting the planet, Venus, placed in the second house. The most malefic planet, Venus, is exactly on the most effective point of the second house and afflicts both the second and eighth houses seriously endangering the longevity. The affliction of Mars, becoming prime determinant of health in this chart, and severe afflictions to the Moon and Venus are indicative of acute health problems to the native to the extent of endangering the longevity as explained above. The severe affliction of Venus creates an impact on badly placed Mercury as the later is placed in the mooltrikona sign of Venus. During the sub-period of Mercury in the main period of Rahu, the native started complaining of pain in the renal area. The problem remained undiagnosed up to the sub-period of Ketu in the main period of Rahu. It was only in the sub-period of Venus in the main period of Rahu when it was diagnosed that the kidney bones had started shrinking causing acute problems to the native. The parents of the native sought astral remedies as medical treatment was not showing permanent satisfactory relief. The native was advised both propitiatory astral remedies for the functional malefic planets and wearing of a Kavach for strengthening the weak functional benefic planets in an auspiciously elected time. The performance of the astral remedies did show improvement and checked further aggravation of the problem. The afflicting aspect of the most malefic planet is more severe than the malefic impact of Rahu and Ketu.

GALL BLADDER REMOVAL

Chart 86

Male born 24th August, 1960, 1246 Hrs. New Delhi, India.

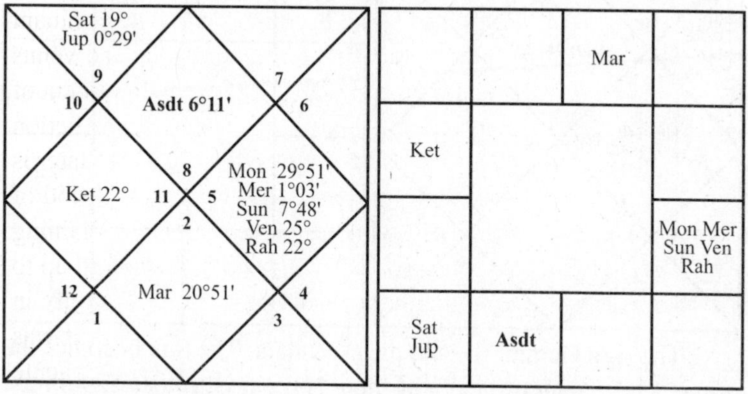

		Mar	
Ket			
			Mon Mer Sun Ven Rah
Sat Jup	Asdt		

Left chart (diamond):
- Sat 19° / Jup 0°29' — 9, 10
- Asdt 6°11' — 7, 6
- Ket 22° — 8, 11
- Mon 29°51' / Mer 1°03' / Sun 7°48' / Ven 25° / Rah 22° — 5, 2
- Mar 20°51' — 12, 1, 3, 4

The sign Scorpio rises in the ascendant. Mars becomes the prime determinant of health in this case as there is no mooltrikona sign in the ascendant. Mars, Venus, Rahu and Ketu act as functional malefic planets. Scorpio rises in the ascendant of shashthamsa. No planet is in debilitation in shashthamsa.

Mars is weak due to debilitation in navamsa. Venus turns weak as it is under the close affliction of Rahu, Ketu and Mars. Jupiter is weak as it is in utter infancy. Mercury, too, is weak as it is in infancy and combust. The Moon is weak as it is in extreme old age. Saturn placed in the second house is weak due to weakness of its dispositor and is closely afflicted by Mars and Rahu. The Sun is strong and provides some relief to the weaknesses and afflictions in the chart. The weakness of Mars, Mercury, the Moon, Saturn and Jupiter and the affliction of Venus and Saturn resulted in a number of physical ailments, frequent fevers and inflammation of gall bladder. During the main period of Rahu and sub-period of Ketu, the native was operated for removal of gall bladder. The native was advised both propitiatory astral remedies for the functional malefic planets and wearing of a Kavach for strengthening the weak functional benefic planets in an auspiciously elected time.

Chart 87

Male born 29th April, 1950, 1030 Hrs. Gurgaon, India.

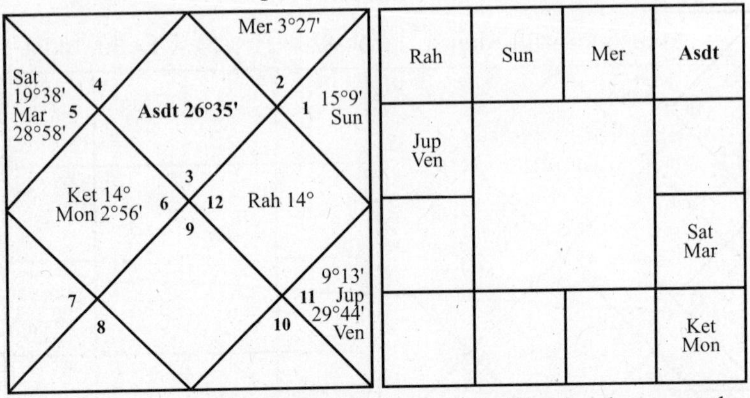

Rah	Sun	Mer	**Asdt**
Jup Ven			
			Sat Mar
			Ket Mon

(Left diagram — South Indian style chart:)

Sat 19°38'
Mar 28°58'
Asdt 26°35'
Mer 3°27'
15°9' Sun
Ket 14°
Mon 2°56'
Rah 14°
9°13' Jup
29°44' Ven

(House numbers: 4, 5, 2, 1, 3, 6, 12, 9, 7, 8, 11, 10)

The sign Gemini rises in the ascendant. The Sun becomes the prime determinant of health as there is no mooltrikona sign in the first and sixth houses. Rahu and Ketu act as functional malefic planets. Virgo rises in the ascendant of shashthamsa and Mercury becomes the additional prime determinant of health. Venus is in debilitation in shashthamsa.

The Moon and Mercury are weak as they are in infancy. The dispositor of the Moon is additionally weak as it is badly placed. Mars and Venus are weak as they are in extreme old age. The Sun, Saturn and Jupiter are weak due to the weakness of their dispositors. The weakness of the various planets in the nativity resulted in health problems from time to time. The native suffered from acute pain in the sub-period of Ketu in the main period of Jupiter and was operated for removal of gall bladder. During the sub-period of Venus in the main period of Jupiter, the native suffered from a relapse and was admitted in the hospital in a serious condition. Astral remedies were suggested at this stage, the performance of which helped in the success of symptomatic treatment. The native was advised both propitiatory astral remedies for the functional malefic planets and wearing of a Kavach for strengthening the weak functional benefic planets in an auspiciously elected time.

Chart 88

Male born 20th June, 1993, 1547 Hrs. Gidhni, India.

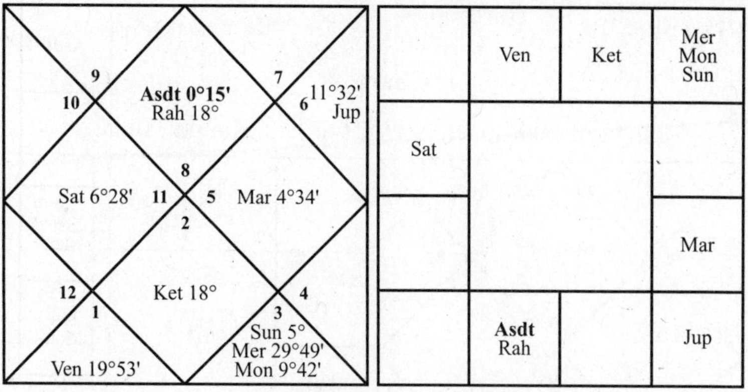

	Ven	Ket	Mer Mon Sun
Sat			
			Mar
	Asdt Rah		Jup

South Indian chart (left):

- 9 / 10 — Asdt 0°15' Rah 18°
- 7 / 6 — 11°32' Jup
- 8 — Sat 6°28' 11 / 5 Mar 4°34'
- 2
- 12 / 1 — Ven 19°53'
- Ket 18°
- 4 / 3 — Sun 5° Mer 29°49' Mon 9°42'

The sign Scorpio rises in the ascendant. Mars becomes the prime determinant of health in this case as there is no mooltrikona sign in the ascendant. Mars, Venus, Rahu and Ketu act as functional malefic planets. Libra rises in the ascendant of the shashthamsa and Venus becomes the additional prime determinant of health. No planet is in its sign of debilitation in shashthamsa.

Venus ruling the house of losses is placed in the house of health and indicates loss of good health. The Sun, Mercury and the Moon are badly placed in the eighth house and become weak. Mercury is additionally weak as it is in extreme old age. The functional malefic Mars is close to the most effective point of the tenth house and mildly afflicts all the houses occupied and aspected. Venus is weak as it is badly placed, debilitated in navamsa and its dispositor is weak.

The placement of Venus in the sixth house and weakness of Mercury resulted in the problem of hernia and the native had to undergo operation twice in the sub-period of Saturn in the main period of Rahu. To overcome the recurrent problem of ill health the parents of the native sought astral remedies. Both propitiatory astral remedies for the functional malefic planets and wearing of a

Kavach for strengthening the weak functional benefic planets in an auspiciously elected time were advised.

PILES

Chart 89

Male born 20th June, 1933, 2140 Hrs. Kanpur, India.

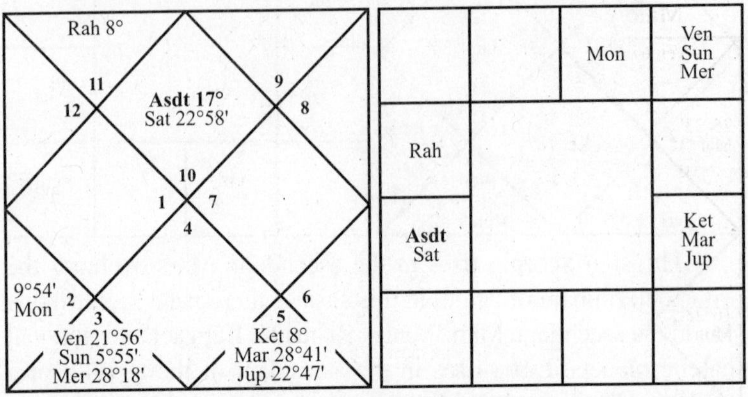

		Mon	Ven Sun Mer
Rah			
Asdt Sat			Ket Mar Jup

The sign Capricorn rises in the ascendant. The Sun becomes the prime determinant of health as there is no mooltrikona sign in both first and sixth houses. The Sun, Jupiter, Rahu and Ketu act as functional malefic planets. Capricorn rises in the ascendant of shashthamsa. The Moon and Ketu are debilitated in shashthamsa.

The Sun is weak due to bad placement and it is closely afflicted by Rahu. The Moon is in its sign of exaltation in the nativity but weak due to debilitation in shashthamsa so far as the health affairs are concerned. The planets Venus, Mercury, Mars and Jupiter are badly placed and weak. Mercury and Mars are additionally weak as they are in old age. **The placement of three planets in the house of diseases, in itself, is indicative of acute health problems.** The native is suffering from a number of health problems including piles. Whenever the lord of the eighth house goes to the sixth house or is under the severe affliction of the sixth lord, the native is vulnerable to the disease of piles or fissure. The native sought astrological remedial measures when the medical treatment was providing temporary symptomatic relief with constant and continuous medication. The native was advised both propitiatory astral remedies for the functional malefic planets and wearing of a Kavach for strengthening the weak functional benefic planets in an auspiciously elected time.

Chart 90

Male born 21st March, 1959, 0625 Hrs. New Delhi, India.

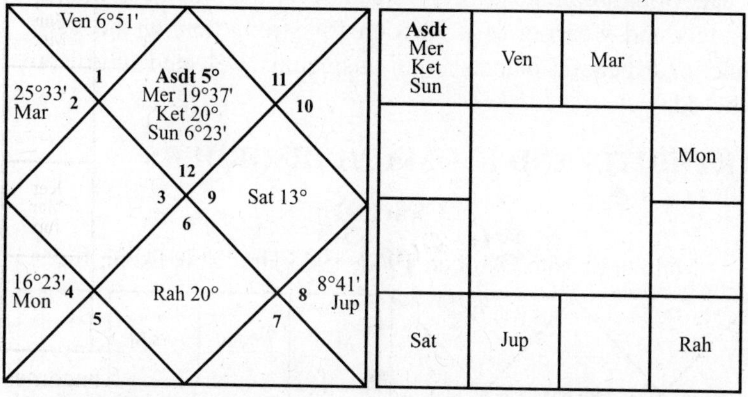

Asdt Mer Ket Sun	Ven	Mar	
			Mon
Sat	Jup		Rah

Chart (left diagram): Ven 6°51'; 1; 25°33' Mar 2; Asdt 5° Mer 19°37' Ket 20° Sun 6°23'; 11; 10; 12; 3; 9; Sat 13°; 6; 16°23' Mon 4; 5; Rah 20°; 7; 8; 8°41' Jup

The sign Pisces rises in the ascendant. The Sun becomes the prime determinant of health as there is no mooltrikona sign in the ascendant. The Sun, Venus, Saturn, Rahu and Ketu act as functional malefic planets. Libra rises in the ascendant of the shashthamsa and Venus becomes the additional prime determinant of health. No planet is debilitated in shashthamsa.

Mercury is weak due to combustion, debilitation and severe affliction of Rahu-Ketu axis. The close affliction of the Sun to the most effective point of the ascendant and the seventh house inflicts ill health on the native during its sub-periods. Venus is weak as its house of placement is afflicted by itself and its dispositor is weak. Mars is weak as its mooltrikona house is under the close affliction of the most malefic planet, Venus, and is in old age. The Moon is weak due to debilitation in navamsa.

The native suffered from acute depression, had to stay separated from the spouse and suffered from number of infections connected to the parts of the body in the lumbar region. The separation from the spouse is seen because of severely afflicted Mercury and the placement of the most malefic planet on the most effective point of the second house. The astral remedies were sought by the parents of the native for good health and greater mental peace. Both propitiatory astral remedies for the functional malefic planets and wearing of a Kavach for strengthening the weak functional benefic planets in an auspiciously elected time were advised.

ARTHRITIS AND STOMACH DISORDERS

Chart 91

Male born 16th October, 1948, 1945 Hrs. New Delhi, India.

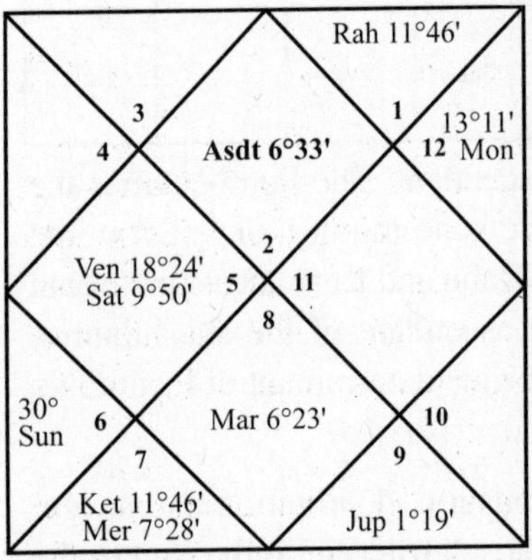

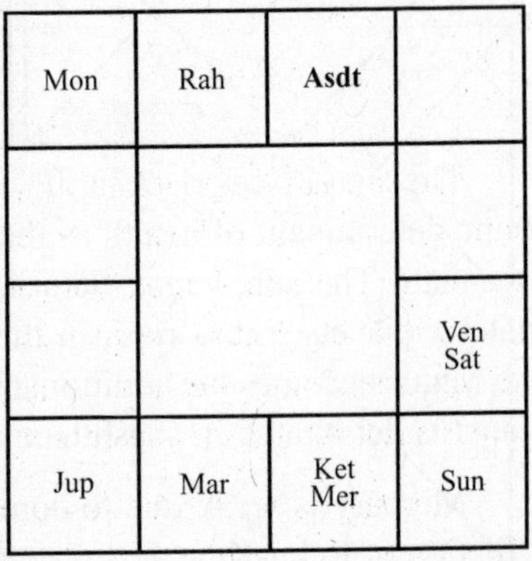

Mon	Rah	**Asdt**	
			Ven Sat
Jup	Mar	Ket Mer	Sun

Chart details:
- Rah 11°46'
- Asdt 6°33'
- 13°11' 12 Mon
- Ven 18°24' Sat 9°50'
- 30° Sun
- Mar 6°23'
- Ket 11°46' Mer 7°28'
- Jup 1°19'

The sign Taurus rises in the ascendant. Venus becomes the prime determinant of health as there is no mooltrikona sign in the ascendant. Venus, Jupiter, Mars, Rahu and Ketu act as functional malefic planets. Scorpio rises in shashthamsa. No planet is in debilitation in shashthamsa.

Venus is well placed but is weak due to debilitation in navamsa and weakness of dispositor. The functional malefic Mars exactly afflicts the most effective points of the seventh, tenth, first and second houses. Jupiter is weak as it is in infancy. The Sun is weak as it is in extreme old age and its dispositor is combust, badly placed and afflicted. Rahu and Ketu are badly placed. Saturn is weak due to the weakness of its dispositor, close affliction by Rahu and close affliction to its mooltrikona house. The weakness of the Sun, significator for stomach, and bad placement of the lord of the fifth house gave the persistent problem of stomach disorders. The weakness and severe affliction of significator of joints, Saturn, gave the problem of arthritis. The native was advised both propitiatory astral remedies for the functional malefic planets and wearing of a Kavach for strengthening the weak functional benefic planets in an auspiciously elected time for providing a cover against further deterioration and greater success of medical treatment.

Chart 92

Male born 11th August, 1966, 0350 Hrs. Gurgaon, India.

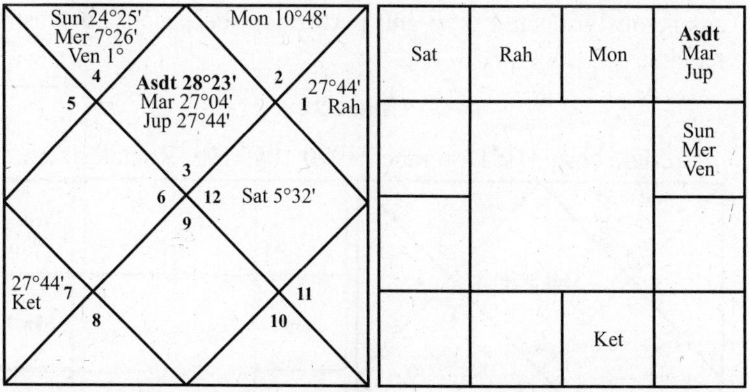

The sign Gemini rises in the ascendant. The Sun becomes the prime determinant of health as there is no mooltrikona sign in the first and sixth houses. Rahu and Ketu act as functional malefic planets. Virgo rises in the ascendant of shashthamsa and Mercury becomes the additional prime determinant of health. No planet is in debilitation in shashthamsa.

The Moon is badly placed in the twelfth house and is weak. Venus is weak due to afflicted mooltrikona house, infancy and weak dispositor. Mars and Jupiter are weak due to afflicted mooltrikona house, afflicted house of placement, exact affliction from Ketu and old age. Ketu causes severe affliction to Mars and Jupiter by way of an exact aspect. Rahu-Ketu axis is near the most effective points of the houses and afflicts all the houses occupied and aspected. This nodal affliction turns Mars, the Sun, Venus, Jupiter and Saturn weak. The weakness of the lord of the fifth house and affliction of Ketu to its most effective point resulted in acute stomach disorders to the native. During the sub-period of Ketu and main period of Rahu, the native suffered from a severe accident and continued to suffer even in the sub-period of Venus due to undiagnosed problems for more than three years when astral remedies were sought. The performance of astral remedies helped in correct diagnosis of the problem and an operation conducted in March, 1997, helped the native by giving permanent relief. The native wore a Kavach with special strengthening powers prepared under our guidance in an auspiciously elected time and performed the propitiatory astral remedies.

Chart 93

Male born 31st December, 1970 1855 Hrs. Rohtak, India.

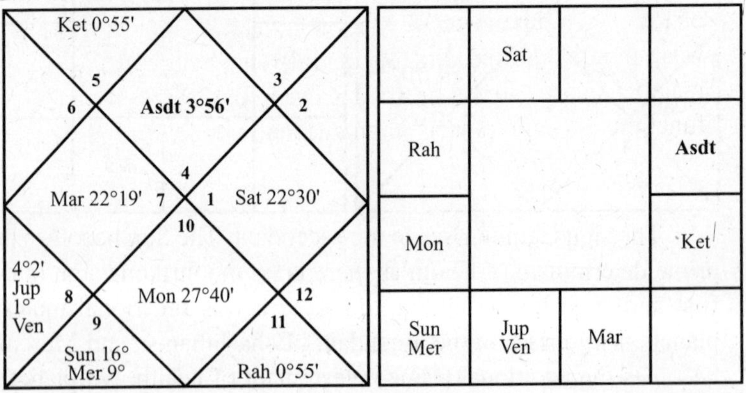

	Sat		
Rah			Asdt
Mon			Ket
Sun Mer	Jup Ven	Mar	

Ket 0°55'
5
6 Asdt 3°56' 3 2
4
Mar 22°19' 7 1 Sat 22°30'
10
4°2'
Jup 1°
Ven 8 9 Mon 27°40' 12 11
Sun 16°
Mer 9° Rah 0°55'

The sign Cancer rises in the ascendant. The Moon and Jupiter become the prime determinants of health. Jupiter, Saturn, Rahu and Ketu act as functional malefic planets. Libra rises in the ascendant of shashthamsa and Venus becomes the additional prime determinant of health. No planet is in its sign of debilitation in shashthamsa.

Rahu-Ketu axis is near the most effective points of the houses and afflicts all the houses occupied and aspected. The functional malefic Jupiter causes severe afflictions to all the houses aspected and occupied as it is near the most effective point of the fifth house. The most malefic planet, Saturn, exactly aspects and afflicts Mars. The Moon is weak as it is in old age and its mooltrikona house is exactly afflicted. Venus is weak as it is in infancy and its house of placement is exactly afflicted. The Sun and Mercury are weak due to bad placement and weakness of dispositor. Jupiter is weak due to afflicted house of placement and infancy. Mercury is additionally weak as it is combust. The weaknesses and afflictions indicate acute health problems to the native.

The severe affliction of the most malefic planet to the lord of the tenth house resulted in problems of joint pains in the main period of Rahu and sub-period of Mars at a very young age. The native was advised both propitiatory astral remedies for the functional malefic planets and wearing of a Kavach for strengthening the weak functional benefic planets in an auspiciously elected time.

LOSS OF VISION

Chart 94

Male born 11th March, 1995, 1145 Hrs. Ludhiana, India.

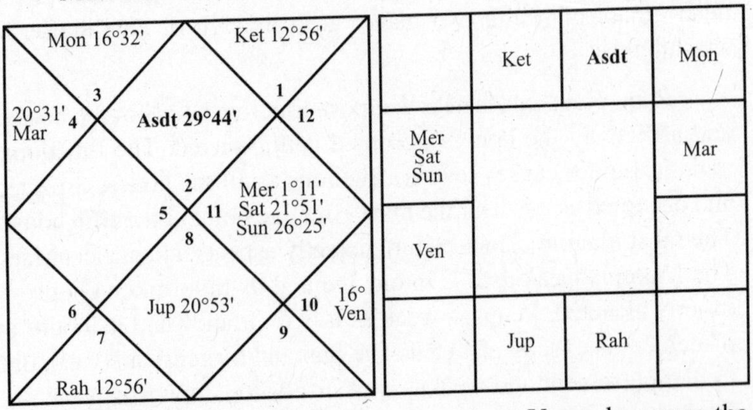

	Ket	**Asdt**	Mon
Mer Sat Sun			Mar
Ven			
	Jup	Rah	

The sign Taurus rises in the ascendant. Venus becomes the prime determinant of health as there is no mooltrikona sign in the ascendant. Venus, Jupiter, Mars, Rahu and Ketu act as functional malefic planets. Pisces rises in shashthamsa. No planet is in debilitation in shashthamsa.

The most malefic planet, Jupiter, exactly aspects and afflicts the lord of the twelfth house, Mars. The functional malefic Mars closely aspects and afflicts the lord of the sixth house, Venus, and the lord of the tenth house, Saturn. Mercury is weak as it is in infancy. Rahu and Ketu are badly placed in the chart. Jupiter and Saturn are debilitated in navamsa. The affliction to the lord of the twelfth house by the most malefic planet and the affliction to Venus resulted in loss of vision to the native at the time of birth. The parents of the native, who were staunch believers of astrological remedies, sought astral help for the eyesight of this child. Both propitiatory astral remedies for the functional malefic planets and wearing of a Kavach for strengthening the weak functional benefic planets in an auspiciously elected time were advised. The performance of the astral propitiatory remedies and use of the

Kavach with special powers helped the native respond to treatment. The astral remedies were administered in April, 1996, and there was a great improvement in eyesight by the end of August, 1996. The preventive astral remedies continued for protection against further health hazards.

CHAPTER 11

PEARLS OF WISDOM FOR SPIRITUAL GROWTH

God lives in the hearts of those who have no lust, anger, arrogance and pride and those who are without greed, excitement, aversion or attraction and are free from fraud, hypocrisy and deceit.

God lives in the hearts of those who always think God as their master, companion, father, mother, preceptor and everything.

For peace and enjoying the bliss, we can follow the Pearls of Wisdom.

1. Patience is very important in life and at all times.

2. If there is a mistake or misunderstanding one should not hesitate to accept.

3. There is always scope of learning.

4. Wise people ignore the acts of foolish persons.

5. Anger, greed, encroaching tendencies, pride and lust make a person blind.

6. For literary/intellectual understanding/creativity one requires:

   • Intelligence

   • Imagination

   • Exploratory mind

   • Concentration

- Patience

- Confidence

- Objectivity

Some more pearls from Ramayana, the epic:

1. While describing the character of saints (holy persons) and those who are unholy, Sant Tulsidas, the writer of Ramayana, says that the holy persons give happiness to others while the unholy persons live for making others unhappy. So, those learning and practicing astrology should follow the conduct of holy persons.

2. Ramayana says that without going into the merits of advice or sayings, one should follow the advice of one's parents; guru (teacher) and god, as this always blesses the person with happiness and peace.

3. Those who do not respect or heed to their parents and God and those who seek service from holy persons are just demons. Such persons always cause sufferings to others and perish after experiencing sufferings in life.

4. While patience and self-control are necessary for being successful and peaceful in life generosity remains a virtue, above all.

In Ramayana, lord Rama says, "Only those who are simple find me. I do not like those who are involved in manipulations and cheating."